IN CASE OF EMERGENCY

In Case of Emergency

How Technologies Mediate Crisis
and Normalize Inequality

Elizabeth Ellcessor

NEW YORK UNIVERSITY PRESS

New York

NEW YORK UNIVERSITY PRESS
New York
www.nyupress.org

References to Internet websites (URLs) were accurate at the time of writing. Neither the author nor New York University Press is responsible for URLs that may have expired or changed since the manuscript was prepared.

Library of Congress Cataloging-in-Publication Data
Names: Ellcessor, Elizabeth, author.
Title: In case of emergency : how technologies mediate crisis and normalize inequality / Elizabeth Ellcessor.
Description: New York : New York University Press, [2022] |
Includes bibliographical references.
Identifiers: LCCN 2021027790 | ISBN 9781479811625 (hardback ; alk. paper) |
ISBN 9781479811632 (paperback ; alk. paper) | ISBN 9781479811663 (ebook) |
ISBN 9781479811656 (ebook other)
Subjects: LCSH: Public safety—Moral and ethical aspects. | Emergencies—Social aspects. | Emergency management—Moral and ethical aspects. | Emergency communication systems. | Discrimination.
Classification: LCC HV549 .E45 2022 | DDC 363.1—dc23
LC record available at https://lccn.loc.gov/2021027790

New York University Press books are printed on acid-free paper, and their binding materials are chosen for strength and durability. We strive to use environmentally responsible suppliers and materials to the greatest extent possible in publishing our books.

Manufactured in the United States of America

10 9 8 7 6 5 4 3 2 1

Also available as an ebook

CONTENTS

FIGURES

Introduction

Mediating Emergency, Maintaining Normalcy

When Michael Hickson contracted COVID-19 in 2020, his doctor advised the cessation of life-continuing measures because "as of right now, his quality of life—he doesn't have much of one." Hickson's wife, Melissa, replied, "Because he's paralyzed with a brain injury?"[1] This clarification was not only for her benefit; unknown to the doctor, she was audio recording the conversation on her phone. Melissa's recording did not prevent Michael's death, but it was circulated by advocacy groups and covered by news outlets as a clear demonstration of the potential disparate impacts of COVID-19.[2] Through the production and circulation of media evidence, this individual case testified to COVID-19 as an emergency on a societal level, with compounding, intersectional effects on those already marginalized. Hickson was a Black quadriplegic man who had required ongoing medical attention since 2017. The doctor's words concretized the fear of many disabled and marginalized people that their lives might not be considered worth saving in a worsening pandemic.[3]

The same summer weekend that Michael Hickson died in Austin, residents of San Antonio, Texas, received a Wireless Emergency Alert, a text message distributed using dedicated federal alerting infrastructures to all smartphones in a given geographic area. It read:

EMERGENCY ALERT

> STAY HOME. The COVID-19 virus is spreading rapidly across Bexar County. Local hospitals are approaching capacity. Protect yourself and your family. Stay home except for essential activities and wear a face covering and avoid gathering with people outside your household. STAY SAFE. For more info visit covid19.sanantonio.gov.

While COVID-19 was disproportionately killing Black Americans and other people of color, thousands of people were simultaneously engaged in national Black Lives Matter protests against police violence, catalyzed by the deaths of George Floyd, Breonna Taylor, and Ahmaud Arbery. These protests were routinely characterized by police overreach in the forms of arrests of journalists, violence against protestors, and little oversight of (often armed) white supremacist counterprotestors. Like COVID-19, police brutality, racism, and protests themselves were constructed as emergencies by protestors and government agencies, respectively, all using the media tools at their disposal.

As the pandemic dragged on, public school districts across the country chose to start the school year virtually, relying on online meetings using the Zoom videocall platform. On the first day of school in a Florida district, a ten-year-old girl was attending class on Zoom when her mother was shot and killed by an ex-boyfriend. The girl's teacher described hearing a commotion, muting the girl's audio and seeing the child put her hands to her ears. The screen then went blank, as the school laptop was hit by debris.[4] A chilling emergency in one location became, through livestream, a farther-reaching form of shared trauma.

These examples can only begin to capture the extent of the overlapping, recoiling, and ubiquitous states of emergency that characterized the United States in 2020. What these examples do show, however, is the centrality of media to constructing a set of circumstances as an *emergency* and the variability of this process. Melissa Hickson's recording enabled her husband's death to be publicized as an instance of potential medical bias in responses to a public health emergency, identifying the coronavirus as a particular kind of emergency for Black and disabled people. The Bexar County alert used emergency infrastructure and language to attempt to lend gravity and produce compliance in matters of public health, after months in which such guidance had been lacking. The emergency of racist policing was shown and recognized through the circulation of videos and exposure to social media activism that emphasized the humanity of Floyd, Taylor, Arbery, and others. Witnessing lethal domestic violence via Zoom transformed a routine—if remediated—school day into an extraordinary shared trauma. In each case, mediation was central to a situation *becoming* an emergency. What is—or is not—an emergency is a matter of technological specificity, of interpretation, of perspective, and of politics, and mediation is central to these determinations.

Mediating Emergency

This book is about how mediation participates in the construction of the very concept and experience of "emergency." The mediation of emergency replicates and entrenches differences of power and access, which nearly always disadvantage those already marginalized by race, disability, geography, poverty, gender, or age. This book is not about how media represent emergency; it is not primarily about news coverage, fictional film or television, or the endless array of true-crime content. Instead, its focus is on the media technologies to which someone might turn when faced with extreme circumstances, through which people understand and take action. These are what I refer to as "emergency media," technologies that mediate experience in order to produce or react to emergency.

The quantity, variety, and ubiquity of media now available to be used by individuals to prevent, make others aware of, or respond to emergency are staggering: telephone calls and text messages to 9-1-1; localized emergency systems such as arena loudspeakers and tornado sirens; home, car, and other security alarms; baby monitors for the young and fall monitors for the elderly; television, radio, and text messages conveying public alerts about weather conditions; dedicated safety apps and wearables; and social media that allows one to mark one's self "safe" on Facebook or use Twitter to communicate from the sites of natural disasters. The speed, interconnection, and everydayness of digital mobile media have created virtual "panic buttons" at our fingertips, offering protection through direct connection to traditional emergency services, to social networks, or to specialized for-profit service providers.

Emergency media such as these are, crucially, cultural. They produce and circulate meanings about what is valuable, what is tragic, and how we ought to respond. These meanings, in turn, have political, social, and economic consequences in terms of how lives are lived and societies organized. When media systems construct some moments as *emergencies*, they render other moments ordinary and undeserving of attention, assistance, or critique. When media systems designate some moments as *non-emergencies*, they cut off resources and assistance, with sometimes tragic consequences.

To understand how mediation shapes understandings of emergency, with what consequences, and how this might be done differently, this book treats emergency media as specific articulations of technology, culture, state and local power, medical authority, and people's routine media practices. It explores the innovations brought to emergency media by digitization and mobile media technologies, particularly through the use of smartphones. It considers the legacies of preexisting technological, legal, and information infrastructures. And most crucially, it considers the unevenness with which mediated emergency is produced and made useful to different groups of people. Emergency media—mediated emergencies—are an important part of the way that extraordinary circumstances are managed and ordinary life is made unremarkable. Their inclusions and exclusions clearly illustrate which lives are considered greivable and which are repeatedly marginalized as unworthy of care or even emergency attention.[5]

At the heart of my argument is the claim that emergency media are cultural, producing meanings and effects that are felt in the structures of power and experiences of everyday life in the United States during the early twenty-first century. As such, emergency media represent a site of articulation through which varied technologies and multiple discourses are brought together to function (materially and ideologically) as one within specific contexts and contingent arrangements of social power.[6] Emergency media function as articulations through which technologies, bodies, populations, and infrastructures are brought together and made meaningful in connection to state power, conceptions of the public, values of health and safety, and the variances of identity that shape individuals' encounters with these systems. Crucially, what emergency media is now is not what it must always be.[7]

In Case of Emergency couples this focus with an emphasis on how the very processes and technologies of *mediation* function to produce a cultural discourse of "emergency" that delimits understandings of life, value, normalcy, and care. I engage the contextual and political imperatives of cultural studies to better understand both the current dynamics of that mediation and where we might locate the agency and energy to change it.

To study mediation is to focus on the complicated and interrelated dynamics that characterize the relationships between technological and social actors. Within medium theory (following Marshall McLuhan), "media are understood as environments in which social life unfolds"[8] and through which the operations of culture and power are organized. This is not to say simply that "the medium is the message,"[9] but to emphasize the interrelations of bodies, technologies, and power that emerge and change through mediation.[10] In other words, mediation focuses attention on processes and relationships, including the embodied and affective sensations of pain, fear, uncertainty, and transformation that may characterize emergencies.

Mediation—via audio, text, video, signal, telephone call, or other means—is key to how emergency is or is not recognized, communicated, felt, and acted upon. The mediation of emergency participates in discourses about responsibility, access, and state power, but its central meaning is one of *normalcy*. The core ideological work of emergency, reinforced through its constant mediation, is to uphold the existence of a "normal" state of affairs and to offer a path to restore such normalcy. Of course, such normalcy is not universally available; insofar as emergency is defined in terms of normalcy, it entrenches and extends inequalities that marginalize many who are the most vulnerable in American society. To understand emergency, we must consider normalcy.

The Normalizing Ideology of Emergency

Emergency has long been defined in opposition to normalcy through the language of exception. In fact, the "state of exception" described by philosopher Giorgio Agamben, in which the rule of law is suspended due to extreme circumstances, is referred to in the United States as a "state of emergency." The state of exception is one in which "the sovereign must stand above law and order and take control,"[11] an exercise of power over morality which can justify nearly any decision. Ideologically, emergency is that which is not normal; its difference is what justifies different exercises of power or shows of support. Through difference, it reinforces the central and seemingly inevitable nature of what is usual, expected, or unremarkable. Yet, as Hardt and Negri write, "the state of exception has become permanent and generalized"[12] through ongoing military engagements, climate crises, and social crises. The exceptional state of emergency is supposed to function as the radical alternative to routine ways of life and forms of government, justifying them in their routine actions. But for some people that emergency never ends, and many emergency measures become permanent, casting us into a "new normal."[13]

The dialectical relationship between emergency and normalcy is evident in official responses to emergency, which are predictably invested in the restoration of the prior state of affairs imagined to be "normal" (and normative). Aid is regularly dispersed not on the basis of actual people's needs, but on a priori standards such as insurance value or lost wages.[14] The 2020 federal pandemic assistance, for instance—$1,200 per adult—reflected a calculation based on the federal minimum wage and an assumed short duration of need. The reality—that many people care for others on their individual salaries, that unemployment continued to rise, that rent continued to be collected, and that restrictions on mobility, employment, childcare, and resources would continue for upwards of six months—meant that federal assistance distributed through a logic of normalcy could not begin to address actual needs.

Political theorist Jennifer Rubenstein's work is highly useful in its attention to the structure and uses of "emergency claims" with respect to normalcy. She argues that to call something an emergency and have that status accepted, events must be presented in a way that conforms to a single narrative: "(i) some person(s), thing(s), or state(s) of affairs are valuable, but (ii) they are threatened with imminent harm or destruction, yet (iii) human agency is capable of preventing or reversing at least some of that harm or destruction."[15] Rubenstein thus introduces value as a core dimension of emergency; to claim that there is an emergency requires an embedded claim that there was a previous (normal) state of affairs that was valuable and should be preserved or restored. This means that many forms of ongoing misfortune or oppression—such as gun violence, climate change, and disability—do not serve as the basis for emergency claims, as they are understood to be part of a normal state of affairs rather than a discrete, fixable set of circumstances. For Rubenstein, this is an indication that emergency claims are, in fact, regressive, disqualifying anyone who was already in dire circumstances and exacerbating hierarchies of power and resources.[16]

To see this at work, we could consider one of Rubenstein's examples of a failed emergency claim. Rubenstein writes, "Imagine that a mid-level executive emails his colleagues: 'I'm sorry, but I can't make the meeting today. We have a family emergency—my daughter has severe autism and every day with her is incredibly difficult.'"[17] Certainly not all illnesses or disabilities would fail in this way—"my spouse is having a heart attack," for instance, might succeed—but disability, like poverty and racism, is a powerful example of how the frame of the "emergency claim" constrains interpretations and responses by implicitly valuing and attempting to restore a form of normalcy that excludes oppression and chronic conditions.

In many ways, the exclusionary and restorative logics of emergency and normalcy recall what disability studies scholars have identified as an ideology of "cure."[18] Rosemarie Garland-Thomson describes the ideology of cure as fixated on "changing bodies imagined as abnormal and dysfunctional rather than on changing exclusionary attitudinal, environmental, and economic barriers."[19] Cure prefers a proof-of-concept exoskeleton over a wheelchair, because the former "restores" a normal state of walking. The ideology of emergency is similarly normalizing in its attempts to address moments of ill fortune by restoring the (assumed) status quo, rather than considering alternative values and ways of being in the world.

Scholars in disability studies have long defined their work not only through its topic, but in terms of a broader critique of social norms and the harms they may cause. In literature and cultural spaces such as freak shows, disabled people have often been used as a counterpart, an Other against which people may reassure themselves of their own normalcy (and value).[20] Thus, Lennard Davis's foundational study of the roots of "normal" explicitly argues that the task of disability analysis is to "reverse the hegemony of the normal and to institute alternative ways of thinking about the abnormal."[21] This is what scholar Julie Avril Minich describes as the *method* of disability studies: the "scrutiny of normative ideologies . . . with the goal of producing knowledge in support of justice for people with stigmatized bodies and minds."[22] The more we know about normalcy—and its exclusions—the more we can recognize and oppose its operation. Emergency is one such normative ideology, and *In Case of Emergency* is fundamentally informed by this approach to an intersectional disability studies that highlights connections between disability, gender, sexuality, and race through the shared project of documenting and demonstrating the harms of a society based around a normative idea of a white, male, heterosexual, and nondisabled body.[23]

We cannot understand the normalizing operations of emergency without attention to both disability and race; emergency upholds not only the normal state of affairs, but the normatively of nondisabled, white supremacy.[24] In their recent formulation of "feminist-of-color disability studies," Sami Schalk and Jina Kim call for a method and field that "highlights the ideological and rhetorical deployment of ableism within legacies of eugenics, colonialism/neocolonialism, counterterrorism, welfare reform, war, urban re-development, and other oppressive practices and structures that route life-sustaining resources away from populations of color."[25] Emergency—and emergency media—are fundamentally racialized: the poverty, debility, and violence in communities of color do not register as emergency claims;[26] the majority of people killed by police violence are also disabled;[27] Black communities are targeted for enforcement by predictive policing and "innovative" apps. All of these examples reveal how "individuals located perilously at the interstices of race, class, gender, and disability are constituted as non-citizens and (no)bodies by the very social institutions . . . that are designed to protect, nurture, and empower them."[28] Schalk and Kim identify the operations of state violence as a key concern to feminist-of-color disability studies,[29] locating this violence in prisons, police, schools, and welfare systems. This violence is also visible in the operations of emergency ideologies and systems.

A poignant example of this reality is the way that Black families have attempted to protect their disabled children from emergency media's normalizing ideology and articulation to police and carceral power. In 2016, Nevada mother Judy McKim painted her garage door with the phrase "Autistic man lives here" and added additional yard signs, one of which read "And he's Black, too" following a call to police that reported her son was "in a rage," and led to an assault and charges against the police officers involved.[30] Smaller protective acts include parents who ask neighbors to never call 9-1-1, or who preemptively install security systems in order to record any encounters with authorities. Calling 9-1-1 for help in an emergency is not safe—and thus not accessible—for everyone.

Tempting as it may be to advocate for more inclusive emergency media, that is not my goal. We have seen efforts to increase, for instance, the accessibility of emergency information by offering American Sign Language translation or captions. These measures rest on policies that use the exceptionalism of "emergency" as a justification for inclusive media practices.[31] Yet, the access afforded by accessible media communications in disaster contexts is at best partial. While the content of a mayoral address about an impending hurricane is conveyed to a d/Deaf audience, for instance, by a live American Sign Language interpreter, neither that audience nor other disabled audiences are informed of any resources that would address their specific needs during or after the disaster itself.[32] Will the evacuation routes be wheelchair accessible? Will the shelters have power available for ventilators? Will there be accessible print materials or digital interfaces for accessing relief services? Media accessibility does not make the message culturally accessible and continues to center the needs and perspective of an audience assumed to be nondisabled.[33]

Even in emergency contexts, in which common sense suggests that access should be prioritized, we can and should be critical of the scope and forms of access and assistance that are made available (and those that are not). In this respect, this book is a work of critical access studies.[34] Too often, access and accessibility imply granting entrance to a system that already exists, via an assimilationist logic.[35] Critical access studies asks, instead, how we might think of access in terms of transformation; how could the experiences and knowledges of disabled people and disability culture enhance what we "know" about the physical, mediated, and ideological systems in which we regularly participate? Similarly, how could race, ethnicity, or sexuality offer resources for rethinking not only the conditions of access for existing emergency media, but their transformation?

Such questions are particularly important in attempting to think beyond normalizing ideologies such as cure or emergency. To the degree that emergency is defined in terms of its difference from and restoration to a state of normalcy, it is inherently about the restoration of white supremacy, ableism, and related exclusions of those whose bodies and lives are marginalized. In the words of disability activist Alice Wong, "'Normal' was actually not great for a lot of people."[36] We must think about ways to challenge, reshape, and upend normalcy; one way to do so is to critically consider emergency.

Defining Emergency

To state that mediation can transform a moment into an emergency, we must have some sense of what characterizes "emergency" as experience and category. For the purposes of this book, I define emergency as *a circumstance that disrupts a person's or community's everyday life, producing an affectively intense experience of the present and demanding that something be done to prevent further harm.* Emergency is often conflated with related concepts like "disaster," "accident," or "crisis," which can help to inform and differentiate this definition of emergency.

Emergency disrupts everyday life. Actions that are taken for granted may become impossible or dangerous during an emergency—for instance, the creek in which children wade can, after an overnight thunderstorm, flood onto the surrounding plains. Disruption has been foundational to sociological definitions of *disasters* as "a form of community disruption that occur and then are over."[37] Conceiving of emergency or disaster in terms of disruption centers its function as an opposite to normalcy. Something, after all, must be disrupted. More recent understandings of disaster emphasize that a disruption may be whatever prevents a society from fulfilling its essential functions, and that disruptions may be of long or recurring durations and may be connected to societal issues such as poverty or racism.[38] Disasters have also been conceptualized through a "hazards approach," which centers environmental risks—hurricanes, earthquakes, floods—and links them to social vulnerabilities or resilience.[39] This approach tends to locate the source of disruption as "outside" the normal flow of life, and outside the control of any person or group. As such, it is too narrow to be applied to "emergency," which we often understand to include very localized and potentially actionable circumstances (discussed below).

Emergency is relevant at the level of the individual or community, not only the governmental, national, or global. Many understandings of disaster and the state of emergency have focused on the scale of global politics and phenomena. The very origins of both disaster research and the field of emergency management are grounded in Cold War–era U.S.

civil defense; the disaster (or emergency) that shaped their work was the threat of nuclear war.[40] Yet disaster researchers—who were largely funded through civil defense initiatives—quickly found that local civil defense personnel tended to focus on specific and local concerns, with general disinterest in national security measures.[41] The use of "emergency" in the field of emergency management (why not "disaster management"?) may be understood as a continuation of this dynamic, in which emergency management personnel are localized, serving a specific region or community.

This focus on community characterizes more recent understandings of disaster and offers a useful reminder that neither disaster nor emergency is self-evident, but both are constructed in context. E. L. Quarantelli, a leading figure in disaster research, defined disasters as primarily social (not spatial or temporal) phenomena in which "vulnerability is socially constructed by relationships in the social system and disasters are based in the notion of social changes."[42] In this framework, events such an earthquake are the source of change, but disaster itself stems from how that change affects people within a given social system.

Finally, beyond the level of the community, it is common to use the word "emergency" for individual experiences that would not typically be described as "crises" or "disasters." If I slip and injure myself on a remote hiking trail, few would disagree that I faced an emergency, but it would be unusual to describe such events as a crisis or a disaster. These terms suggest a larger-scale geographic or population event. A landslide on that same trail that caused greater or ongoing harm to a larger number of people might more easily be termed a disaster or crisis.

Emergency is affectively intense. Emergency is not a neutral experience but is characterized by a potent mix of feelings, potentially including fear, confusion, pain, adrenaline rush, eerie calm, panic, anger, pressure, and other reactions. An emergency—disruption—is a situation of incoming or arrived threat. Thus, it is affectively intense in that it produces many felt potentialities, some of which may materialize into action and other which may leave us in what Lauren Berlant refers to as "an affectively intense cul-de-sac" of multiple feelings, sensations, and possibilities.[43]

Furthermore, emergency may be felt into being; we know it is an emergency because it feels like an emergency. Affect theorist Brian Massumi describes the logic of preemption as "when the futurity of unspecified threat is affectively held in the present in a perpetual state of potential emergence(y)."[44] Preemption, in other words, works because the actions that it prompts in the present are based on felt fears and expectations of a future that may never occur. Should preemption succeed, the threat will never materialize. Massumi's focus in the theorization of preemption is threat, understood as a global or militaristic capacity. However, his affective analysis of future threat and present preemption is equally useful to understanding experiences of emergency as affectively intense. Like threat, emergency can be "felt into being";[45] the affective experience of fear, or worry, is real, which, in turn, makes the possible threat or emergency real as well.

Emergency is located in the present tense. Closely connected to the affective dimensions of emergency, its temporal orientation is toward the (extended) present. The "nowness" of emergency separates it from theorizations of "disaster," "accident," or "crisis."

Disaster research and response has historically focused on aftermath, and current emergency management literatures identify "phases" of preparedness, response, recovery, and mitigation, cycling into one another without mention of any catalyzing circumstance or moment. The disaster (or emergency) is everywhere and always, but also nowhere and never. Similarly, theorizations of the "accident" suggest that its temporality is most firmly located in the past (though it may inform the future). Media scholar Greg Siegel argues that the accident—that which "just happens"—was historically problematized and thus made solvable through the cultivation of safety.[46] Evidence of past accidents provided the negative image of risk through which to identify and enact safety measures designed to prevent future accidents, or at least to minimize the risk and likelihood of accidents.

Such perpetual possibility of accident contributes to conditions of generalized accident or perpetual crisis, always and never arriving.[47] What theorist Paul Virilio calls the "generalized accident" is everywhere at once, disrupting communication, economic, and political systems on a grand scale.[48] Similarly, cultural critic Steven Shaviro describes *crisis* under neoliberalism to be less a turning point and more "a chronic and seemingly permanent condition."[49]

Emergency, by contrast, is not defined by its possibility and avoidance, but by its *happening*. The moment of the accident or disaster—"the punctual 'now'"[50]—might be said to be the moment of emergency. Rubenstein suggests that an emergency is "an impending disaster that can be warded off, at least to some extent,"[51] indicating that it is arriving, in progress, not completed. Like extended temporalities of crisis, emergency is happening and felt in the present tense. It is temporally set apart from normal time, an intensified and even extended present, with an eye toward the "near-future."[52] In emergency, there is the possibility of action, indicating that it is neither past nor future, but available for immediate intervention, leading to the final component of my definition above.

Emergency demands that something be done. Unlike the accident or disaster, emergency demands action or intervention to stop or reduce harm; in its present-oriented temporality, emergency offers what Rubenstein describes as an "opportunity for helpful action."[53]

The need for action characterizes philosopher Elaine Scarry's understanding of emergency as well. Scarry poses that "the emergency requires that 1) an action must be taken, and 2) the action must be taken relatively quickly."[54] The emergency requires a response, not merely a recognition or endurance. Emergency, she argues, does not require that people stop thinking and take orders. It requires deliberative, democratic cultivation of actions and habits before emergency occurs; such steps can prepare people to take meaningful action in emergency. One of her examples, the widespread teaching of CPR, illustrates how intentional thinking and procedures are taught, publicized, and practiced such that members of the public may be able to perform CPR when confronted with that particular emergency. Again, nothing about learning CPR will preempt the potential threat of this health crisis; it is a technique of emergency preparedness, enabling action when needed.

"Emergency" is a complex, ongoing, active, felt, and contextual phenomenon. The characteristics above help to differentiate it from its near synonyms and lay the groundwork for this book's exploration of the *mediation* of emergency. How, given this understanding of emergency, do media produce, extend, and respond to emergency?

Emergency Media Systems and Their Dynamics

Emergency media are those technologies and mediated communications to which individuals turn in order to express, justify, and enable the affective experiences and concrete actions that belong to the intensi-fied "here and now" of emergency. They do not represent or report on emergencies—those are media *about* emergency—but instead offer to manage how we feel, what we do, and what might be the outcomes of an emergency experience.

Some examples of emergency media are obvious: 9-1-1, for instance, is explicitly designated for people to call in the event of an emergency. Similarly, the use of the Emergency Alert System on television or radio or the blaring of a midwestern tornado siren may be understood as directly mediating emergency in the moment. These examples have a commonality, in that they would likely fit the U.S. legal definition of emergency information, which is "intended to further the protection of life, health, safety, and property, i.e., critical details regarding the emer-gency and how to respond to the emergency."[55] To provide emergency information is to mediate a circumstance such that it takes on the cul-tural meanings of emergency and potentially causes people to feel and behave in accordance with instructions.

There has been little critical scholarship devoted to the media sys-tems that are dedicated to emergency usage. A notable exception, Greg Siegel's analysis of CONELRAD (the precursor to the U.S. Emergency Broadcast System and now Emergency Alert System), offers detailed historical analysis of CONELRAD as a "radical alternative"[56] to com-mercial and public broadcasting, an exceptional exertion of govern-ment control that ultimately upheld "'normal' broadcasting practices, policies, and political economies."[57] Conversely, the theorizations of emergency and related concepts explored previously have very little to say about media. While disaster research has begun to address the changing role of centralized communications in an age of social media,[58] there is less available research that works to understand the media systems, platforms, and labor that participate in moments of crisis and the role that such mediation plays in constructing knowl-edge and experiences of emergency.[59]

Media scholars Lisa Parks and Janet Walker recently addressed a similar gap in their theorization of "disaster media," which they de-scribe as "a heuristic, or approach, that recognizes the ways 'natural' and human-made disasters are communicated about, constructed, and vari-ously exacerbated or relieved through media means."[60] Their conception of disaster media focuses on how media are used to produce varied temporalities and meanings in experiences of disasters (particularly ecological disasters). In fact, Parks and Walker's claim that "media are co-producers of disastrous events that form in and through the inequities they deepen and the earthly disruptions they so often accelerate" is quite similar to my own understanding of emergency media. However, as "disaster" and "emergency" are differentiated above, "disaster media" and "emergency media" place their emphases on different situations and scales of mediation.

Emergency media may be characterized as infrastructures that delimit and produce experiences as emergencies (or not) through their technological, cultural, and labor functions. As infrastructure, emergency media might be understood to be part of the background of everyday life, only rising to consciousness for most people when they are needed and appear as "just there, ready-to-hand."[61] The policies, technologies, labor practices, and material circumstances that enable wireless emergency alerts, fire alarms, and other emergency media systems to function are generally rendered invisible, ignorable, or unappealing.[62] By addressing the infrastructural dimensions of emergency media, I hope to make them visible and thus available for critique and, ultimately, change.

Scholars of science and technology studies have long argued that material and information infrastructures are slow to change due to the many linked systems and practices they may encompass. Thus, in the case of emergency media, many public systems are marked by slow change and an inability to keep up with the public's expectations of digital media. In this gap, many for-profit companies have seen an opportunity to innovate and reshape emergency and safety around consumer expectations. Claims of innovation, which hyperbolize newness and change while devaluing the crucial work of maintenance and reliability, attract attention (and users) that legacy infrastructures may not.[63]

Safety surveillance is one form of innovation that technology companies have introduced to the mediation of emergency. Similar to other forms of extractive for-profit surveillance, safety surveillance involves allowing others (people or companies) to undertake constant surveillance of a person's body or location, ostensibly in the interest of ensuring their safety. Of course, merely watching cannot prevent or respond to emergency; most of the time, safety surveillance technologies are collecting data and providing reassurance to those interested in safety (often not the person being monitored). The threat of emergency here is used to introduce new forms of capitalist surveillance and to intensify relations of power within and among friends and family who may monitor one another. Safety surveillance is deeply invested in reassurance, a reassertion of normalcy and denial of emergency.

Innovations in emergency media include not only consumer media platforms, but what technology scholars Matthew Fuller and Andrew Goffey call "gray media," technologies that recede from view even as they extend the workings of bureaucratic power.[64] There are growing numbers of apps and platforms offering both emergency service providers and end users novel forms of emergency information and intervention, from data-driven computer-assisted dispatch platforms to wearable devices equipped with multiple health and safety alerting functions and multipurpose safety platforms offering suites of digital services to governments, corporations, and individuals. As such, these platforms shape the infrastructure of emergency media without often rising to public view or critique.

The role of technology in emergency media infrastructures is perhaps most clearly illustrated in the ongoing inability of internet-enabled systems to make direct calls to 9-1-1. This has been an issue since the rise of Voice over Internet Protocol (VoIP) systems in the late 1990s, because VoIP calls lacked a stable, physical "location" for the call's origin. This meant that 9-1-1 could not discern the local dispatch center and direct calls appropriately. Later laws attempted to address this problem, but their most visible effect was that VoIP services began including warnings that these systems could not be used for 9-1-1. Twenty years later, the same problem has emerged for many smart devices; Amazon's virtual assistant Alexa, for instance, cannot call 9-1-1 directly.[65] Instead, there is a wealth of advice about how to set up Alexa "skills" (essentially apps for the Alexa platform) that allow you to alert preselected family or friends of an emergency or suggest how you might set up a local police non-emergency number in your contacts. For both VoIP systems and smart home technologies, there is a gap between the innovations of new technologies and the capacities of legacy emergency media infrastructures. New features emerge—and, in the case of Alexa, subject users to near-constant surveillance "just in case" the device is summoned—but they may not integrate well with existing systems, ultimately degrading the functioning of the system as a whole.

Often, we are not well informed about how (or how well) emergency media function, at a practical level. Instead, these media systems are omnipresent in references and cultural representations. News broadcasts, weather reports, true-crime television or podcasts, disaster films, medical dramas, postapocalyptic video games, and other cultural artifacts represent emergency and often incorporate emergency media as information or evidence, as in the 9-1-1 calls used in countless true-crime podcasts. From such sources, people cobble together assumptions, many rooted in childhood, about how emergency media works. Americans who grew up with the bleating of the tests of the radio and television Emergency Broadcast System, watched Saturday morning cartoons in which Sonic the Hedgehog explained 9-1-1 and discouraged prank calls,[66] or participated in nuclear attack, tornado, or fire drills at school may have a deep (but backgrounded) awareness of the media systems we are expected to rely on in emergency.

I use the phrase *infrastructure of feeling* to highlight how such cultural and material messaging can solidify affective understandings of safety or emergency, understandings which may come to deviate from how technologies of safety and emergency actually do or should operate. In using this term, I am obviously drawing on Raymond Williams's classic "structure of feeling," which scholars of affect often point to as a starting point for theorizations of intangible, felt elements of a culture.[67] Infrastructures of feeling concretize once-emergent structures of feeling by solidifying local policies, labor practices, and material artifacts in such a way as to render them more dominant, more persistent, and more tightly intertwined with surrounding cultures. The infrastructure of feeling around a given form of emergency media offers affective reassurance to its most-privileged audiences that can function as a distraction and uphold emergency's normalizing function. The effectiveness of infrastructures of feeling in providing reassurance or feelings of safety can, in turn, make it more difficult to recognize and change systems that are not functioning or may be functioning in such a way as to exacerbate the problems they claim to solve.

Emergency media do not operate autonomously, but through people's performance of what I call *emergency media work*. Emergency managers, 9-1-1 dispatchers, information technology specialists, and communications officers are just a few of the workers who produce and maintain emergency media, forging infrastructure as an assemblage of standards, material components, and human labor. Studies of information labor have made clear the infrastructural role of telegraph boys, telephone operators, and commercial content moderators and others whose labor is often invisibilized to foster an illusion of reliability or automation.[68]

The infrastructural labor of emergency is similar, but I argue that we have to move beyond conceptions of information work and processing to consider these jobs as *media work*. By media work, I mean to capture those kinds of labor that are fundamentally completed through media systems and involve the interpretation and production of media messages. Drawing on studies of media work within film and television studies, I argue that emergency media workers are performing similarly interpretive, creative, and communicative labor. When an emergency manager determines that an approaching snowstorm represents a threat and writes the brief message to be distributed by wireless emergency alert to all cell phones in her geographical area, her description, language, intensity, and instructions are deliberately chosen for the desired effect of encouraging people's action in what her message will declare to be an emergency. This is not an automatic process, but one in which best practices, personal style, and cultural competency can greatly affect the message's content and impact.

Through the technological, cultural, and labor dimensions of emergency media's infrastructures, it becomes clear that emergency media form a bridge between people's experiences and the feelings, actions, institutions, and responses that are possible. They are a point of articulation, a fulcrum between the individual and systemic, and the affordances and limitations of these media systems are conduits that shape the forms of aid and interaction that can occur. Though emergency media are often taken for granted, there is nothing inevitable about their technological, institutional, or cultural functions. They can be changed.

Researching Emergency

To document and make sense of contemporary emergency media requires multiple forms of information and analysis. This book draws on the following sources, in addition to secondary and critical literatures: media policy documents; popular news and entertainment texts; discursive and technological readings of hardware, apps, and technological infrastructures; in-depth interviews with professionals in government, emergency operations, and emergency app development; and archival research. Additionally, data from student focus groups conducted as part of a collaborative research project at the University of Virginia have been analyzed in chapters 2 and 3.

In presenting this qualitative research, I would be remiss not to the note the ways in which my particular standpoint has shaped the collection of materials, and particularly in the collection of interview data. I am a middle-aged, nondisabled, cisgender white woman who spent most of her life in the Midwest and is married with children; I am, in short, the very kind of person that many emergency systems in the United States are designed to serve. As a "nice white lady," I have undoubtedly had an easier time gaining access to some spaces and conversations than others would, and I have also likely not been able to access other knowledges about the workings of emergency media. In the process of doing this research, therefore, I have interrogated my qualitative data and my interpretive instincts through processes of triangulation.

Throughout, I supplement qualitative research on contemporary systems with analysis of historical examples. As cultural theorist Jennifer Darryl Slack argues, "contemporary uses often invoke ancient meanings,"[69] and today's emergency media often remediate or position themselves in opposition to earlier systems. Thus, to understand current emergency systems I have often looked backwards, to fire alarms, informal phone trees, and infamous personal emergency response systems ("I've fallen and I can't get up!") among other touchstones. This is not a comprehensive history of emergency media—that work remains to be done—but historical examples have evocative and explanatory value. Furthermore, this work is already historical, in one sense, because of its integration of material related to COVID-19. I have included analyses of such examples because they can speak to larger themes in the cultural meanings and functions of emergency media. Equally, however, these appear as a form of preemptive archiving, ensuring that the maps, contact trackers, and social media content that characterized life in the United States in 2020 and 2021 are recorded in a fashion.

In Case of Emergency is organized according to a loose typology of emergency media: alarms, maps, alerts, reports, and testimony. These categories attempt to separate various mediating functions in order to explore their relation to the production (and construction) of "emergency." As such, there are definite overlaps; a single technology of emergency media may contain multiple functions, as in the case of personal emergency systems, which are both alarms and locative systems. Furthermore, the media environment of emergency is not uniform. People's choices about models of smartphones, integration of smart home technologies, and granular decisions about apps and social media construct highly variable technological environments. Geographic location, ownership of spaces and technologies, embodied differences, and accessibility create divergent relationships of access.[70] These different arrangements highlight the importance of thinking deeply about emergency media in the contemporary American environment. These differences, chosen or enforced, can mean significant differences in the availability, effectiveness, and accountability of emergency services. My focus on mediating functions in the following chapters allows for the integration of wide-ranging forms of emergency media, from the well-known to the forgotten, in hopes of speaking to a range of emergency media assemblages.

Chapter 1 asks how media construct emergency. What makes a moment an emergency, and how do media figure in this moment? To answer, this chapter focuses on alarms. Alarms demonstrate emergency media's logistical function in constructing "emergency" by producing an intense affective "here and now" that demands action. Drawing on theories of logistical media and affect theory, this chapter begins to develop the concept of safety surveillance, a dynamic through which people enter into surveillant relationships with other people, companies, and technologies that are justified through "safety" and the avoidance (if not prevention) of emergency. These relationships often have the effect of disempowering the person whose safety is monitored, figuring them as always at risk, never safe or fully autonomous.

Safety surveillance is expanded in chapter 2, which focuses on maps as emergency media. Maps mediate emergency by indicating likely locations of impending danger, as in the case of weather maps showing the trajectory of a storm. In so doing, maps can construct the temporality and locality of emergency and provide affective reassurance of "safety" through contrast. Location and safety become, in some ways, equivalent. The use of location sharing and personal safety apps, most of which represent users on maps, further entrenches the imbalanced power relationships that characterize safety surveillance.

Chapter 3 focuses on alerts, informational messages that often come from authoritative sources attempting to define circumstances as emergencies in order to produce specific public actions. In addition to their affective power, alerts are informative, even instructive: "Traditionally, 'alerts' have been used to indicate that something significant has happened or may happen."[71] The first half of this chapter deals with official alerting systems, such as the federal Wireless Emergency Alert system and alerting systems in corporate or educational contexts, while the second turns to the novel uses of alerts for public health and protest during 2020. This chapter is the first to delve into the labor practices by which emergency is mediated, considering the emergency managers, communications officers, and other figures who decide when and how to alert their publics. I position this as the media work of interpretation and production, using critical literature based in media industries to suggest that even this most hierarchical form of emergency mediation is open to various forms of intervention and negotiation.

The focus on infrastructure and emergency media work carries into chapter 4, which uses reports (particularly via 9-1-1) to illustrate how media systems and their workers actively coproduce the phenomenon of "emergency." Reporting is shaped by technological and interpersonal means, meaning that some reports are recognized and treated as emergencies, some emergency reports (claims) are denied, and some reports are racist fabrications that produce disastrous outcomes. Thus, this chapter proposes that we consider infrastructures of feeling—the prominence, ubiquity, or reassurance offered by reporting systems—as hypervisible affective distractions from infrastructural failures and alternatives to emergency's normalizing function.

Finally, in chapter 5, I argue that some forms of emergency mediation may be understood as testimony that makes a bid for recognition of circumstances as evidence of a structural emergency. Often communicated by individuals, and often distributed and circulated on social media, testimony provides evidence in hopes of receiving attention or assistance from people other than official government bodies. This power of such testimony is such that many social media platforms have attempted to incorporate these functions, capturing them within ecosystems of data and safety surveillance. Yet, as seen in examples drawn from the Movement for Black Lives and mutual aid groups during the coronavirus pandemic, users' testimony and its emergency bids exceed the frames that these technology companies attempt to provide. Drawing from theorizations of media witnessing and testimony as well as historical examples, this chapter explores how testimony can challenge structures of emergency claims and response. In so doing, they can also define and enact emergency differently.

This destabilization of emergency's normalizing ideology is the focus of the conclusion, which looks to several more practical steps by which to engage with and reform emergency media, thereby denaturalizing the meanings of emergency. Emergency media are articulations of material and ideological forces that—to date—have promoted normalization and upheld structures of state, carceral, and social power. It is an articulation, it is a hinge. Unpinning mediations of emergency from their current legacies and rebuilding them with attention to care, vulnerability, and justice is one way to change not only our media, but our broader culture.

1

Alarm!

The Intensified Affect of Emergency

When Michael and Jessica Hughey were awakened by the sound of their four-year-old daughter screaming via a baby monitor, they assumed she had woken up from a nightmare. No fun, but likely not an emergency.

As the Hugheys walked to their daughter's room, a hallway smoke detector began to blare. Now, there was an emergency.

Fortunately, the Hugheys had recently established a fire safety plan. Their daughter stayed on her bed and called for her parents, enabling them to quickly remove her and use a fire extinguisher to put out the fire (caused by a malfunctioning humidifier). Michael Hughey observed, "How lucky we were that the monitor was on. . . . And [that] the smoke detector works. If those two things for whatever reason wouldn't have worked, it would have been a terrible situation that we don't even want to think what the future would look like."[1]

Both baby monitors and smoke detectors are easily ignored or even forgotten much of the time. Operating as a passive form of in-home surveillance, baby monitors are often understood as technologies of care, enabling parents (like the Hugheys) to be "good parents" by extending their awareness of their children's needs.[2] Smoke detectors, silent except in operation or when in need of maintenance, are home safety technologies that protect people and property by triggering loud blaring noises and sometimes flashing lights in response to smoke. Under normal—safe—circumstances, a smoke detector or fire alarm is silent, apparently inactive while monitoring.

The combination of passive surveillance and extreme display in activation is key to those emergency technologies—like baby monitors and smoke detectors—that we might categorize as *alarms*. Alarms offer awareness, not instructions; had the Hugheys not developed a fire safety plan with their daughter, she may have done any number of other, potentially dangerous things. Alarms act logistically, orienting a person or public spatially and temporality to a new state of shared events, affect, and activity. They attempt to produce an affective transition from normalcy to the intensified present of emergency. Alarms assert an intense "here and now," activating previously dormant affects based in risk, fear, or preparation for potential emergencies.

This chapter considers the functions and histories of alarms. I understand *alarms* to be nonlinguistic forms of emergency media—sounds, lights, buzzes and vibrations, ringing telephones—that can quickly foster a shift from normalcy into emergency through their activation. I draw on examples ranging from early fire alarms to burglar and home security alarms, late twentieth-century health monitors, and the multitudes of smartphone alarm systems. There are obviously important differences between types of alarms (and relevant time periods); today's surveillant, data-driven consumer home security systems, for instance, reflect a very different arrangement of ownership, agency, and power than do government-operated tornado sirens that hail and secure masses of people. Our ability to opt in, to control, to be served and simultaneously serve as producers of valuable data can seem both empowering and dystopian, offering increased safety while facilitating disengagement from public services and resources and handing unprecedented control of domestic space to distant corporations. Although emergency alarms certainly differ from one another, I examine them collectively in order to highlight the logistical and affective functions of alarms and the inequalities they may foster.

Logistically, alarms attempt to organize social life and flows.[3] They fulfill this logistical function, however, without communicating explicit information. From the simple alarm clock to municipal tornado sirens, the medium may be the message. Like McLuhan's illustrative electric light, visual, sonic, or haptic alarms may be said to lack "content."[4] Yet still, they are meaningful technologies, shaping "how things are in the world and how things are known."[5] They are not simple unitary signals, but complex, culturally situated artifacts. As such, alarms are a key form of emergency media for considering the role of affect—the ineffable potentialities that circulate among people and things—in emergency. An alarm can produce multiple overlapping affective states in its audience, some of which are the "toxic" emergency affects of fear or panic.[6]

But alarms function unevenly. Home security systems predominate in affluent neighborhoods where racialized fears of crime and the sheer value of property promote a desire for constant luxury surveillance and immediate awareness. When alarms sound frequently, they are nearly universally ignored, a phenomenon known as the "car-alarm effect." Furthermore, while alarms may monitor the world, they may also be turned on bodies—our own, or those of other people. The Hugheys' baby monitor, for instance, stood sentry over a child so that her parents could register and respond to the alarm. This is an example of what I refer to as *safety surveillance*, in which individuals are technologically monitored "for their own good" even as the alarm serves and empowers *others* to act and potentially objectifies or disempowers the person being monitored, reifying interpersonal or institutional power dynamics.

Sounding the Alarm

The bleating smoke detector that transformed a normal night at the Hugheys' into an emergency is a common safety feature in contemporary homes, businesses, and public spaces. Its noise is insistent and meaning seemingly obvious, but the function of such alarms ought not be taken for granted. A brief history of fire alarms and related devices demonstrates that while these alarms are nonlinguistic, they are nonetheless reflective of culturally situated knowledges about who is to be protected and how.

Fire alarms were among the first implementations of mediated emergency (and surveillant and normalized forms of safety). Early Gamewell fire alarms used the telegraph to transmit messages from stand-alone fire alarm boxes to local fire stations.[7] By the late nineteenth century, fire alarm designs incorporated push button bells that could replicate signals over distance, striking multiple bells throughout the system or even in firefighters' homes.[8] In the twentieth century, telephonic fire and police call boxes "were topped with lights that would flash upon activation" alerting not only authorities but the public of a state of emergency.[9]

Though public call boxes such as these functioned as alarms, their usage was neither obvious nor equitable. As media historian Rachel Plotnick demonstrates, knowledge of how to use a technology such as a push button was concentrated among those with the means for electrifi-

Figure 1.1. A man demonstrates activation of a telephonic fire callbox, ringing a physical bell and moving a handle, for an audience at the 1933 Indiana State Fair. Indiana Historical Society, P040.

cation or the opportunity to use such technologies in their workplace.[10] A photograph from the 1933 Indiana State Fair (fig 1.1) features a representative of Indiana Bell Telephone demonstrating proper operation of a telephonic fire alarm that has a bell, a light bulb, and a pull handle installed for simultaneous warning of the public and the fire department. The display and demonstration of this technology suggests there was a need for public education in the mediation of emergency; its uses were not self-evident. Furthermore, these alarm systems were not necessarily intended for public use. Even as call boxes proliferated on city streets, they were initially controlled through the limited distribution of callbox keys to trusted (white, male) citizens.[11]

The cultural education that occurred around fire alarms belies the naturalized view of alarms in much semiotic scholarship. Semiotician C. S. Peirce categorized signs into three categories: likenesses or icons, indications or indices, and symbols.[12] A fire alarm is an indication that shows "something about things, on account of their being physically connected to them."[13] Through this "pure demonstrative application of the sign,"[14] the fire alarm becomes useful. Its proximity to a fire itself—or even automaticity, in the case of modern smoke detectors—is precisely what makes it effective and what suggests that such signs sit outside the forms of meaning-making that characterize symbols or icons. Indications, for Peirce, garner attention but do not properly communicate.

Similarly, Valentin Voloshinov dismissed "signals" as fixed things that cannot "stand for anything else, or reflect or refract anything, but [are] simply a technical means for indicating this or that."[15] Unlike signs, which he considered a site of contestation and evolution of meaning in language and ideology, signals were merely "recognized."[16] Alarms— bells, horns, whistles, lights—were thus positioned semiotically as free from cultural or ideological content, taken for granted in their obvious connection to a phenomenon (such as fire).

The seeming obviousness of alarms ought to suggest not that they are free from ideological meaning, but rather that "the depth, the habituation, and the near-universality of the codes in use" in these systems can "produce apparently 'natural' recognition."[17] Alarms function logistically and affectively because their meaning is so deeply ingrained that it can be difficult to think of them outside of this context. Even in instances where sirens are incorporated into musical performances, for instance, "when we hear the wail of a siren, we understand it as a warning."[18] Thus, their use—whether in Black Sabbath's "War Pigs" or Beyoncé's "Ring the Alarm"—is often affectively literal, conjuring a sense of danger, intensity, conflict. Alarms may be a medium without a (semiotic) message, but alarms have nonetheless functioned to materially change what McLuhan refers to as "patterns of perception"[19] such that they produce cultural meaning.

Yet, the "near-universality" of such meanings is not totalizing. The establishment of alarms as indications of "danger" or "warning" occurred through uneven historical processes such as those that guided the deployment and usage of fire alarms through callboxes, push buttons, and later technologies such as smoke detectors.[20] Furthermore, alarms can fail. Their warnings can be missed, misinterpreted, or disregarded. This often happens through overuse, as anyone who has casually ignored a fire alarm after countless drills or false alarms can attest. It can also happen through inaccessibility, as alarms that rely on one or more senses may exclude and endanger people on the basis of disability or sensory capacity.

As indicated by the old phrase "sound the alarm," alarm systems often rely on sensory—especially audible—media. The loose public created among those who hear the alarm and enter a state of emergency is not merely geographically constituted, but sonically so; military fanfares, royal trumpeters, and church bells characterize the etymological history of "alarm."[21] Alarms are often predicated on a presumption that everyone will hear them and be made aware of relevant circumstances or required actions. What, then, happens to people who cannot hear an alarm?

The experiences of d/Deaf and disabled people indicate the limitations of even modern fire alarms in equitably warning people and enabling action in an emergency. For example, a deaf woman staying at a Norwegian hotel in 2007 explicitly confirmed with hotel staff that she would be informed by staff should a fire alarm occur, as the hotel did not have accessible alarms. Yet, she reports that "the fire alarm went off in the middle of the night and no one came to warn me,"[22] leaving her to wake up terrified and confused by fire trucks outside the building.

In the United States, the Americans with Disabilities Act addressed circumstances such as the hotel fire alarm by introducing requirements concerning the height and usability of alarm pulls, the positioning of audible warning alarms, and requiring the installation of strobe lights as supplementary visual alarms.[23] These visual strobes were required in public places and common areas, and compliance with requirements for visual alarms resulted in the need for more alarms (as light often cannot travel as far as sound within a building) and additional power supply.[24] Multimodal alarms (see figure 1.2) are now commonplace, but such ac-

Figure 1.2. Author's photograph of a fire alarm. A red casing houses a round speaker at the top, with a clear light housing below, and the word "FIRE" written in white at the bottom.

cessibility fixes do not negate the normalizing expectations built into alarms and the emergencies they indicate.

Fire alarms' meaning—a warning and implied demand for action—may also be disrupted when one cannot take the expected actions. American disability activist and wheelchair user Emily Ladau recalls

a frightening moment in high school when a fire alarm went off, but since I wasn't sure if it was a drill and I couldn't use the elevator, I had no choice but to shelter in place. While I watched every other able-bodied student file outside to safety, I sat there contemplating the fact that there was no plan in place to evacuate me.[25]

The association of the alarm with danger was not only clear but intensified for Ladau; without specific evacuation plans, the alarm signaled danger amplified by futility. Thus, alarms not only produce cultural meaning unevenly, but also produce variable affects, as explored in the following section.

Here and Now

In the mediation of emergency, alarms are a first stage, a calling-into-being of a state of danger, a warning about what is to come. As such, alarms offer an opportunity to think about the logistical and affective dimensions of emergency media. When they are "on," they create *an intense present of the "here and now."* When they are "off," they might as well not exist. Alarms are intrusions, reminders, prompts specifically designed to rupture the normal state of affairs and to constitute "emergency publics" that experience and make sense of an emergency through available information and social structures.[26]

In doing so, many public alarms act as what John Durham Peters calls "logistical media," which set "the terms in which everyone must operate."[27] In their logistical functions, alarms "coordinate, capture, and control the movement of people, finance, and things,"[28] prompting evacuations, sheltering in place, and other pauses in the operation of business as usual.

To say that a medium is logistical is not to deny its cultural impact, but to highlight a specific component of its functionality and meaning. The example of the clock tower, which Peters explores in detail, is instructive; its function is temporal and spatial, orienting those in its surroundings to particular arrangements of time and geographical relationships. Clock towers are not neutral in their presentation or function; they, and other logistical media, "encode a subtle and deep political or religious partisanship."[29] Often tied to religious contexts or governmental buildings, clock towers themselves may be expressive of relations of power, cultural priorities, or even artistic and architectural schools of thought. In other words, how logistical media structures time and space, normalcy and emergency, varies according to the needs, expectations, and institutional powers of their context.

This variance in logistical function is clear in the evolution of the simple alarm clock with respect to temporality. Mechanical alarm clocks featured a small hammer that struck dual bells when the analog clock reached the selected time. The ringing bells disrupted sleep and brought one into chronologic time, a time of hours and minutes, school and work, outside of the timelessness of sleep or drowsing.[30] The introduction of the clock radio altered the logistical functions of the mechanical alarm clock, as one awoke directly in "the time of the radio, in the time of the media."[31] The alarm refigured temporality, extending beyond the individual or chronologic to initiate a simultaneous "immediate now" of broadcast media.[32] Today, both mechanical and clock radio alarm clocks are rare; many people rely on smartphones' alarm features or dedicated apps to not only awaken from sleep but to initiate sleep, monitor it, and improve it.[33] One is encouraged to optimize sleep, but more importantly one may structure waking around an "algorithmically determined 'smart wake up.'"[34] Unlike a circadian rhythm, a chronologic time, or a media time, the "smart wake up" professes to determine and enact an optimal alarm based on the use of various technologies to monitor sleep and determine "easy" or appropriate timeframes for waking. Both individuated and technologically dependent, the smartphone alarm offers new logistical features, a temporality initiated by the alarm system itself.

When an alarm sounds (or blinks or vibrates), it initializes an emergency affect based in an *intensified here* and *now*. At times, this connection is so intense that the distance between the emergency and its mediation seems to disappear: "Though I never saw a tornado, the siren's roar was terrifying. To me, the siren was the tornado."[35] The tornado alarm here triggered the *"affective fact* of the matter,"[36] a real sense of fear, anticipation, or panic in the face of warning that is experienced *whether or not* the tornado should ever materialize or strike. As argued by theorist Brian Massumi, affectively, an alarm is "immediately performative."[37] It calls into being a web of potentialities and emotional responses that contrast with a normal state of affairs. An alarm's mediation initiates a process of becoming otherwise, via what Patricia Clough calls the "imperceptible dynamism of affect"[38] that circulates between bodies, objects, and encounters. The alarm makes the emergency real by making it felt.

If the alarm's cultural signification is one of warning, its affect is one of *intensity*. Feminist theorist Sara Ahmed uses "intensity" to describe social spaces of heightened feeling, in which "shared feelings are at stake, and seem to surround us. . . . But these feelings not only heighten tension, they are also in tension."[39] Even when an emotion is given the same name, it is experienced differently and relationally by those involved. Thus, while alarms may conjure affects of fear or panic, such affect is unevenly distributed and experienced (recall young Emily Ladau waiting out a fire alarm with no means of evacuation).

While many affective states may be produced in the intensity of alarm, a dominant affect is likely that of fear or panic. Silvan Tomkins describes fear as a "toxic, emergency affect,"[40] an "overly compelling persuader" designed for crises.[41] Fear is unsustainable, or dangerous when sustained. Should it become panic—"affect with urgency but little discrimination"—it is unpredictable, isolating, and dangerous.[42] The space of fear is also a space of decisions. In finding shelter, evaluating options, following or avoiding a crowd, the intensity of fear or panic may produce actions that would otherwise be impossible or unthinkable.

The siren wails, the tornado is coming—or is it already here? Fear has both spatial and temporal dimensions; it is a feeling of fear coupled with anticipation of injury or threat. Fear "presses us into that future as an intense bodily experience in the present,"[43] creating an intensified and extended "now" with a focus on the near future. This "now" both is and is not "live," "immediate," and "ongoing." The "liveness" of broadcast media offers an immediate now, but it is also always already constructed as a "story," an attempt to narrate and thus place in the past.[44] Alarms do not narrate; in the absence of narration they offer duration, an ongoing warning of incoming threat. Digital media and flows foster a "real time" of immediacy and instantaneity,[45] in which flows of data and content stream in a mode of constant, placeless newness. Alarms are socially and geographically situated—often place-bound—and function as interruptions in the normal course of life; they are always "on" (monitoring) and nearly immediate, but their sounding marks a change rather than a continuity.

The *here* produced by alarms is often constructed through sonic space. The bell tower, historically a geographic center of many communities, was "traditionally used as a summons or alarm, for marking states of emergency"[46] that extend to all those who heard it. A tornado siren standing sentry at a centralized location in the Midwest is, like a clock tower in older times, positioned to sonically call its population to attention and action in case of emergency. Tornado sirens are civil defense technology repurposed for local use; the threat of tornado was much more salient than that of nuclear war for much of the central United States.[47] Since 1970, outdoor sirens have accompanied tornado warnings issued via broadcast media (and now text messages and weather apps).[48] Today, tornado sirens use a variety of tones of at least seventy decibels over a one-kilometer range.[49] Through sound, tornado sirens establish a shared spatial "here" of emergency affect, before and regardless of the danger of which they warn.

The spatiality of emergency's affect is as important as its temporality. As Ahmed indicates, "There is a relationship to space and mobility at stake in the differential organization of fear."[50] The tornado warning, with its implicit demand that people seek shelter in basements, hallways, or cars, attempts to produce fear (or caution) and restrict mobility in the interest of safety. Yet, some people feel the warning differently—rather than seek shelter, storm chasers use the information in a tornado warning to seek out, watch, or document the tornado itself. Fear produces a retreat or shrinkage of space; its absence enables expansion in space.[51] And just as power differentials enforce different experiences of time,[52] different relationships to structures of state, institutional, and interpersonal power may alter one's experience of space and location. When a tornado siren wails, those who live in mobile homes or impermanent shelters do not have the option of retreat to a secured basement. Fear here meets futility, a combination which can either intensify into panic or negate an emergency affect. When the danger cannot be avoided, what is the point of being afraid?

Theorizations of the ongoing or permanent temporality of emergency have tended to focus on a global scale: climate change, wars without end, disasters viewed from afar.[53] Such a scale undergirds what Richard Grusin terms "premediation," in which broadcast and online media attempt to preview and play out possible futures to prevent the unknowable immediacy of "real time."[54] Anders Ekström argues that contemporary media foster ever-closer connections between communications technologies and warning systems (as if they were ever truly separate), blending temporalities of forecast and suspense.[55] The shared, mediated emergency creates a kind of collective now and never, similar to what Massumi identifies as the temporality of preemption, in which threats are identified and nullified before they materialize.[56]

The intense here and now of emergency, however, may also be an individualized temporality, experienced alone or by only a few. The "now" "is not a reductive or single state but is multiple, diverse, different and differentiated, a series of compressed and paced qualities."[57] As argued by media theorist Sarah Sharma, technologies mediate "the relationship between culture and power, specifically in terms of time,"[58] constructing varied relationships to speed and slowness, waiting and acting. Time is not experienced uniformly but in specific relations to power and possibility.[59]

The "now" of emergency hits differently depending on access to aid or financial resources, the possibilities and constraints on action, and the commonality of crisis in one's daily life. For instance, emergency is less random, less ignorable, and more present in the lives of many disabled people than it may be to able-bodied or otherwise socially empowered individuals; so, too, then, is the ability to respond to emergencies in care and community a skill that can be built by those inhabiting recurrent times of emergency.[60] This is the burden and gift of "crip time," which "bends the clock to meet disabled bodies and minds,"[61] but which nonetheless necessitates a break from usual chronologic and cultural assumptions about daily life and the life course.[62]

Watching and Waiting

When an alarm sounds, its culturally situated meaning as warning is transmitted along with an affective construction of emergency as intensified here and now. We are warned, we are afraid, we are hailed into a time and space of possible danger that requires action and awareness. However, the affective dimensions of emergency are not only in play when an alarm is active. Like the historic bell towers, which became understood as "catastrophic places of danger, emergency, and death"[63] even when silent, alarm systems also participate in a circulation of affect that extends and persists beyond mere moments of use.[64] An alarm is normally silent. In times of non-use, they contribute to the construction of normalcy itself through the absence of the (exceptional) alarm and its affective emergency. If the alarm is emergency, is its absence safety?

Many alarms function as what Charles Acland and Haidee Wasson have termed "useful media," acting as "a tool that makes, persuades, instructs, demonstrates, and does something."[65] Though they focus primarily on cinema adapted to useful ends, Acland and Wasson provide a compelling reminder that when media are made useful, they often act in the interests and at the discretion of existing institutions of power. "Useful" is, as Sara Ahmed describes, "an adjective with a job description."[66] Useful media has things to do, and alarms are certainly useful in providing warning, protecting people or property, and producing affect and action.

But during periods of silence, an alarm might be thought of as "unused" or "out of use." In tracing these and other states of use, Ahmed demonstrates that objects move in and out of use, are used and worn down, or may be strengthened through use. Things that are unused, she argues, might be "yet to be used," but they could also "become unused" when their use is stopped.[67] Alarms seem to become unused—out of use, retired—in their silence, as they have stopped (or not yet started) making themselves known.

Of course, an alarm that is not sounding is still "in use," meaning that it could be used even if it is not currently being used.[68] It is simply in a different mode, waiting. Waiting to sound is, in fact, the most common state of an alarm. Waiting, media scholar Jason Farman argues, is not merely an in-between time but is a time and space of becoming;[69] as we wait alongside our alarms, for a signal that has not (yet) arrived, we collectively become assured of a kind of safety. Through their silent sentry, alarms become naturalized parts of everyday life, unremarkable and silent signals of safety that repel the fearful affect of emergency. If, as Massumi argues, the instant alarms "'show,' we are startled,"[70] perhaps when they hide themselves, unused, we are reassured that all is well.

Media scholars have approached questions of use from the perspective of non-users, people who opt not to use a given media for various reasons.[71] Non-users may resist a technology and never use it, stop use voluntarily or involuntarily, or be excluded from use by cost or other barriers.[72] Non-users are generally marginal to media studies literatures; non-use may be even more so. Why, after all, study a medium that is not or cannot be used? Sally Wyatt argues that by overanalyzing use and users, "we implicitly accept the promise of technology and the capitalist relations of its production"[73]; focusing only on use assumes that use (or access) is inherently beneficial. To ask about media non-use, or media that is unused, is to ask about where media fails, how, and with what effects.

Use is therefore a fruitful perspective to apply to alarms and other emergency media systems. Their benefits are attached to their waiting, watching, sensing, and surveillance as much as to their sounding. In an ideal world, alarms might never sound, unused; that they are nonetheless available, ready to spring into use, allows us to stave off feelings of uncertainty or danger, as the surveillant, out-of-use alarm offers its protection. Furthermore, some alarms are themselves based in the un-usability of other media. Interruptions in mediation may signal the need for a warning or produce the warning in question via an automated alarm.

The history and operation of tornado sirens offers an interesting example of how unused media can be productive of alarms and emergency. In 1883, Edward S. Holden proposed a tornado warning system in *Science*, which was tested experimentally but never implemented. Instead of relying on decrees from a weather service or other authority, Holden's system attempted to discern and act upon "a wind of a destructive force."[74] It consisted of

> a line of telegraph wire around the west through south-southwest directions from a town, at a radius of 2 to 2.5 miles. The line would be grounded at each end, and connected to a battery at the telegraph office which would provide a constant current through the line. The telegraph line would also have a connection in houses within the town, to an apparatus containing a bell, which rings using a coiled spring (similar to an alarm clock), and a magnet that prevents the bell from ringing as long as current flows through the wire. If the circuit were broken, the current would stop and the bell would begin to ring.[75]

Should the wind exert sufficient force to break the circuit by blowing a board attached to the telegraph pole far enough to snap a wire, the bells would begin to ring (or a cannon could be fired, warning people outdoors).[76]

Holden's system was based on rendering a media infrastructure literally unusable in order to trigger a sonic alarm system and provide warning of dangerous winds or a tornado. While it was not implemented, its logic persists: today, weather-related interruptions of electric lines that do not resolve themselves ("lockouts") are taken as a strong indication of the need to issue a tornado warning.[77] Here, unusable media itself becomes an indication of emergency; the emergency is the alarm.

When alarms are understood as functional useful media, active but not sounding, they convey not emergency but assurance. In short, the alarm is waiting, and is watching; when it is on but not active, in use but not being used, the alarm fosters a surveillant normalcy that can be interpreted as safety. Such "safety surveillance" and its affect of reassurance is the focus of the final section of this chapter. In the case of personal health alarms, how—and for whom—does reassurance provide a sense of safety?

Safety Surveillance and Non-Use

Many private alarms—home smoke detectors, smart wake up apps, and varied health and fitness monitors—are designed for non-use. They require little setup or maintenance, and are then expected to wait, to watch, and to fade into the background when not in use. For instance, in 2016, Apple Inc. was granted a patent for a feature that could turn an iPhone or other device into an active health monitor and alarm system. Titled "Care Event Detection and Alerts," the patent proposed that when a "care event" transpired—such as a vehicular accident, lost child, fall, or mugging—the system could contact a user-defined "care list" including family, friends, and emergency services, even if the user was incapacitated.[78] The patent, illustrated with a sketch of a jogging woman in addition to several technical flow charts referring to a "cooperative electronic device," seemed designed for implementation into the Apple Watch.[79] It suggested a future in which the Apple Watch would enable individuals to not only track their daily activities, but to actively protect and ensure a particular form of safety for its users by sounding the alarm when users could not.

In its operation, this Apple patent strongly resembled an older form of personal alarm technology, the personal emergency response system (PERS). Best remembered through unintentionally campy advertisements—"I've fallen and I can't get up!"—PERS devices were sold by companies such as LifeCall, Lifeline, and several others during the late twentieth century.[80] These systems used a wireless radio transmitter (often worn as a pendant) to connect individuals to a monitoring center via their landline telephone. The monitoring center would have a file of information on subscribers, including telephone numbers for local emergency services and contact information for family or neighbors, enabling them to send help quickly.[81] Several PERS companies are still in operation, and many now offer smartphone apps as well as the classic pendant system.

Both the Apple and Lifeline systems foster a form of ongoing surveillance that offers to protect the wearer with little action on their part; non-use—or a "passive alarm"—is a valued component of these alarm systems. In a 1976 patent for an "automatic telephone alarm system," James Dibner—often considered the inventor of the PERS—suggested that an alarm system might rely on a twenty-four-hour timer and magnetic tape player attached to a telephone handset.[82] If a user went a full twenty-four hours without lifting the telephone handset, the system would trigger a phone call to local authorities and the tape player would play a prerecorded message requesting help at the appropriate address.[83] This patent structured the emergency alarm entirely around an absence of mediation; like the snapped telegraph wire of Holden's tornado alarm, the interruption in mediation would initiate an emergency. Regular telephone use was the normative foundation of this design, reflecting a world in which 95 percent of American households had landline telephone service and telephone calls were commonplace.[84]

While landline telephone use is no longer so standard, there are many similar passive alarms that promise to provide safety and assurance to elderly adults through common technologies, recognizing the fear of accident or emergency that might be felt by "old or infirm people who live alone . . . unable to summon help, and perhaps expiring or suffering irremediable damage because they may not be found for days."[85] Apple Inc.'s 2019 patent for fall detection in a wearable device (like an Apple Watch) features a system in which a mobile device would detect a fall, connect to the user's information in the cloud, and send notifications to "one or more users (e.g., caretakers, physicians, medical responders, emergency-content persons, etc.)."[86] Like the PERS, this feature is intended to allow "the aging and infirm to live independently without this fear"[87] of injury, emergency, disconnection.

But while promising to assuage the fears of users, there is some evidence that monitors like this actually provide reassurance and a sense of safety to *others* through the silence of the alarm. The "user" of the PERS or the Apple technology is more precisely understood as the "wearer," subject to a safety surveillance that extends beyond the device to include a group of responsible parties: professionals, family members, corporate representatives. These others are also "users," empowered to track and react to the information conveyed by the health monitor. The techno-

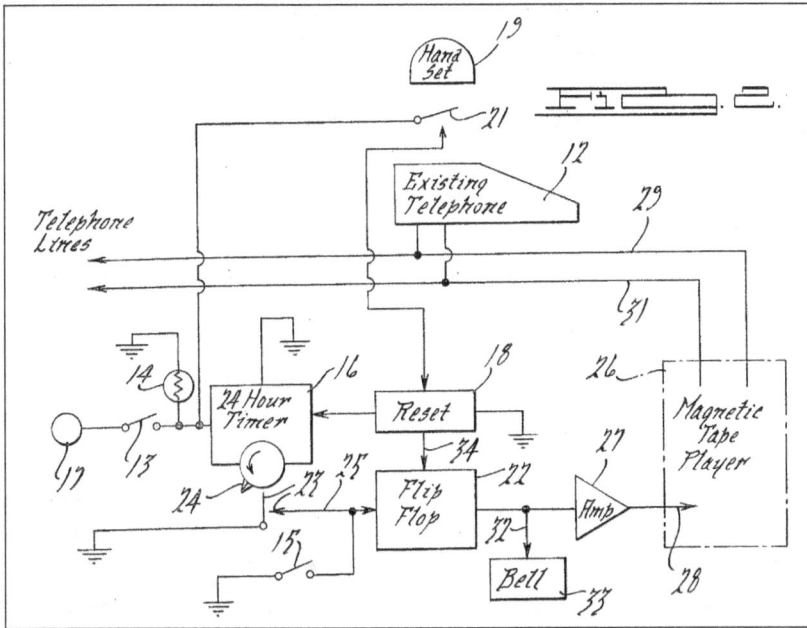

Figure 1.3. Image from 1976 patent for an "automatic telephone alarm," showing a twenty-four-hour timer integrated with the telephone infrastructure.

logical surveillance is tightly connected to a social system and attendant power dynamics.

The marketing of PERS systems illustrates this imbalance, as it was aimed primarily at families, caregivers, or residential institutions that surrounded the wearer. Sandy Markwood, the CEO of the National Association of Area Agencies on Aging, explains that many inquiries about PERS devices "come from the caregivers asking what would happen to Mom or Dad if they fell. . . . These devices provide a sense of relief for them."[88] The confidence and relief invoked in such statements are likely meant to reassure adult children that a PERS could ease their feelings of worry or unease technologically. This contrasts with the feelings of the primary users (wearers), who often objected to the look, feel, or invasive nature of the device.[89]

In such statements lies what surveillance scholar David Lyon identifies as a tension between "care and control,"[90] as individuals who adopt these technologies become subject to a form of technologically enabled social surveillance that monitors their bodies while producing copious amounts of data to which wearers often lack access. Even the emergency alarms triggered by these systems are not always for the wearer, but for the benefit of those chosen to be reassured of their well-being. The elderly parent who wears a device is not only a user but is also and primarily the phenomenon being monitored; the silence of the alarm for others offers reassurance that all is well.

Herein lies the crux of what I call *safety surveillance*. These are opt-in services (often for-profit), justified in terms of "health and safety,"[91] that involve ongoing passive surveillance punctuated by alarms or other activations should an emergency be detected. Safety surveillance is intensely social and affective; it is often entered into collectively, with the intent of mutual care. Nonetheless, power dynamics of the family or community color safety surveillance, as some individuals become targets of benign surveillance and others take on a surveilling role in concert with the technology.

In this way, it resembles what internet scholar Tama Leaver calls "intimate surveillance," which involves "close and seemingly invasive monitoring" of infants by their parents.[92] Leaver argues that infant wearables (such as the Owlet foot monitor) normalize "the idea that digital surveillance of infants equates with care and good parenting."[93] Affects of care and protection are marshaled to justify intimate surveillance, which in turn fosters the production and collection of data by corporate parties. Leaver is particularly concerned that these dynamics might persist throughout a child's life, with unknown effects; in the history of the PERS, however, it is clear that the linkage of care and surveillance via technology had already been long applied to elderly family members. Like intimate surveillance, safety surveillance employs an affective rhetoric of care, and is invested in the reassurance of those other than the person being surveilled; the silence of the Owlet, the PERS, and the Apple Watch is a sign of normalcy and safety.

Safety surveillance is thus reliant on the use and non-use of its alarms. While the reassuring sense of safety offered by unused alarms would seem to be a bulwark against the affective state of emergency, it simultaneously fosters awareness of possible threats and their affective facts. Such surveillant alarms may thus both stoke and calm fears, requiring people to acknowledge the possibilities of danger in order to protect themselves from it. This is complicated by the power dynamics inherent in family and other close relationships. As feminist surveillance studies reminds us, issues of domestic violence alter the nature of privacy and surveillance;[94] the automatic notification of a former partner or angry family member in the event of a health crisis is a site where safety surveillance might become malign. I further explore the uneven power dynamics and datafied nature of safety surveillance in the next chapter, in which maps are similarly used to reassure people of the safety of their loved ones.

Conclusion

This chapter has explored how alarms' meaning and affective circulation produce emergency and normalcy (sometimes simultaneously). In an alarm—a light, a wail, a buzz—we are made aware of circumstances that may justify affectively moving into a time and space of emergency. Many of the examples in this discussion were historical, illustrating the continuities of alarm media in their mediation of emergency. However, these dynamics not only persist but may be intensified in an environment of rampant datafication and consumer convenience.[95]

The Hugheys credited their baby monitor and fire alarm with their safety, springing into use when needed. However, the Hugheys did not appear to have fully integrated the technological logics of safety surveillance into their home, as seen in the integrated emergency media infrastructures of smart home systems. Exemplified by services such as Google's Nest Protect, Amazon's Ring technologies, or the SimpliSafe package of sensors and cameras, smart home security systems bring together features of burglar alarms, smoke detectors, and security cameras, along with thermostats, locks, and smart appliances (including baby monitors). With such integration, the alarm may be deferred, but safety surveillance and its logics of fear and reassurance extend into daily life.

A fire alarm becomes avoidable: Nest Protect (owned by Google) offers a pricey smart smoke alarm and carbon dioxide detector that uses wirelessly connects to a Nest app on the user's phone. In the event of an alarm, it first contacts the user via phone, enabling one to quickly turn off the siren in case of accidental activation. Rather than the automaticity of alarm and warning, the user has the option to preempt the alarm's sounding. Similarly, the Ring Alarm Smoke and CO Listener offers a makeshift solution. Not a sensor but a listener, this device sends smartphone alerts when it registers the sonic alarm of existing smoke and carbon monoxide alarms, enabling someone to know of an alarm even when they are not in the space of emergency.[96]

A home security system becomes constant reassurance: SimpliSafe and Amazon Ring both offer doorway cameras that enable constant sight and on-demand recording. This form of luxury surveillance is clearly appealing to those with wealth to protect, using discreet cameras rather than more overt signs of security.[97] As always, these systems stoke "fantasies about reasserting control over domestic space" in often racialized and classist ways,[98] even as they justify themselves through rhetorics of care and protection of those closest to you. These systems, ostensibly optional consumer goods, generate extended infrastructures through which Ring camera footage appears on sites like Ring TV for public consumption and is easily shared with police departments.[99] The expansion of Ring is not a matter of individual decisions, but of an expanding infrastructure of police surveillance; once again, the user is only nominally empowered by safety surveillance that extends far beyond their home and personal technology. These systems depend on and produce fear in order to sell reassurance, and customers who buy in find themselves part of obfuscated data regimes that perpetuate structural violence.[100]

Smart alarms render emergency—and safety—potentially available for constant interaction and concern. These systems are so usable, so available, so seamlessly integrated into a landscape shaped by consumer technology that reassurance requires not simply non-use but the possibility of constant (or at least regular) use to produce the same affective safety. Rather than waiting for the activation of a fire alarm by a waiting smoke detector, the Nest Protect allows me to click and check: Is it on? Is it working? Is anything happening? As these technologies integrate more and more features to be checked—SimpliSafe now offers warnings of home flooding, for instance—they foster a form of safety surveillance that constructs safety not only through silence but also through constant technological vigilance. If the alarm never sounds, because we have watched and been watched by it so efficiently, is the emergency nowhere or everywhere?

Historically, alarms have functioned as a warning, moving people into a time and space of emergency, with all of its attendant logistical and affective implications. This transition has been facilitated by the combination of alarms' moments of non-use and their soundings; a normalcy of silence and reassurance, punctuated by moments of sensory input and emergency. Increasingly, however, alarms' times of non-use are being captured and displayed by digital technologies, enabling reassurance itself to become the focus of these emergency media. Here, safety surveillance emerges as a new dynamic of emergency media, which monitors individuals' bodies and surroundings ostensibly for their own safety but equally for the reassurance of others and the enrichment of the technology companies who collect and store data in the name of safety.

2

Maps and the Affective Surveillance of "Safety"

When the Category 4 Hurricane Florence approached the coast of North Carolina in September 2018, the National Weather Service advised residents to evacuate in advance of what would become the ninth-most destructive hurricane to hit the United States.[1] In the days leading up to landfall—and the weeks that followed—many used social media to document their evacuation, their time away, their eventual return, and recovery from Florence's damage to local homes and infrastructures. As part of this documentation, many users of Instagram—a social media site already based on sharing photos—repurposed images of online or televised weather maps, adding slight adjustments and original captions.

One Instagram user chose a still image of a radar weather map (uncredited and undated) that showed the strength of rains throughout North and South Carolina, and into Tennessee and Georgia. On this image, the user drew a purple circle using annotation features either within Instagram or native to their phone, indicating a place on their route where they had barely made it through a flooded city. The use of the map lent credibility to their own description of a weather-related emergency, bolstering observations and feelings with data, through the evidence of location. Although the map alone would have been useful to the user (and others) in the moment in which it was live, its later repurposing for social media content reveals the ongoing relevance of maps, which foster overlaps of information and affect, conveying not only what happened but how it felt.

Maps—and locative data displayed as maps—are omnipresent features of mobile media. The integration of GPS technology in smartphones and attendant apps has made the collection and use of location data commonplace, as telecommunications and technology companies—and whomever they sell data to—harvest and make use of locational information.[2] From getting real-time directions to using a phone's location history to track events, photos, and social media behavior, the extraction and redisplay of locative information is a core smartphone feature. Most commonly, these technologies display locative data in either static or real-time GPS maps, segmented to center the user's position on a screen-sized rectangle, providing little broader context. Countless third parties collect and repurpose location data as well, enabling a rise in mapping as a means of representing what is happening and where by countless services, including traffic apps, weather apps, social media platforms, and apps and services that focus on emergency warning, services, and prevention.

Heavily naturalized through their familiarity and repeated use, maps are nonetheless deeply political in their construction. As design and information critic Johanna Drucker argues, maps "construct normative notions about time, space, and experience that become so familiar we take them for accurate representations rather than constructions."[3] Maps make information actionable, informing our decisions and feelings. This amplifies their normalizing function, as they are not merely images but contexts for action. The weather map of Florence, recontextualized on Instagram, might have previously influenced decisions about whether and when to relocate and influenced the user's choice of driving route, only to be used retroactively to express the fear of that experience. Broadly speaking, maps can affect our sense of our own and others' safety, and are routinely used to justify personal, institutional, and governmental decisions about what is and is not evidence of emergency. They are interpretations that shape knowledge and actions in the face of emergency and that feed our desire for reassurance and feelings of safety.

Maps function as both informational and affective forms of emergency media, conveying not only what is (or may be) happening, but how we might (or ought to) feel about it. Informationally, maps are visualizations of time, space, and their relationships to other forms of data. Affectively, maps may indicate literal approaching danger, activating fear and the intensity of emergency affect. They help to produce the affective "here" of emergency, though their temporal orientation may reflect the past, present, or (hypothesized) futures. Maps can convey where (and sometimes when) emergencies are likely to occur, as in the case of maps that forecast dangerous weather systems. Maps can also be powerful visualizations of normalizing ideologies of danger and safety, as mapping makes sense of space in relation to social values. Thus, maps may mark areas as more or less safe, as in mappings of crime statistics, red light districts, school districts, or wealth distribution, though such maps should always be interrogated for how they conceive of risk, and for whom. Alternative sets of social values may also be expressed through maps, as in projects that crowdsource accessible or trans-friendly bathrooms, using cartography to link locations to local knowledge for the use of people who need access to such spaces.[4]

This chapter considers maps as a form of emergency media. First, I examine smartphone features and apps that use maps to express locative safety (and its opposite, emergency); drawing on qualitative research with young adult users of these systems, I interrogate the dynamics of reassurance and power that are evident in safety surveillance facilitated by maps. These real-time mapping systems often build on (or replicate) static maps of safety features. Thus, I next turn to the historical maps and infrastructures of blue light emergency phones on college campuses. These phones, and their mapping, produce what I call "infrastructures of feeling," hypervisible media infrastructures that build in ideologies about emergency, safety, and social dynamics, making them affectively powerful and difficult to change. Finally, I turn to weather maps and the maps used to visualize various rates and risks of COVID-19. Easily dismissed as purely informative, these maps also contribute to the felt dimensions of emergency experience.

This chapter, in addressing maps as emergency media, ranges across very different forms of mapping, each with their own contexts, logics, and ideological histories. By addressing them together, as a form of emergency media, I do not mean to diminish these differences or to suggest that they all operate in the same manner. Differences in how maps are created and in what context, in their degree of authority or availability, and in their intended and actual audiences abound, and all of these differences are tied to the different relations of power that various maps may exert. By bringing varied forms of mapping together to discuss their function as emergency media, I attempt to demonstrate commonalities in their growing use as mediations of emergency. Ultimately, this chapter asks how maps set the terms of engagement for daily life and how they might undermine it, putting people at risk.

Maps as Reassurance

The rise of GPS-enabled locative media services that "rely on information about location in order to function and provide the user with an augmented sense of space and place"[5] has led countless apps and built-in smartphone features to use this data as the basis for safety or emergency applications. Many forms of locative media offer self- and social surveillance for navigational, entertainment, social, and commercial purposes; it is no surprise they should also be used for safety surveillance. For instance, Apple's built-in iOS app "Find My," which combines earlier "Find My Phone" and "Find My Friends" apps, allows iPhone users to give one another ongoing access to their phone's location data, expressly to "keep in touch with one another, coordinate around an event, or know when a family member has arrived home safely."[6]

Locative media routinely collect data about users' location and movement and use mapped displays either to provide reassurance through evidence of normalcy or to indicate emergency through evidence of unusual behavior. These maps can offer reassurance that a space is safe, or that someone is where they are "supposed" to be, where they are known to be safe. When that normalcy is disrupted, technologized forms of safety surveillance often infer a state of emergency and encourage users to do the same.

Use patterns surrounding locative safety media illustrate the centrality of affects of emergency and reassurance to this technology. In 2019, as part of an interdisciplinary research project focused on technology and perceptions of safety on college campuses, colleagues and I conducted eight focus groups and three in-depth interviews with undergraduate students at a mid-sized public university.[7] In these conversations, young adults reported routinely using Find My, as well as family apps such as Life360, the mapping features of Snapchat and Facebook Messenger, and location-tagged Instagram posts to communicate location information to their friends, particularly on weekend nights.

Often, the choice to take up technologies of safety surveillance was made on the basis of *possible* emergencies. Research participants routinely explained their own and others' choice to use this technology in terms of either specific cases of violent crime, or with vague language that invoked the threat of crime.[8] For instance, Ella explained that she would share location information with friends and acquaintances before going out on the town, later looking "to make sure that everyone's on the map. So at the end of the night you can be like, 'Okay, everyone's in their dorms. There's no one, like, far away in a river.'"[9] Ella's explanation invokes a vision of danger familiar from fictional or true crime stories, a bogeyman against which the map provides affective reassurance of ongoing safety and normalcy. As told by young adult participants, their parents' rationales for safety surveillance via locative technologies more often included specific details of crimes committed in local areas or against college students. Among young people themselves, the threat of emergency was often minimized or described flippantly, while the ability to offer map-based reassurance was presented as evidence of care for others.

Safety surveillance via locative safety services was commonly justified as a form of care. Being able to see others' locations was described as a source of "comfort" or as a way of preventing "scary" situations in which someone's whereabouts were unknown. Many students expressed having acquiesced to safety surveillance explicitly because they knew it would be reassuring for their parents (particularly mothers). As one young white woman explained, "My mom, she uses [location tracking], and I realize it's for safety reasons . . . it's just for, like, her comfort, to know this is where I'm at."

Among minoritized participants, dynamics of care were particularly important justifications for engaging with safety surveillance; knowing where people were was a means of caring for them within a campus or community space perceived as potentially unsafe. Members of close-knit communities, such as campus ethnic and religious clubs, described routinely activating Find My features to be sure that they could check up on one another (and particularly on younger students). One young woman of color described using Snapchat maps because it reassured her of her friends' safety, but also because "it makes me feel safe too if I see more of my friends around the area." Locative maps enabled minority students to map out spaces that were "theirs," where they felt at home and safe, versus spaces that were perceived as "belonging" to the majority-white student body. This recalls Germaine Halegoua's findings that marginalized populations were most likely to describe their use of mobile navigation in terms of "alleviating fear, feeling safe, and managing risk."[10] Locative surveillance, for Halegoua's participants, enabled them to construct a sense of safety by providing them with knowledge of their surroundings. Safety surveillance similarly constructs safety through location, promoting knowledge of *others' locations* as that which will enable people within families, friend groups, or communities to exhibit care for one another's safety and well-being with the help of digital technologies. Not only a spatial self but a spatial *us* can be created through locative safety technologies.[11]

Yet, for all of the reassurance offered by locative safety services, it is important to remember the other side of safety surveillance; its justification in terms of care can easily slide into an overreaching exercise of power by those already empowered within family or community relationships. In a fairly benign example, one male participant explained that his mother routinely checks on family members' locations. Thus, when he overslept one morning (missing a usual activity), his mother called immediately to ask why he was still in his apartment. In this case, the mother was not worried about danger, per se, but nonetheless took the map's evidence of an abnormal morning as an indication of circumstances that required action (a possible emergency). When "normal" behavior was absent, an affect of emergency was triggered, leading to what many could consider an overreach into her son's private life.

Such oversight reinforces the unequal power dynamics of most safety surveillance technologies, which position some users as "watched" while others "watch." The "watchers" are most commonly those with a higher degree of financial or social capital within a relationship, who are looking over others for "their own good" even as doing so may be affectively self-serving, enabling them to demonstrate care and receive reassurance. Unsurprisingly, focus group participants were more comfortable talking about themselves when in the role of watcher, caring for friends, than when discussing the possibility that they were also being monitored in this way. Safety surveillance empowers the watchers; participants rarely expressed feeling safer because they knew that others were actively monitoring their locations.

These dynamics led some student participants to reject safety surveillance, using alternate means to communicate, "forgetting" to turn on location sharing, or more forcefully objecting to be watched. Many students described agreed-upon uses of social media that avoided ongoing surveillance in favor of discrete choices to share information. For example, students would prearrange to text one another either when arriving or departing from their homes. Others, particularly women, also described using their phones to call friends, parents, or partners while walking home at night because it "made it feel less spooky." In these moments, the text or phone call functions as an indication of safety without necessitating location sharing with peers or third-party technologies, or even disclosure of where the person in question actually was and why. By relying on active choices to inform one another of location and safety, these practices worked against the assumptions about normalcy, space, and emergency that undergird many personal safety technologies.

Several participants, notably, framed rejection of safety surveillance as a matter of care or maturity. One woman of South Asian descent explained that her parents would worry if they saw her actual comings and goings, so she turned location sharing off for their own good. For other young people, rejecting safety surveillance serves as a sign of maturation, as suggested by Tama Leaver's research on the datafication of childhood.[12] Reviews of the Life360 app, a family-oriented location and information sharing platform, demonstrate this disavowal. A sizable minority of reviews by what seem to be teenagers and young adults ask how to turn off tracking, decry the app as invasive and creating "a toxic environment within families," and leave corresponding one-star reviews. Research participants raised Life360 as something that they were "put through" and were grateful to be done with, even as they continued to use Find My and social media platforms to monitor peers' locations in the interest of safety.

Given the power imbalance in safety surveillance, the reassurance that it offers can easily be abused, disempowering those who are being monitored by making them into objects of data collection and often invisible surveillance. This makes it a particularly insidious form of surveillance, easily converted to manipulation or even domestic violence, as in examples of literal gaslighting in which abusers remotely tracked their partners and then used smart home technologies to manipulate lights, temperature, or locks.[13] Safety surveillance can replicate and retrench power dynamics of the home or other institution, as employers watch workers, universities their students, and so on. This dynamic of safety surveillance raises questions about the efficacy and ethics of commercial and institutional safety apps, such as the safety software suites colleges and universities increasingly rely on to manage a range of safety-related resources. These platforms, such as LiveSafe or Rave Guardian, offer alerting and reporting features for campus officials, as well as student- and public-facing apps through which people can contact police, find resources, and more.[14]

Many of these platforms offer an escort feature, in which a user can select another person to "watch" them walk home, either in-app or via text messages that link to an external map application. Escort features generally enable the watching party to see as the user's location changes, a blue locative dot gliding across a street map. The escort feature is presented by these companies as a map-based remediation of normalized earlier behaviors—such as calling and talking to someone as you walk home at night—that builds engagement among users who otherwise might avoid an app advertised as only for emergencies.[15]

Stand-alone safety escort apps have also emerged, often incorporating additional biometric monitoring via data from smartphones' accelerometers and gyroscopes. This enables tracking changes in speed, falls, and pauses; these departures from "normal" spatial and temporal progress along a route are interpreted as possible emergencies. These incidents trigger countdowns during which the user can disable an automatic call to either 9-1-1 or preselected emergency contacts. If the user does not stop the countdown, the app makes automatic calls, initializing an emergency response. Such features are obviously ill equipped to recognize differences due to disability, gait, pace, mobility devices, or other physical and material features that affect one's movement through space. The result is the potential to trigger emergency states due to misalignment of the individual and the locative data.

Escort apps rely on normalcy to recognize emergency. In doing so, they often rely upon a normative, nondisabled vision of the user, and upon racialized and gendered notions of safety. This is evident, for instance, in advertising for a now-defunct app called Companion, developed by students at the University of Michigan in 2015. In all promotions, the user of the escort service was imagined as a young woman, reinforcing assumptions that women are at particular risk of violence (especially sexual assault) when in public after dark.[16] If college women were understood as victims, from whom were they at risk? Companion constructed risk through its interface and marketing as being anything *not* associated with a university environment. The app asked users to indicate places or behavior that seemed "sketchy"—itself a racially and economically loaded term—and was working toward data sharing with local police departments to increase policing of such "sketchy" areas.[17] The benevolent safety surveillance promised by the app's marketing transitioned seamlessly into a form of police surveillance carried out via consumer technologies.

Safety apps and escort features deploy maps as means of reassurance and treat deviations from expected behaviors as signs of emergency. They rely on normalized forms of identity in terms of how they construct risk, danger, and movement through space, and demonstrate how what mobile media theorist Jason Farman calls our "sensory-inscribed experiences" of locations have "everything to do with the representations we interact with of those spaces."[18] The relations between bodies, spaces, and technologies in relation to safety and crisis are shifting, and locative media concretizes them through maps in such a way as to comfort some and objectify others for intimate or carceral surveillance. We might ask of this technology: who is to be kept safe, and from whom?

Campus Maps and Infrastructures of Feeling

Many of the safety apps that serve universities or target young adults invoke an earlier technology of safety surveillance: according to the *New York Times*, they "seem like digital updates of 'blue light' poles, the campus phone stations that college students have used for years to summon help or report an emergency—often after a problem has already occurred."[19] These phones, installed beginning in the 1980s primarily in outdoor, high-traffic areas, often featured a blue light atop a pole that housed either a telephone or push button that directly connected the user to campus or local police (see figure 2.1). This highly visible infrastructure served—and still serves—not only to assuage concerns about campus safety (particularly sexual assault) but to concretize that once-emergent structure of feeling in such a way as to render it more dominant, more persistent, and more tightly intertwined with local campus cultures.

Tracing the history of blue light phones requires the use of a broad archive of materials related to campus life, including student newspapers, funding records, maintenance archives, student council discussions, and publicity materials.[20] Maps, however, are a particularly evocative demonstration of how a technology of safety surveillance grew and became normalized while instantiating particular ideas about who was and was not safe, where, and why.

The location of emergency "call boxes" on a 1987–88 bicycle safety map produced by the University of Colorado Boulder is typical of early installations, emphasizing placement of phones (and thus assumptions about possible emergencies) in high-traffic, low-visibility locations such as on the path through the quad, at the alumni center, near the student recreation center, and on a road near large athletic fields.[21] Figure 2.1 shows a simplified version of this map, with two new phones added to the east side of campus. This placement reflects the often linked concerns about safety, lighting, and sexual assault that drove many conversations about student safety and emergency technologies through the 1980s and 1990s.[22]

Such placement of blue light phones is also evident in the historical maps of blue light emergency phones at other institutions.[23] In 1994, for instance, George Washington University had twenty blue light phones installed and a safety map issued in a university police brochure indicated that they were clustered in high-traffic public areas near central campus buildings.[24]

The placement of emergency phones on urban campuses such as George Washington and University of Pennsylvania was further directed by a desire to protect students from surrounding communities that were perceived to be a source of danger. On urban campuses, the blue light towers were associated with (often racialized) fears of mugging or property crime in addition to sexual assault. A 1997 article in the *Washington Post* explained that local universities installed blue lights "for students in distress" and closed-circuit television cameras "to thwart criminals in the act,"[25] suggesting that the dangers of the urban environment were prime justifications for these security additions.

The University of Pennsylvania more explicitly associated blue light phones with urban crime, likely because the university's location in West Philadelphia was understood as inherently dangerous by many students, parents, and administrators. Penn installed blue light phones throughout campus during the 1997–98 academic year and followed up with an

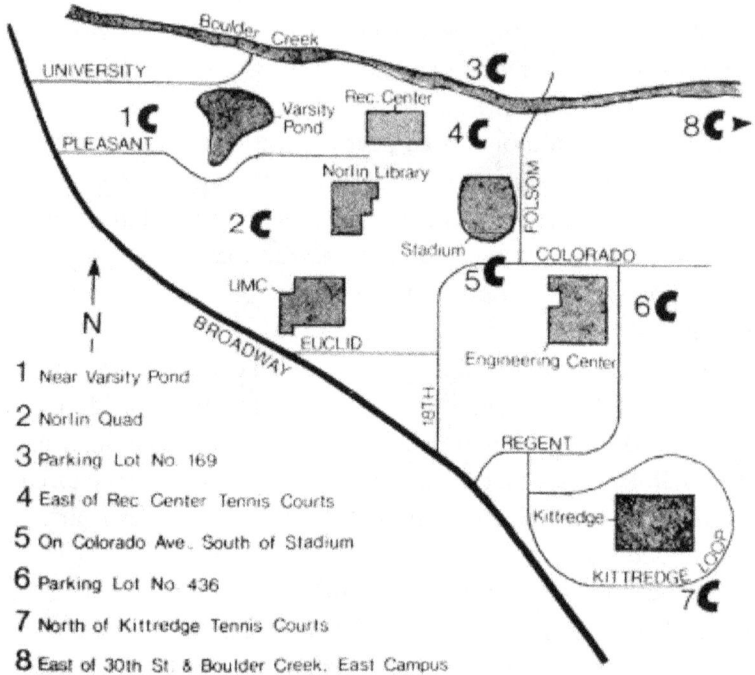

UNIVERSITY OF COLORADO

CU Police Department: 492-6666   Emergency: 911

Boulder Creek

UNIVERSITY

3 **C**

8 **C** ▶

1 **C**

PLEASANT

Varsity
Pond

Rec Center

4 **C**

FOLSOM

Norlin Library

2 **C**

Stadium

COLORADO

N

UMC

BROADWAY

EUCLID

5 **C**

6 **C**

Engineering Center

18TH

1 Near Varsity Pond

2 Norlin Quad

3 Parking Lot No. 169

4 East of Rec Center Tennis Courts

5 On Colorado Ave. South of Stadium

6 Parking Lot No. 436

7 North of Kittredge Tennis Courts

8 East of 30th St. & Boulder Creek, East Campus

REGENT

Kittredge

KITTREDGE LOOP

7 **C**

EMERGENCY CALL BOXES

Figure 2.1. Excerpt from a 1989 wallet-sized map of campus emergency phones. University of Colorado Boulder Chancellor's Office records, COU:2347, box 317, folder 1, Special Collections and Archives, University of Colorado Boulder Libraries.

"aggressive program" of investment "in the safety and security of our surroundings" by expanding the number of phones and other security measures "throughout the campus and adjacent neighborhoods,"[26] indicating that there was a perceived threat beyond campus. This threat was named in the *Philadelphia Inquirer* in 1995, which reported that "Bobbie Kase, a parent from Phoenix, had expected pavement and city clamor around Penn's buildings or worse, a ghetto next door."[27] But ultimately, "reassured by scores of blue-light emergency call boxes around the Penn campus and the university escort services, Kase said, 'I would want my son to come here.'" Thus, the phones functioned as what feminist media scholar Carrie Rentschler terms "environmental security" that promotes "one form of safety consciousness—strangers are dangerous—by largely disabling another: university members are dangerous."[28]

This disavowal of the risks of campus, strengthened through the affective infrastructure of the blue light phones, was evident in the juxtapositions of a 1992 "Crime Awareness and Public Safety" report issued by Georgetown University. The booklet includes a map of thirty-five blue light emergency phones placed throughout campus, around academic buildings, parking lots, and dormitories, and describes them as to be used "to summon assistance in case of emergency." Yet, a table summarizing crime reports and arrests between 1989 and 1991 proclaims zero rapes, one aggravated assault, and zero drug or alcohol violations.[29] This source, thus, tells multiple stories of risk. There seems to be no (acknowledged) emergency to respond to, and yet the technologies of safety that other institutions installed precisely in response to sexual assault and student activism are present. There is a dual effort here to reassure, through the statistics and the phones, and to deny the possibility of emergency.

Having established a material network of lighting and telephony and linked it to existing institutions such as campus police forces, campuses embarked on promotion of this technological infrastructure in order to create feelings and experiences of "safety" where previously there may have been fear or doubt. Maps, like brochures, annual reports, and campus tours, were vehicles through which to communicate the institution's commitment to "solving" the problem of campus safety. This public face, however, contrasted with the realities of blue light emergency phones, which university administrators understood—from the beginning—to be of limited utility.[30] If the phones were rarely used, then their function was not instrumental but affective—institutions installed them precisely to produce feelings of reassurance by signifying safety (non-emergency).

In this function, blue light emergency phones constitute an *infrastructure of feeling*, a material or representational instantiation of particular ideological and felt elements of a society. Drawing on Raymond Williams's classic formulation of the "structure of feeling" as "a particular sense of life, a particular community of experience hardly needing expression," I argue that these intangibles are often concretized through the media systems that they produce.[31] The infrastructure of blue light emergency phones was intended to produce affective experiences of "safety" among students, parents, and administrators, reassuring them that these sentries would allow reporting of emergencies, or deter incidents altogether.

Blue light emergency phones arose in a particular context, but then became a fixed referent that held the promise of safety. They took on the invisible nature of the strongest infrastructures (and ideologies). Feminist ethnographer Ara Wilson sees such invisibility as a resource for feminist and queer analyses of infrastructure, itself a "baggy" framework within which to analyze social and material relationships without falling into determinism.[32] For Wilson, telephone systems link infrastructure to frameworks of intimacy, connecting embodied voices via technology.[33] "Affect" offers a similarly loose conceptual vocabulary, a means of capturing the potentialities of bodies as they encounter outside forces or stimuli, propelling moments and movements that are formed with (but not entirely by) the social.[34] Blue light phones share Wilson's intimate and infrastructural dimensions, additionally carrying with them affective dimensions of embodied experiences of fear (or safety) concerning sexual assault.

While Williams's notion of a structure of feeling attempts to capture a temporally changing phenomenon, on the edge of consciousness, that characterizes the lived experience of a particular time period or generation, an infrastructure of feeling can function spatially as well. College and university campuses are loosely bounded geographies, often with distinct cultures that are both part of and set apart from their surroundings; there are elements of campus tradition, local knowledge, specialized forms of communication, and durable values that persist across generations of students. In order to bring newcomers into a campus culture, a degree of instructional communication is necessary to convey the proper interpretative framework and set of expectations for daily life in that spatial and cultural context. Thus, blue light phones function similarly to the time-biased media theorized by Harold Innis;[35] the infrastructure of feeling is localized and taught, a means of bringing people into a particular culture and its attendant affective dimensions.

The persistence of this infrastructure of feeling is evident in the replication of blue light maps and repurposing of blue light infrastructure in current campus safety platforms, which often include maps of existing safety resources. While these maps integrate GPS to produce a location-aware map of safety resources in one's immediate vicinity, they are otherwise not dissimilar to the printed maps of prior generations. They usually retain the location of blue light emergency phones, but do not display the locations of other technologies of safety and safety surveillance. The jurisdictions or common locations of campus police officers or other safety personnel are rarely indicated. The locations of security cameras not only do not appear in these maps but are often treated as sensitive information, not available to the public. The maps do not illustrate known incidents of crime or violence, either, resulting in an ostensibly dynamic map that in fact replicates static paper maps of safety infrastructure. The goal, again, seems not to be preventing or responding to emergency, but providing reassurance that all is well, all is safe, all is normal. In fact, such reassurance has been one of the leading arguments against removing blue light emergency phones; in the words of one alert system sales representative, these "hangover technologies" remain "great for perception, make parents feel good." Given the affective strength of this media system, many campuses have decided to retain the phones but to simultaneously repurpose them as mounts for security cameras, speakers (as seen in figure 2.2), or Wi-Fi beacons that facilitate informational forms of emergency mediation.

The infrastructures of feeling established by blue light emergency phones and reinforced through paper maps and locative apps demonstrate the affective power of maps in creating safety (and staving off emergency). Next, I turn to meteorological maps; no less affective, these maps' power is in their authoritative source and dynamic display of information. When that information—and authority—is disrupted, emergency itself is called into question.

Figure 2.2. Author's photograph of a contemporary emergency phone tower (blue light phone) at Georgetown University, 2018.

Weather Maps and Apps as Habitual Information

Weather maps function affectively as emergency media, as when an impending storm on the map signals a need for action in an intensified here and now, but they are also important information infrastructures of daily life. While mapping weather traces back at least as far as the late nineteenth century, in which military and shipping operations had significant interests in chronicling and forecasting conditions,[36] the rise and spread of radar maps as a routine part of news and weather television broadcasting and now as foundational elements of mobile weather applications has ensured that there is nearly always a weather map at the ready. These familiar maps usually show a local area—a city and its surroundings, half of a state, a coastal region—centered on either the broadcast market or location data of the phone in question. Atop this map, colorful indicators of precipitation and its intensity—green for rain, yellow for heavy rain, pink for snow, and so on—move and demonstrate the past and likely future paths of weather systems.

Despite its near-ubiquitous appearance in printed newspapers, television and cable shows, and mobile apps, the weather map is rarely studied within media studies literatures. Studies of weather media, such as the multiple perspectives offered by Julia Leyda and Diane Negra's *Extreme Weather and Global Media*, tend to focus on the mediation of weather more broadly, particularly the sensationalization of weather as media spectacle and the connections between weather media and the "conditions of permanent crisis" that characterize many components of life in an age of climate crisis.[37] Weather forecasts in news programming, cable outlets like the Weather Channel, and news coverage of weather disasters are forms of "ordinary television"[38] that attract little notice, even as they encourage audiences to understand themselves as living in a dramatic, near-apocalyptic weather landscape that, nonetheless, requires no serious changes in behavior or governmental support.[39]

The affect of emergency that characterizes much media coverage of weather disasters is less obvious in daily uses of weather maps. While televised forecasts—and their accompanying maps—were long the most common means of checking the weather, smartphones are now the primary vehicle for this information.[40] Many smartphones have weather apps preinstalled, in addition to a wide range of third-party weather apps available,[41] indicating that checking the weather is a core use of these technologies. In their everydayness, pulled up upon waking to plan the day, smartphone weather apps are a prime example of "mundane" media technology, incorporated into "the rhythms, routines, and rituals of daily life."[42] Yet, as media theorist Wendy Chun suggests, perhaps "our media matter most when they seem not to matter at all";[43] habitual use of weather maps as sources of information that structure daily activities masks our reliance on these systems and their potential limitations in moments of emergency. Weather maps (and the media systems that circulate and display them) are part of the "information orders" of everyday life, setting the terms of knowledge by which people operate.[44] When weather maps—or weather apps—are revealed as fallible, this dependability is shaken.

Much of what we see in mediated weather maps comes from the same sources of information; the National Weather Service, radar maps based on satellite data collected by the National Oceanic and Atmospheric Administration (NOAA), and a host of local weather observations. Mathematical modeling systems convert this data into projected forecasts (which may differ from one another), which are then represented in the familiar maps. So, what happens if this information is revealed as not only incorrect (as often is the case in weather forecasting), but directly subject to alteration or manipulation? If the map is not dependable, how might we know if there is a weather-related emergency? These questions underlie the outrage and mockery that surrounded the "SharpieGate" incident in 2019.

"SharpieGate" was the name given to a briefing during which then president Donald Trump presented a NOAA National Hurricane Center map forecasting the path of Hurricane Dorian from the Caribbean toward Florida. On the physical map, it appeared that someone had used a black permanent marker to draw a semicircle extending Dorian's path into Alabama. It seemed that the map had been altered in order to provide retroactive support for Trump's earlier tweet about the storm's impact on Alabama. The Birmingham National Weather Service quickly debunked Trump's tweet, but it had already potentially spread panic among people who had not previously believed themselves at risk.[45]

SharpieGate was of a piece with many other false claims and ludicrous cover-ups attempted by the Trump administration.[46] The media's breathless coverage of this as yet another Trump lie likely intensified a back-and-forth narrative about who did what when, as Trump and others denied the alteration or even knowing that the map was altered, while anonymous officials seemed to confirm that Trump made the change himself.[47]

These news stories generally failed, however, to address the possible effects (and affects) of altering the map. Changing or falsifying government weather forecasts is criminalized precisely because this kind of disinformation has affective and logistical impact, causing people to potentially alter their behavior in ways that are not in their best interest.[48] Internal emails from NOAA indicated that personnel were explicitly asked not to respond to Trump's original tweet, and that they were not informed prior to the appearance of the altered map; yet agency employees saw a need to correct misinformation to "calm the nerves of citizens" and to uphold the scientific and civic authority of the agency.[49] These behind-the-scenes discussions indicate an awareness of how seriously weather maps are taken as informational and affective media, and thus how vulnerable they are to a crisis of confidence. If altering official weather maps became commonplace and people lost confidence in what they conveyed, all kinds of safety and evacuation procedures would become much harder to implement. The disruption of a single map via SharpieGate reveals both the taken-for-granted strength of such routine and emergency mediation in ordinary times and its vulnerability to bad actors or interference.

Under normal circumstances, use and confidence in weather media is high; one survey found that over 80 percent of respondents checked smartphone weather apps at least once per day, and that over 70 percent of respondents were confident that the hourly forecast, severe weather alerts, and rain notification alerts given by their apps would be more or less accurate.[50] Yet, weather apps are not simply sources of information; they, like most apps, are in the business of both providing and extracting information.

For weather apps, one of a few categories in which location data is central to an app's operation, collecting and selling users' location data has been a lucrative strategy. This became contentious in 2019, when The Weather Channel app was sued by the City of Los Angeles under California's Unfair Competition Law for inadequately disclosing to users how their location data would be shared or sold.[51] The Weather Channel app, which at the time had forty-five million active users, was accused of not only collecting and selling location data, but of actively working to link weather conditions to shopping patterns, providing a rich source of data on consumers' activities based on a foundation of routine information-seeking behavior.[52] The case was settled in 2020, with an agreement by the app's operator, TWC Product and Technology LLC, and owner, IBM, to revise the disclosure screens to more accurately communicate how location data might be used.[53]

Just as alteration of weather maps may shake confidence in maps' authority, the data and business practices of the Weather Channel and other apps may shake confidence in the neutrality or utility of the apps. In fact, avoiding ads was one of the main motivating factors in users choosing to move to new smartphone weather apps.[54] If your weather app appears more interested in selling you rain boots, for instance, than in quickly telling you if it will rain today, there has been a compromise in the core functionality and a reveal of the surveillance capitalism that underlies even technologies of mundane and emergency information.[55]

Visualizing Data, Mediating Emergency

In addition to cartographic and meteorological maps, maps are commonly used to visualize other forms of data. These maps, too, can mediate emergency, conveying areas of greater or lesser risk, danger, or change. Maps have been used to represent the spread of disease, in particular, since John Snow's 1854 representation of cholera cases in London, which illustrated clusters of disease around drinking wells.[56] Similarly, during the COVID-19 pandemic, maps at a variety of scales have demonstrated incidence of the coronavirus, fatalities, testing rates, exposure likelihoods, and other forms of data related to the spread of disease. As information graphics, they are "visualizations based on abstractions of statistical data."[57] Such visualization can make data more understandable and affectively powerful for people with little knowledge or interest in the underlying data or statistical modelings. Precisely because of the effectiveness of such forms of data presentation, it is crucial to remember that these are not simply presentations but *representations* of data, what Drucker calls "arguments made in graphical form."[58]

The power of data visualization maps as mediations of emergency stems from their use of the familiar map format, which enables them to draw on its informational and affective power. Just as one might watch a weather map of an approaching storm, watching the shifting maps of COVID-19 infections might create a sense of impending emergency, the affective state of fear that Ahmed describes in terms of danger that comes closer (but may miss).[59]

Maps were a dominant form of visualizing rates of COVID infections, hospitalizations, fatalities, and patterns of spread. Some of the most high-profile maps, widely referenced and reproduced throughout 2020, were those produced by Johns Hopkins University of Medicine (JHU).[60] JHU described the maps as a "resource to help advance the understanding of the virus, inform the public, and brief policymakers in order to guide a response, improve care, and save lives."[61] In short,

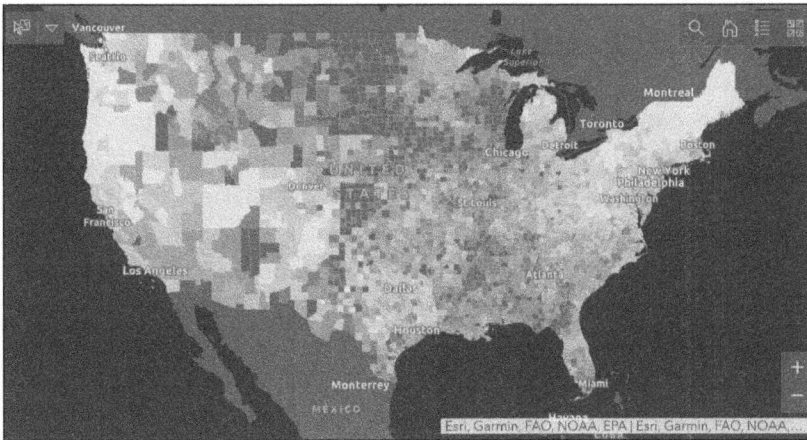

Figure 2.3. Author's screenshot of the JHU COVID-19 U.S. map, November 21, 2020.

the mapping was explicitly intended to guide decisions on the basis of reliable information presented in an approachable format.

The JHU maps, as seen above (fig. 2.3), used a familiar flattened map in the tradition of the Mercator projection and emphasize national and subnational borders as units of knowledge and illustration. The U.S. map seen here assigned each county a color value between a light yellow (indicating fewer than 1,306 confirmed cases per 100,000) and deep maroon (indicating more than 6,256 confirmed cases per 100,000), with gradations of orange and rusty red in between. This use of color saturation enables a nonexpert viewer of the map to easily infer where emergency conditions might be found, though this was not always true of the highly variable arrangements of colors and emergency levels put together in individual states.[62] Judging by this illustration, the upper Midwest was a hotbed of infection, while the Northeast appeared relatively "safe."

Such color-coded maps offering information-at-a-glance are complicated by several factors. For instance, JHU's site notes that there are areas of the country, including New York and Utah, where data is reported differently than elsewhere (presumptive COVID deaths are not included in New York's totals).[63] Furthermore, factors of population and space affect this presentation just as they do infographics of electoral college votes in U.S. elections; the large spaces in North and South Dakota, filled in with a dark maroon, are easily visible while smaller geographic regions may fade into their surroundings (as is the case for New York City). Additionally, the low populations of some counties mean that the rate of infection reported by cases per 100,000 is higher than the actual numbers of cases, while populous regions experience the infection rate as an averaging of a higher number. Thus, in November 2020, Middlesex County in New Jersey showed a rate of slightly over 3,000 cases per 100,000, and has had over 27,000 confirmed cases; Benson County, North Dakota, by contrast, had a rate of nearly 10,000 per 100,000, but has had only 689 confirmed cases.[64] Thus, the quick view of the map offers only a partial understanding of the disease, requiring a deeper reading of the data to understand how to contextualize these colored polyhedrons.

In spring 2020, early iterations of COVID data maps inadvertently revealed the exclusions and assumptions made by rendering data geographically. Several areas, such as Leesport County, Pennsylvania, showed relatively high rates of infection that were largely attributable to congregate housing within their borders. In Leesport County, for instance, a nursing home was the site of twenty-four of thirty-three infections.[65] Nursing homes and prisons were both early loci of infection among people likely to have preexisting conditions, poor access to medical care, or both. Yet the outcry about the ways in which this affected mapped visualizations relied on ableist logics of exclusion, which argued that such infections and deaths should be discounted in order to lift restrictions for others in the area.[66]

These deaths, it seemed, not only did not matter but were perceived as obstacles to a larger normalcy; a black eye on the counties in question, as mapped data emphasized the preexisting and worsening states of health in carceral and long-term health settings.[67] Subsequent data visualizations, including a *New York Times* map updated beginning in May 2020, offered mappings of *only* nursing home data, reinforcing a segregation of elderly and disabled people from the general population and participating in a eugenicist logic by which those already most at risk of death from coronavirus were also perhaps the most expected or accepted victims. Reflecting evergreen concerns about who is left out in collections of big data,[68] the invisibility and effects of prisons and nursing homes of COVID maps speak to how geographic interpretations of disease may simplify or misrepresent lived conditions.

The dangers of such simplification are more pronounced in mapped visualizations that offered not only representations of data, but interpretations of risk and recommendations for readers' subsequent actions. The Ohio Department of Health, for instance, offered a county map of the state that used a series of darkening colors to indicate "levels of emergency" and associated instructions. In fall 2020, most of the state appeared red, corresponding to a "Level 3 Public Emergency: very high exposure and spread. Limit activities as much as possible."[69] Its actionable advice orients a nonexpert audience to reading it—and possibly similar-looking maps—as a straightforward progression from "better" to "worse." Furthermore, the map offers no possibility of representing a county outside of the public emergency framing, with even the lightest yellow counties categorized as level 1 emergencies in which there is "active exposure and spread," but without any instructions for residents.[70] The map, in short, presents an argument for COVID as an all-encompassing emergency even as it facilitates a hierarchal reading of conditions as determined by county boundaries which may have promoted a false sense of security in the "level 1" areas.

When we make decisions based on representations of data, such as COVID maps, "the map becomes the territory; the projection incites a course of action that can lead to its own realization."[71] Tony Sampson and Jussi Parikka describe the often-reproduced "curve" of COVID infections as part of an "operational loop" in which policy actions build on certain models and these actions feed back into the data the models claim to represent.[72] COVID maps similarly both represent and influence the phenomenon under study; a county shaded as a "level 3 emergency" may result in choices that reflect and extend the declared state of emergency through local policies and individual behavior. The operational loop is strongest when visualizations are naturalized, and particularly when simulations or speculative data becomes mapped in a way that resembles observational data. A map released by scholars at the Georgia Institute of Technology purported to show the risk of at least one person at a holiday gathering being positive for COVID.[73] Though it had been operational for several months, the map gained popular traction leading up to Thanksgiving 2020, as people looked for information on which to base decisions about travel and family gatherings. The power of an operational loop here becomes clear; if an area appears to have low risk, there is the possibility that many people will then decide to go there or host gatherings there, resulting in higher (but unforecasted) risks of COVID infection.

As a result of the seeming ease—and serious consequences—of interpreting mapped visualizations, many scholars have called for renewed attention to data and media literacy in the age of COVID-19.[74] As Alexander Campolo argues, as data visualizations circulate "their parameters, assumptions, and underlying uncertainty may be concealed or even naturalized."[75] Many people online already engage in "map critique," demonstrating misreadings and presenting alternative visualizations, and such content could potentially be useful in educating the general public in how to understand and act on the basis of mapped data.[76]

However, the power of COVID data maps is not simply in their presentation of information; they are powerful because they adopt a format familiar from other forms of emergency information and thus draw on the affective power of maps as indicators of danger and safety. A bar chart is also a visual interpretation of data, but it does not have the same effect. Maps have a history as mediators of emergency, and COVID-19 is but one window into how maps disseminate information and produce affect in their construction of health, safety, danger, risk, and emergency.

Conclusion

Considering maps as a form of emergency media provides a useful articulation of the affective and informational dimensions of emergency mediation. Maps communicate what is happening, where, and sometimes even when; often, maps also tell us how to feel about these events and what actions might be required. Maps of physical space (both static and dynamic), of weather forces, and as data visualizations serve to provide information that is both quickly available and actionable.

Maps are increasingly implicated in the dynamics of surveillance, power, and care that characterize safety surveillance: surveillance is normalized in the name of safety and care; power dynamics are enforced rather than challenged through the arrangements of data and access;

and reassurance is central to the affective purpose of the technology. Maps of safety infrastructures, such as blue light emergency phones, defibrillators, police outposts, medical facilities, and so on, can illustrate what a community considers important and what kinds of access are (and are not) provided to various community members. The areas that are protected, the use cases that are highlighted, and the styles of a map's presentation all speak to ideas about what constitutes safety and emergency, and for whom.

Yet, maps do not have to be inherently normalizing; maps of safety and emergency do not need to center the perspectives of law enforcement, privileged communities, or those safe at home watching disaster unfold. Alternative mapping projects offer a provocative means of engaging with data differently, often restoring the human dimension to data, using crowdsourcing to construct data and interpretations apart from official sources, and retracing the contours of physical and historical geography.[77] Thus, I offer one final map to close this chapter: the Anti-Eviction Mapping Project.

The Anti-Eviction Mapping Project (AEMP) is a free and open-source resource that uses crowdsourced data to produce a map illustrating housing legislation and housing justice actions around the world.[78] It, like the Data for Black Lives and COVID Racial Data Tracker, is a subaltern map of the COVID-19 crisis.[79] The AEMP is familiar in some of its choices; national and subnational borders dominate, and a grayscale color theme moves from light to dark, recalling the better-to-worse uses of color in many other visualizations. The map also includes icons that pinpoint housing justice actions around the world. In its reliance on crowdsourced data and invitations for viewers to become part of a larger community working toward housing justice, the AEMP is an example of mapping that goes beyond "compliance mapping" of applicable laws and standards to "recognize marginalized experts" and "redefine data."[80] Many of the red icons reflect organized tenant's rights groups, but many are also posted by individuals calling for others to join in local rent strikes.

Beyond these challenges to "official" mapped visualizations, a core intervention of AEMP is the reframing of the commonsensical meaning of emergency itself. This map does not present correlations of housing protections and rates of infection; the emergency is not COVID itself, but the resulting economic conditions that have made many people's housing precarious. AEMP describes itself as "an emergency response project," and it offers not medical but political advice. Through this alternative framing of emergency, the AEMP map suggests that as we mediate emergency differently, we may begin to experience it differently.

Maps as emergency mediation create affect and inform action. The use of maps to convey information about weather, events, or data often functions as an official declaration of a kind of emergency: this is happening, pay attention, take action. Presenting information about or in case of emergency demarcates some circumstances as different from others, and in doing so reifies an unmarked experience of normalcy that tends to support the status quo. This hierarchical and informational deployment of emergency to produce action in a population is further expanded on in the next chapter, which focuses on alerts.

3

Alert

Interruptions, Instructions, and Authority

BALLISTIC MISSILE THREAT INBOUND TO HAWAII.
SEEK IMMEDIATE SHELTER. THIS IS NOT A DRILL.

On January 13, 2018, residents of Hawaiʻi received this emergency alert. Its content and capitalization indicated urgency, while its brevity made it difficult to confirm whether this threat was legitimate. Upon receipt of the message, some people panicked, others found shelter, some locals ignored it completely, and some people rushed to spend their last minutes on the beach. Thirty-eight minutes later, residents of Hawaiʻi received a second alert: "There is no missile threat or danger to the State of Hawaii. Repeat. False Alarm." The affective experience of emergency initiated by the first alert was ended by the second. While the threat was illusory, attributed to a worker's mistake, the impact of the emergency alert on people's experiences, fears, and behavior was quite real; a false alert (or alarm) can still produce the affects and actions of emergency. For thirty-eight minutes, there was a state of emergency produced by the mediation of state power.[1]

This chapter examines emergency mediation through *alerts*, which are information-centric, hierarchical forms of emergency mediation that rely heavily on trust in the alerting authority. Alerts illuminate how media systems have defined and been defined by the normalizing ideology of emergency, as the power of alerts often stems not from their specific contents, but from the very designation of circumstances as an "emergency" outside of the normal state of affairs. This definitional power allows those in positions of authority to designate a moment as an emergency and attempt to modify the behavior of a public. By activating a frame of "emergency" to justify exceptional measures and direct public actions, alerts function as a site of exception from otherwise normal life and mediation.

Throughout, I draw on a wide range of emergency alerts, including those sent as part of the federal Wireless Emergency Alert (WEA) infrastructure, those sent by opt-in third party systems on behalf of municipalities or institutions, those sent by consumer safety apps, the alerting practices of COVID-19 contact tracing apps, and the legacies of interpersonal alerting systems such as phone trees. Most emergency alerts have similar goals—providing information as emergency prevention or mitigation—and many of them rely on a legacy of broadcast media and federalized civil defense or emergency management practices.

The authoritative nature of alerts makes them easily misread as official, neutral, or purely informative but alerts are, in fact, technologically and rhetorically *constructed* messages. Considering them as such exposes the *emergency media work* behind emergency media. The process of crafting and deploying emergency alerts is communicative and interpretive, an act of meaning creation, which occurs within diverse working cultures with multiple goals. The emergency media work of alerting is done by emergency managers, emergency communication specialists, and public officials, but it is also done by app developers, public relations teams, and institutional or corporate representatives. Thus, this chapter draws heavily on interviews with those involved in alerting, both in public and private contexts, to examine the production of this form of emergency media and the production cultures[2] of emergency, which create the messages that are sent to—and potentially acted upon by—various emergency publics.

Information in an Instant

Alerts are information-centric. Often accompanied by an alarm (as discussed in chapter 1), an alert is "a written or verbal message that includes informational content" about a particular circumstance.[3] Alerts function as part of the larger information infrastructure of an emergency, in which they are one of the overlapping media, material, and interpersonal systems by which information circulates and is used by a public to make sense of events.[4]

Alerts are temporally and geographically specific, and sometimes even more narrowly targeted via group membership or social ties. To receive an alert is to be hailed as a member of a public that is collectively at risk. Crisis informatics scholar Megan Finn describes disaster publics in similar terms, as groups of people who are understood to be at risk and in need of information or services. An alert public, then, is a group determined to be at risk in a given moment, and this group is often technologically constructed through databases of contact information, geofencing, or similar means.

The purpose of emergency alerts is "to provide the necessary information to warn the public and effect the necessary actions that will lead to their safety."[5] By including information about what has already happened and instructions about what to do next, alerts partake in the intensified present of emergency by calling people to action. Alerts are thus tightly tied to what philosopher Elaine Scarry describes as the action-oriented nature of emergency;[6] ideologically, this orientation produces an emphasis on pointing out possible dangers in order to preserve or restore as much of the normal state of affairs as possible.

Emergency alerts both declare that an emergency may be happening ("ballistic missile threat inbound") and provide instructions for how people might mitigate its effects on themselves ("seek immediate shelter"). In this didactic capacity, alerts have an intrinsic hierarchical character; they are received from a source of authority, whether that is a government, an employer, or a technology we rely on to inform and instruct us on optimal next steps. The top-down nature of most alerts necessitates a relationship of either direct authority or trust; users may be mandated to follow an alert's instructions, or they may be "nudged" such that they take in the information and perceive themselves to consent to taking next steps.[7] The latter course requires that people trust the source of an alert to be accurate and operating in their best interest.

One of the major challenges for maintaining users' trust in emergency alerts—and thus their willingness to act—is that people can easily become inured to them. Frequent messaging, or messaging about risks that do not materialize, can result in a general tendency to disregard alerts and hope for the best.[8] Such risks are particularly evident when emergency alerts are considered alongside the mundane alerts, or "push notifications," that characterize myriad digital and mobile media apps and interfaces. Alerts are the preferred method of push interaction for smartphone features and applications, many of which ask users to "enable alerts" in order to be actively told of particular events or information.[9] The smartphone or app alert may also be multimodal; an alarm (a sound, vibration, or flash) may accompany the appearance of information on-screen in order to gain attention before conveying information and implied actions.

If an emergency text alert arrives sandwiched between a reminder to exercise, a social media comment, and an update confirming that a sandwich will be delivered in ten minutes, it is easy to miss the potential emergency in a context in which meanings may be flattened by technological similarity and simple habituation to receiving alerts and updates.[10] Studies of haptic alerts suggest that routine alerting results in them becoming simply "signifiers of the technological context of simply needing to be notified," reasserting a user's technologically saturated and always-on context.[11] Alerts may thus be part of ordinary life, even as some alerts—like emergency alerts—attempt to produce a temporal and affective shift into a new mode of being.[12]

In the instant of an alert's mediation, the user is formed as a recipient; the alert asks its audience to take up the temporal and active dimensions of emergency in pursuit of prolonged safety (or normalcy). This is not to say that alerts are necessarily productive of their desired outcomes; many people can and do ignore all kinds of alerts, including emergency notifications. For this reason, it is important to consider not only the alerts themselves as mediation and media content, but also their contexts of production and reception.

Producing and sending emergency alerts is a form of media work, involving decisions about messaging and audiences. Research indicates several themes that may characterize the possible effectiveness of an alert, including "terse messaging and self-efficacy; information level; emotions; space, place, and time; behavioral intentions vs. actual responses; and language expectancy."[13] In other words, there are a number of variables in terms of how alerts are written and received that may result in people being more or less willing to act on their information. Nevertheless, there is wide variation in how alerts are written, approved, and distributed that speaks to forms of professional knowledge that are cultural as well as practical.

Furthermore, the receipt of an alert does not always succeed in the construction of the recipient as a "passive spectator or as a potential victim."[14] There is negotiation possible in the reception of emergency alerts.

Differences of identity and social position affect how alerts are taken up; for example, research on U.S. college campus alerts suggests that men are more likely to adopt vigilante behavior in response to an alert.[15] Furthermore, to the degree that alerts adopt a didactic tone, a measure of resistance or refusal may be expected as a means of reasserting agency or contesting the declaration of "emergency" made by an alert.

This chapter moves through various forms of alerts to consider their dynamics of power and authority, their technological contexts, the media work that produces them, and recipients' diverse reactions. Throughout, I argue that the ability of alerts to "declare" emergency is at best partial, resulting in both dangerous gaps in the information environment and opportunities for less hierarchical forms of emergency information exchange.

This Is Only a Test

Since 2006, federal emergency alerting in the United States has occurred through the Integrated Public Alert and Warning System (IPAWS), which integrated, standardized, and increased the capacity of prior governmental alerting systems, such as the Emergency Alert System, under the authority of the Federal Emergency Management Agency (FEMA). In 2012, the WEA system was integrated with IPAWS. A partnership between the FEMA, the Federal Communications Commission (FCC), and wireless service providers, the WEA enables alerts to be sent to Americans' cellular phones. WEA messages often replicate television and radio versions of the alert message, attempting to reach the growing number of people in the United States who rely on smartphones in place of landlines, home internet access, and broadcast television.[16]

WEA messages are of four main types: "imminent threat" alerts are issued when there is an immediate risk to lives; Amber alerts are issued for missing children in a local area; presidential alerts are intended to allow national reach in the event of a catastrophic disaster; and public safety messages are available to follow "imminent threat" alerts, providing more information or updates as a situation develops. Other categories—such as BLU alerts used to engage the public in police manhunts and similar business, and Silver alerts issued for missing senior citizens—are emerging and may soon be treated as on par with the four existing categories.[17] Cell phone users can opt out of all WEA messages other than presidential alerts.

The ability to opt out is one of several characteristics of the WEA that were shaped through the prioritization of what disaster communications researcher Hamilton Bean describes as the "technocultural values of consumer convenience, autonomy, and control."[18] Yet the emphasis on matching consumer expectations did not extend to creating a system that could meet users' expectations (themselves shaped by commercial technologies). For instance, WEA messages were initially limited to 90 characters, could not include links to further information, and had little support for languages other than English or disability accommodations. While the character limit expanded to 360 in 2019, links are possible, and Spanish-language alerts are now supported, the WEA continues to lack support for multimedia features. Perhaps because of the ability to opt out of alerts and alerts' limited capabilities, public engagement with the systems is low.

Low public engagement is a concern, as a degree of public familiarity is key to establishing not only the authority but the trust necessary for alerts to be trusted and acted on. When the WEA system launched, FEMA developed an outreach plan focused almost entirely on educating alerting authorities, with little attention to public education.[19] In materials for the public, FEMA used the slogan "Get Alerts. Stay Alive." The brusque tone was combined with minimal information, as in a 2012 flyer that read:

> Alerts for the most serious emergencies are designed to reach you at the right time and place.
>
> • Imminent threats in your area
> • AMBER alerts for abducted children
> • Alerts from the President in a national emergency
>
> Look out for these official alerts, so you'll know what to do in an emergency.[20]

Notably absent from this message is any explanation of what these alerts will look like, what information they might contain, or what people should do upon receiving an alert. These "official alerts" do in fact often arrive without indicating the agency that sent them, and there is concern that people find these alerts intrusive or annoying, leading them to opt out and potentially placing them in danger if they do not receive future alerts.[21]

One of the most powerful drivers of awareness, however, would be regular testing of the kind that characterized prior federal alerting systems, including the Emergency Broadcast System (EBS).[22] Put in place in 1973 as a replacement for the CONELRAD radio broadcasts,[23] the EBS partnered with television and radio broadcasters nationwide. To ensure that these partnerships would hold, broadcasters were required to test the EBS weekly, at a random day and time between 8:30 am and local sunset; those stations that did not participate in the EBS were to be off-air for the duration of the test. The participating station would show a visual slide and convey a message (with slight variations) like the following: "This is a test. This station is conducting a test of the Emergency Broadcast System. This is only a test." This would be followed by up to twenty-five seconds of a piercing audio tone, and then a reiteration of the test message and the conclusion of the alert test. Because of the regular daytime testing of the EBS, it became a cultural touchstone, part of the background of broadcasting and likely familiar to Americans of certain generations. Through the regular tests of public emergency broadcasting, the American public was trained to expect to receive mediated information from official media sources in moments of crisis.

The EBS became the Emergency Alert System (EAS) in 1997, broadening the distribution of emergency alerts to including broadcast, cable, and satellite providers. While participants were still required to test equipment weekly, television stations were no longer required to transmit a video message, and scripts were no longer required.[24] Tests occurred in less popular time slots, and combined with the splintering media environment, it became easier to miss routine testing. Additionally, the rise of an "ubiquitous media environment" led decision-makers to rely on commercial media messaging rather than using the EAS in response to the obvious national emergency of September 11, 2001.[25] Twenty years later, broadcast tests are easily missed by cord-cutters, and a fractured and less-trusted mass media environment has created an environment in which American culture is nearly hostile to the use of federal emergency alerts.

The announcement of an October 2018 test of the national presidential alert system (which users could not opt out of), using WEA and IPAWS, was met with disbelief that veered on outrage. Though many Americans were already receiving WEA messages—thirty thousand weather-related imminent threat messages were sent between 2012 and 2017[26]—and the language of the test mirrored EBS messages,[27] the presidential alert test claimed a different kind of authority and demanded a different level of trust. Popular websites provided instructions for blocking or avoiding the alert,[28] often in politicized terms. This degree of reach into one's life—and cell phone—by then president Donald Trump (known for social media abuse and falsehoods) was enough to put many Americans on guard against a perceived intensification of government oversight.

Such objections reflect a lack of trust in the government, and specifically the president, and thus a perceived lack of authority to provide information and declare a situation an "emergency." Technology critic Ian Bogost attempted to shut down fears about misuse of the system following the test, suggesting that the outcry had less to do with this alert than with decades of eroding trust in governmental institutions, aided and abetted by mobile and social media.[29] Bean similarly describes the public response as the result of a struggle for control between officials calling for centralized government control in an emergency and people desiring control of their devices.[30] He contends that federal alerts such as the presidential alert, which lack clear usage guidelines and have low public awareness, "generate the appearance, but not the fact, of control."[31]

Use of WEA or IPAWS alerting systems generates that appearance of control by imposing an "emergency" framing. The claim being made is that an authority—the president, the National Weather Service, local government—has identified an emergency and is calling people into that framing, with its attendant affective and active dimensions. To issue an emergency alert is to make a claim to authority that is supported both by the technological power of the state to reach the public and by the ideologies of emergency that have historically underwritten official forms of emergency media. Recipients are called on to take up the declaration of emergency and act on it; if they do not trust the claim, or the authority of those making it, such ideological buy-in is less likely. The combination of complaint, mockery, and disinterest that characterized the 2018

WEA test further indicates that what could be a valuable public media service is, instead, subject to deep distrust. In these reactions, the test of the WEA system reveals a host of fissures in the technological capabilities, cultural contexts, political mandates, and access conditions that characterize emergent media and understandings of emergency.

Furthermore, the claims of authority and control that are made by broadcast-style national emergency alerts mask a much more fragmented bureaucratic reality. Though IPAWS serves as a gateway for messaging, neither FEMA nor the FCC issues alerts; rather, there are over 1,500 alerting authorities in federal, state, local, tribal, and territorial governments across the United States. The people working in agencies recognized as alerting authorities generate messages in compliance with IPAWS standards, making decisions about geotargeting, timing, and messages. This media work of emergency alerts is done largely by professionals affiliated with emergency management—emergency managers themselves, public information officers, and sometimes public relations professionals, public safety professionals, or even interns—and their work effectively delimits what will (or will not) be rendered an emergency through alerting.

Alerting as (Emergency) Media Work

The crafting and distribution of messages is the fundamental work of alerting, and put in those terms, alerting is a form of *media work* that is both practically and culturally significant. Studies of media work within film and media scholarship have largely focused on entertainment media industries (often Hollywood-adjacent).[32] Yet, framing alerting labor as media work allows us to recognize the professionalized use of media technologies and production of media content that characterize alerting (and emergency management more broadly). These are meaning-making practices to which workers bring their own values and through which they make decisions that refract back onto the construction of ideologies and practices within a larger society. In the case of nontraditional forms of media work—like emergency alerting—workers' influence occurs through the decision-making about what constitutes an emergency and through the communication of actionable information. Following others who have studied labor in atypical media contexts[33] and studies of information labor,[34] I use observational and interview data to explore alerting as emergency media work within the professional context of emergency management.

Emergency management is a broad and growing field, particularly since 9/11. FEMA defines it as "the managerial function charged with creating the framework within which communities reduce vulnerability to hazards and cope with disasters."[35] Emergency managers are employed at all levels of government, in higher education, and in corporate capacities; they routinely generate plans for emergency response, promote disaster preparedness, and coordinate teams of stakeholders in the event of an emergency.[36] Sometimes, emergency management is a "one-man shop," and sometimes there may be a full staff with areas of specialization. Often, emergency management involves diverse and shifting responsibilities. This was clear in 2020, when several emergency managers I spoke with described their work as "all-COVID now," meaning that they (temporality) set aside ongoing or routine projects.

Focusing on emergency management as a media production culture in which practitioners self-theorize to make sense of their work and its role[37] reveals a shift in the field. Many emergency managers have historically come from military or first responder backgrounds and treated emergency management as a second career; this largely white, dominantly male group was routinely referred to as "old school" by interviewees. By contrast, there has been enormous growth in university emergency management degrees in recent decades—with over seventy schools now offering a program—along with many short courses and several certification programs offered by FEMA's Emergency Management Institute.[38] These courses often include training in theories of emergency management, emergency research, and media outreach and social media use. This educational path has resulted in younger emergency managers, who approach it as a first career, and has brought in more diversity (particularly more women). Often, emergency managers who take an educational path learned of emergency management through other forms of public service, such as AmeriCorps or volunteering during a specific disaster, motivated by a belief that emergency management work can "make a difference."

Additionally, emergency management has become more informationalized; while on-the-ground coordination remains important, emergency managers often work from an Emergency Operations Center where they take in information about the nature of events, plan, coordinate, and adjust via communication with various first responder organizations and local groups. Emergency management is being refigured as knowledge and communication work, or specifically what I consider *emergency media work.*

As media work becomes more central to emergency management through the production of alerts, public outreach and education, and data-driven practices of hazard monitoring, many emergency managers have adopted a broader sense of their job as focused on preparedness and awareness, achieved through communications. One municipal emergency manager told me, "I have a communications degree, and let me tell you, I use it more in this job than I ever have in my life" to send out press releases, do radio spots, talk to local reporters, and post on social media. The other strategies are similarly media work, though different platforms and audiences affect the kinds of messaging and targeting decisions that are made.

Within this shifting professional culture, the process of issuing an emergency alert is highly technologized and marked by several decision points at which the cultural and communicative media work of emergency managers and related professionals is in evidence. Whether issuing a university alert or using the WEA to inform a state's population of emergency conditions, these workers are engaged in the interpretation and representation of events (that may be emergencies) for their audience.

The process of issuing an emergency alert is as follows. An alerting authority (such as a state or local government) has likely purchased a commercial software platform, such as Veoci, OnSolve, or Everbridge, that allows them to write and distribute alerts for their jurisdiction. Use of these platforms is driven by the need for technological interfaces to support alerts and the desire to go beyond WEA options in terms of content and events. Often termed "mass notification systems," these technologies enable municipalities, corporations, universities, and other organizations to reach out to their publics with more flexible, targeted, and pervasive forms of emergency alerting (though many also offer integration with IPAWS). These systems often support not only outreach, but internal communications between emergency managers and responders that integrate text alerts, maps, images, and social media sharing capabilities and stand-alone apps that the public can download to receive local alerts or even respond to them. Many companies integrate these software offerings with hardware—speakers, signage, panic buttons—to create a "total alerting environment" as seen in figure 3.1.

This image is taken from a brochure provided by Alertus to attendees at a 2018 information session focused on higher educational contexts. The image shows an illustration of a college campus featuring a central "Activation/Emergency Operation Center," from which an emergency alert can be sent via Wi-Fi, ethernet, FM radio, and telemetry paging. That message then integrates with a range of display and information technologies, including outdoor notification speakers, digital signage overrides, alert "beacons" (dedicated screens), a desktop override on network computers, LED marquees, and an Alertus app that members of the target community may have on personal phones, among other avenues. Alertus further offers to integrate WEA and IPAWS messaging with the campus system, to manage blue light phone systems, and to update and maintain the console through which campus personnel can control the emergency information infrastructure.

Systems such as Alertus offer tremendous capacity for emergency messaging, but these alerting systems are for-profit, niche platforms bought and sold by agencies, not individuals. They are perhaps the grayest of media;[39] there is little public information about the cost, contract terms, data management, or security of these platforms.[40] They are regularly conduits for potentially sensitive information, and they are literally databases of contact information, meaning that gaining access to how local governments negotiate terms, how they are used, and past messaging can be difficult. The hierarchical nature of alerting relies on and facilitates surveillance, as alerting platforms operate on behalf of a public that is asked to opt in to an opaque system in order to receive information that might help in an emergency.

Regardless of the technology being used to issue the alert, the "alert originator" (the person who writes or submits the alert) must make decisions about what merits an opt-in alert, and what merits a higher level of distribution. Using the alerting software, which often has template options in addition to allowing custom text, an alert originator creates a message that is verified by the larger organization, sometimes via mul-

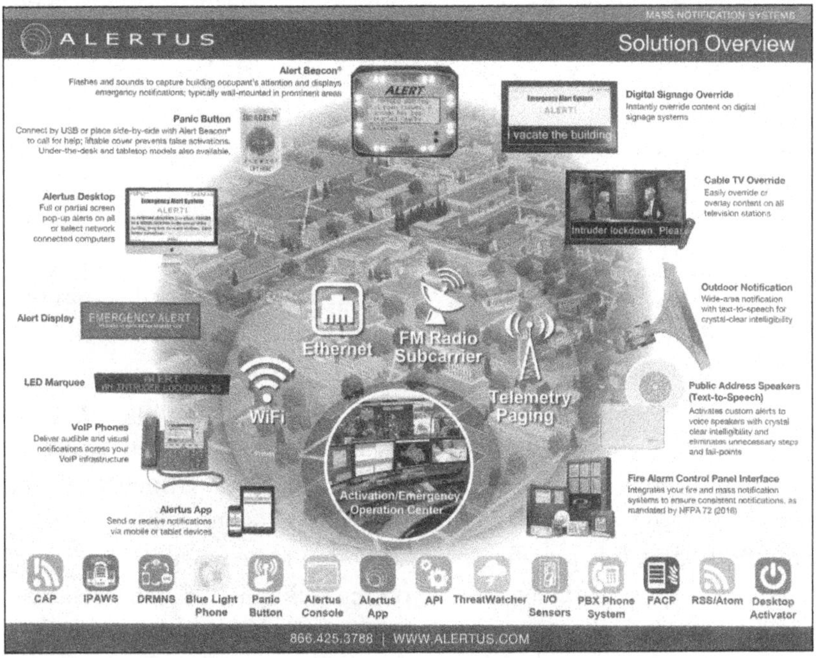

Figure 3.1. Alertus flyer featuring an illustration of a college campus with alert hardware and software options illustrated and noted throughout.

tiple levels of oversight and edits. If using WEA, the alert is then sent to FEMA's Federal Alert Gateway for a compliance check before being distributed to wireless service providers.[41]

The first step in this process is making the decision about what constitutes an emergency and thus justifies an alert, at what level of urgency. The decisions made by emergency managers and others within federal, state, municipal, or private organizational contexts essentially determine what will (or will not) be designated as an emergency. The rubric of "imminent threat and danger" often guides these decisions, perpetuating a bureaucratic perspective on emergency as "necessarily circumscribed in time,"[42] emphasizing emergency as a temporary departure from normalcy. Decision-making processes vary widely, with some emergency managers authorized to make the call personally, and others involved in discussions with local government or law enforcement. In some cases, decision-making rests with a sheriff or others described by one participant as the "boots on the ground, seeing that emergency in front of them." The determination of what is an imminent threat or emergency "can get very subjective," meaning that alerts generally prioritize the most "obvious" emergencies, such as floods, explosions, or armed shooters.

Once a decision is made to issue an alert, either via WEA or via an opt-in system, messaging becomes the focus of alerting's media work. WEA uses the Common Alerting Protocol (CAP), which requires that submitted messages convey an event's urgency, severity, and certainty.[43] These guidelines are supported by research in emergency communications, which suggest that "complete" emergency messages produce better responses, as people minimize their time spent "milling" for more information.[44] A "complete" message includes information about the "message source, hazard identification, hazard location, timeframe, and guidance."[45] Yet even with CAP requirements and guidelines for effective messaging, it is possible for information to be unclear. Emergency managers I spoke with described avoiding colloquialisms, abbreviations or acronyms, or other forms of speech that take for granted knowledge of English or the specific community geography and focusing on ensuring "the language is straightforward and simple." Decisions made about what information to include, how to prioritize content or instructions, how to fit a message into 90 or 360 characters, and how to appropriately address a diverse audience are ultimately decisions about media creation undertaken by professionals in the context of emergency management.

To focus on the specific decisions and effects of alert messaging, the next section briefly explores how the events of 2020 led to unusual uses of alerting, revealing the ongoing importance of the media work that goes into deciding what is (or is not) an emergency, crafting and message, and ultimately connecting with—or being rejected by—an audience that is asked to act.

Culture, Authority, and Urgency in 2020 WEA Messages

In spring 2020, as rates of COVID-19 climbed and states began shutting down for periods of weeks to months, many jurisdictions used WEA messages to keep people up to date on changing restrictions or breaking news. As of April 14, 2020, 177 messages had been sent about COVID-19 by government agencies in twenty-six states, Washington DC, Puerto Rico, and the Navajo Nation;[46] by late September, that message number was over 400.[47] By comparison, between 2012 and 2018, 96 percent of alerts issued through IPAWS were weather-related (primarily hurricane and tornado alerts).[48] Alerts issued in 2020 were thus departures from standard uses of federal alerting technologies. In fact, in early April, the Public Safety and Homeland Security Bureau of the FCC issued guidance that explicitly reminded alerting authorities that the WEA was "available as a tool to provide life-saving information to the public during the coronavirus COVID-19 pandemic."[49] The use of alerts in an unusual circumstances makes them a useful site for considering the how alerts not only deliver information but attempt to declare (or produce) emergency through crafted messages and claims to authority that are not always accepted by audiences.

There was enormous variance in messaging among COVID-related alerts issued between March 14 and April 26, 2020.[50] For instance, Leon County, Texas, issued alerts about each of its first several individual cases: "Leon County has 4th case of COVID-19. Female 70–79 years old in 77871 zip code." Few other jurisdictions offered such detailed information, or even rates of infection via alert. By issuing an alert, Leon County claimed that each case was an emergency, for the full population. This authoritative claim, however, came without instructions or context. It was unclear what recipients should do, meaning that this alert could easily spread fear rather than produce desired behaviors. Furthermore, this and most other COVID WEA messages assumed a healthy and nondisabled audience, rarely pointing to information specific to people who already had COVID, people with preexisting conditions, people living in congregate housing, or others marked by debility or vulnerability. Just as technologically inaccessible messages fail to inform disabled recipients,[51] so do broad messages often fail to account for the information needs of diverse populations.

More commonly, COVID-related alerts adopted a formal tone and provided clear evidence of authority and instructions for recipients. A Michigan alert was fairly typical:

From the Governor's Office: The State of Michigan has extended the Stay Home Stay Safe order until April 30 to save lives. Non-essential travel has been prohibited, but you can still leave for health and safety reasons, groceries and food, outdoor activities, and caring for others. For additional guidance, see www.michigan.gov/coronavirus

This alert, issued on April 9, includes key information, explains it, and links to additional information. Furthermore, this alert makes its authority clear; it is tied directly to the Governor's Office. Should someone have only seen the notification and not opened it—"MI Stay Home Stay Safe order extended to April 30. More at www.michigan.gov/coronavirus"—the link would have replicated this information about source and authority. Messages with a clear sender, or authority, are generally better received than those without, as people can often doubt the provenance of emergency alerts received without clear indication of their source.[52]

In some cases, alert text clearly conveyed cultural priorities. On April 11, the day before Easter, recipients in El Paso, Texas, got an alert reading "Avoid parks/family gatherings this Easter. Stay home, stay safe. Do it for your loved ones." The same day, residents of New Mexico were sent this: "COVID-19 update: Gatherings not safe, even at church. STAY HOME. Info at newmexico.gov." Both messages address their full audience in terms of a Christian religious holiday, indicating a possible fear of superspreader events and an assumption of relevance. Messaging such as this indicates a lack of attention to diversity in the target audience and ignores the possibility that cultural specificity that excludes some people may lead to hostility or distrust of the larger system, leading to less responsiveness to emergency messaging in some sectors. In a similar but less discriminatory example, many jurisdictions issued their alerts using all-caps lettering, "shouting" their message in order to convey urgency, but also reducing the readability of messages for many people and potentially diminishing impact for recipients who became annoyed by such stylistic choices.

In addition to using alerts for COVID-related policies and recommendations, some jurisdictions used WEA messages to announce curfews or other news related to Black Lives Matter protests. These messages attempted to declare a state of emergency and drive desired behavior, and like all alerts were the focus of coordinated emergency media work. However, as local and state jurisdictions do not always coordinate alerting, there were places such as the Los Angeles area where multiple alerts about COVID and protests were being received from different sources (not all of whom clearly identified themselves). Thus, there was increased potential for distrust of alerts and rejection of the government's declaration of emergency, as people became confused and then irritated, or simply rejected the alerts' declaration and definition of emergency. Alerts, like all media, are subject to audience interpretation and negotiation and the use of emergency alerts for curfews and protest control illustrates this variable reception.

In the case of a protest in Dallas, Texas, in early June 2020, a WEA alert about a curfew was sent and received while people were still in the streets: the loud alarm ricocheted among phones, and people shouted "Fuck the curfew!" turning off the alerts and phones to continue the demonstration.[53] Photos, screenshots, and conversations on Twitter attested to the peaceful nature of the protest as the time crept closer to the curfew of 7:00 p.m. In this case, while the authority and messaging of the alert were clear, recipients simply rejected the claim that there was an emergency requiring action. This alert was not received as an authoritative indication of emergency but was understood by protesters as a misuse of authority to target and criminalize protestors (many of whom simply could not have curfewed in time, in any case). They recognized themselves, in some sense, as the very "emergency" that was being invoked.

The declaration of emergency is always political, and the use of curfews to control protests marks a very clear political use of emergency media to control various populations and further the interests of the police, white supremacy, or both. Preemptive curfew alerts were used in Kenosha, Wisconsin, after Black father Jacob Blake was shot in the back seven times in late August 2020. When protests for Blake extended past the curfew, and an armed out-of-state seventeen-year-old white boy shot three protestors and killed two, the Kenosha sheriff implied that protestors' violation of curfew explained their deaths: "Had persons not been out involved in violation of that, perhaps the situation that unfolded would not have happened."[54] To use an emergency alert is to claim an emergency; to have that claim taken up requires a level of trust in the authority making the claim. When that trust is violated, those claims are not believed.

The year 2020 offered an opportunity to see WEA messages evolve in response to events, revealing the precarity of an alerting system based on broadcast media and legacy emergency management behaviors. Questions of trust, authority, and messaging remain relevant, but these examples also show the ways in which conceptions of audience affect how alerts are used, written, and received. Emergency alerting must not be conceived of only in relation to official policies and structures; to think about emergency differently, we must also consider how alerts might function differently.

Alerting Alternatives

Private alerting platforms sell their services to organizations in need of communications tools and security "solutions" through reference to earlier "bad objects" of emergency media. For instance, a wide range of campus safety and sexual assault prevention technologies are promoted as either updates to, or replacements for, existing infrastructures of blue light emergency phones (discussed in chapter 2).[55] Similarly, a number of alerting platforms aimed at emergency management professionals in municipal, higher education, or corporate contexts present themselves as alternatives to outdated "phone trees."[56] In this historical metaphor, we can see an alternative alerting structure that does not hew to the top-down legacies of broadcast media and militaristic emergency management. Instead, the phone tree offers a model of horizontal, peer alerting; the message of emergency remains declaratively urgent and the informational imperative is intact, but there is increased space for interpersonal negotiations and affective connection.

A phone tree, historically, was a prearranged system in which one person would make a telephone call to several others to convey urgent news. These recipients would have their own assigned contacts to whom they would pass the message, these calls would lead to more calls, until a full community was informed. Phone trees have been—and continue to be—used by military bases, religious organizations, public school systems, sororities, neighborhood groups, small business communities, corporate organizations, and emergency responders themselves.

Telephony has been an often-overlooked medium of community and activist organization, no doubt in part because of its ephemeral nature. Telephone calls—to individuals, to hotlines, to therapeutic resources, to information services, or by phone banks—leave little record of their contents.[57] In the context of twentieth-century activism, however, the telephone appears to have been a key technology of information and organization.[58] Reliant on multiple instances of one-to-one communication, phone trees allowed for "distanced intimacy"[59] and relationship formation through the flexible and customizable patterns of conversation that surrounded a given message. Community members shared information, but likely also established shared bonds of friendship or responsibility, as phone trees often "bonded participants emotionally with like-minded people."[60]

In addition to activist contexts, phone trees have been used as emergency media in a variety of contexts. Public school systems established phone trees for communicating about inclement weather delays or accidents; municipalities often used phone trees to share information among first responders; and informal phone trees were activated following disasters such as September 11, 2001.[61] College campuses incorporated phone trees as part of their security apparatus, usually using them to contact multiple campus police officers or to notify members of administration of particular events or threats.[62] Phone trees were also routinely set up as part of corporate emergency management plans, as when local Los Angeles businesses and organizations established emergency communications procedures in anticipation of possible rioting following the Rodney King verdict in 1993.[63] Statistics from the early 2000s indicated that 62 percent of companies maintained phone trees as part of their emergency preparedness plans.[64]

Like the children's game of telephone, in which a whispered message is passed from child to child and inevitably mangled, an emergency phone tree had the potential for missed- and miscommunication. Common criticisms include the fact that a missed call could disrupt the flow of information through a phone tree. Reporting on the shift to automated alerting in the Air Force Reserve Command described older phone tree systems as "quaint" and "messy . . . with participants not knowing what to do if someone doesn't respond, and the tree can turn into low-tech spaghetti code."[65]

Thus, it is unsurprising that the phone tree became a site for disavowal by technologists selling organizations on greater efficiency, speed, or reliability. Robo-dialing platforms, email lists, and now alerting apps have all communicated their benefits through negative comparisons to phone trees, presenting themselves as "the phone tree of the 21st century."[66] In 2013, the City of Napa, California, phased out its phone tree communicating weather threats to local businesses, because "there are more efficient methods available to provide timely information."[67] Napa replaced the phone tree with an opt-in alerting app.

More recently, there has been a reversal. Platforms such as Catapult EMS—an emergency management platform aimed at K–12 schools and developed by a company already in the business of providing educational technology—have integrated phone call features. Catapult EMS features a mass alert notification system in which "alerts are sent to a specified emergency phone tree of district administrators, safety teams, teachers, staff, substitutes, and law enforcement via phone, text and email."[68] In a total alerting environment, automating the humble phone tree is yet another means of duplication aimed at ensuring delivery and promoting action.

While Catapult EMS and similar platforms replicate the phone tree through automation, there are also innovations in mobile emergency media that draw on phone trees' legacies of intimacy and customization. These personal safety apps ask a user to preemptively establish a network of social contacts to be alerted in case of emergency. This mechanism was particularly popular in personal safety apps aimed at women. Circle of 6, winner of the 2011 White House and Health and Human Services "Apps Against Abuse" Technology Challenge (which asked developers to create apps to address dating violence and sexual assault among young adults), built its entire service around asking users to select a "circle" of six other people who could "reach out and protect each other"[69] in a variety of circumstances:

> For example, it's late and you need a safe ride home. Tap the car icon, and a message goes out with your GPS coordinates telling your circle you need to be picked up. Or say a creepy guy has cornered you at a party. Tap the phone icon, and it asks your circle to call you so you can fake an interruption.[70]

What is particularly notable about this description is that the user and not the technology or a professional responder determines what makes an event worthy of sending an alert. The media work of alerting is displaced onto users, in turn potentially empowering them to define emergency in their own terms and to negotiate that definition with friends and family. Where top-down emergency alerts ask people to trust in authority, phone trees and related systems ask people to trust one another in a technologically facilitated relationship. These dynamics have been carried into a new sector of emergency alerting: contact tracing and related apps.

Staying Safe with Notifications

Horizontal alerting systems flourished in the wake of COVID-19 and public protests, as people seek out information about their bodies and communities that is not individually knowable. While some of these apps enable interpersonal connection, as with the messaging app Signal, many of them rely on a wisdom of crowds and ask users to place their trust in the authority of technologies to keep them safe. For instance, Citizen is an Android and iOS app that uses the tagline "Connect and Stay Safe" and promises that users can "get real-time safety alerts and live video of incidents" nearby, assembled from both 9-1-1 data and in-app citizen reports, which can include photos or video.[71] Theoretically, this platform enables individuals to participate in their own definition of emergency through the content that they share, edit, or respond to. However, critics have brought up the fact that law enforcement could easily tune in to Citizen, and that false reports and racially biased claims can be easily made and are difficult to challenge.[72]

As a counterexample, we might consider COVIDWISE, the contact tracing app launched in partnership with the Commonwealth of Virginia and the Virginia Department of Health (VDH). By December 2020, COVIDWISE had achieved a 10 percent adoption rate within the state.[73] While it used Bluetooth exchange, it did not initially integrate directly with the iOS and Android tracking systems; the stand-alone nature of the app may have hindered its further utility prior to integrating with iOS in February 2021.[74] Notably, however, the COVIDWISE system enabled the VDH to input confirmed cases, enabling the authority of the public health infrastructure to confer its legitimacy on the app's emergency alerts. An emergency would be initiated when the VDH confirmed a case (tied to a phone number) and all codes exchanged with that phone would be found, and corresponding phone owners notified via alert.

Exposures

11:06 AM 70%

Exposures

Exposure Notifications

Exposure Notifications On

Manage Exposure Notifications in Settings
Exposure last checked Today at 10:39 AM.

Past Exposures

No Exposures Detected

If this app detects an exposure that meets VDH's criteria, you will receive a push notification and additional information will be displayed here.

Learn More

Learn more about Exposure Notifications at

HOW IT WORKS

Exposures   Notify Others   Virtual VDH   Share   Stats

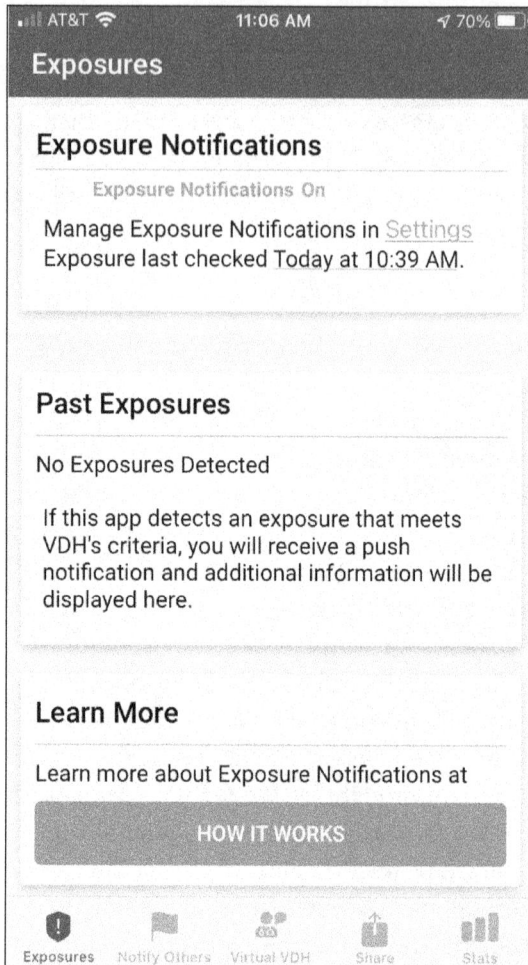

Figure 3.2. Author's screenshot of the "Exposures" screen in COVIDWISE (August 2020). The information on-screen indicates that exposure notifications are on, and there have been no past exposures detected.

COVIDWISE features clear, short explanations of how it works and what do to if you experience symptoms or receive a COVID-19 diagnosis. In addition to sending "exposure notifications" if the user has been in contact with a confirmed case, the app also offers an "Exposures" screen (figure 3.2) that indicates whether a user has notifications on or off and keeps a record of past exposures for reference and in case of missed alerts. Like any app that automates peer-to-peer notifications, there is a possibility that someone who receives a COVIDWISE alert would not understand its source, forget they had signed up for it, or otherwise respond with confusion. To prevent this, COVIDWISE has adopted regular notifications that users have not been exposed. These alerts function as a kind of familiarizing text, reminding users that the app exists and reassuring them of the absence of exposure. Instead of the very presence of an alert indicating emergency, COVIDWISE cultivates a background awareness that may help its alerts to be received and acted on according to recommendations.

The lingering problem with contact-tracing systems such as CO-VIDWISE, however, is what happens after someone tests positive. Without public health and welfare infrastructures to enable people to take off work, isolate, and continue to provide for themselves and their families, a COVIDWISE alert is an emergency in which people cannot always take action.[75] Alerts may declare emergency through their definitional power, but just as recipients may reject the messaging of a WEA message about curfew, they may be unable to act on a COVID notification, leading to illness, anxiety, debility, or even death. These alerts, by themselves, do not mitigate emergency. They do, however, participate in its affective dimensions and in the biopolitics of COVID in the United States.

Conclusion

This chapter has covered a wide range of alerting technologies and contexts in order to highlight the overwhelmingly top-down nature of alerts as mediations that attempt to declare emergency and produce related affects and actions in a public. Due to legacies of broadcast media and federal disaster policies, alerts rely on hierarchical relations of authority to make claims about what is, and is not, an emergency and for whom.

This means that the decisions about what justifies an alert and how an alert is written and distributed are deeply impactful and political decisions that often prioritize dominant institutions and sectors of society. Thus, emergency managers and related staff who generate alerts are in the position of doing important media work, reaching out to audiences with a specific message and desired effect.

Alert recipients, however, can ignore or reject alerts and their implied assertion of emergency. The information provided in an alert may be irrelevant, confusing, contradictory, or simply too much; in such situations, we might expect that recipients are "blasé"[76] and that they might opt out of alerts when possible. But there are more forceful rejections of alerts' emergency claims as well, stemming from mistrust in the issuing authority or a sense that one's interests are not being representing in conceptions of emergency or subsequent alerts. The specific interests of Black people, people of color, disabled people, people who do not speak English or Spanish, and other minority groups are often left out of alerting procedures. The diversification of emergency management and allied fields may be one step toward changing this oversight, as more diverse personnel working in alerting may generate more inclusive alerts.

Additionally, the technological context of alerts deserves serious consideration and possibly alteration. Hamilton Bean demonstrates that the WEA's development was constrained by a dedication to individualist consumer values on the part of service providers and federal agencies. Individualist consumer values have, on the one hand, constrained the federal alerting system through its initial ninety-character limit, lack of support for images, discouragement of links, and lack of support for non-English languages. One the other hand, consumer values did not impact the WEA's development in such a way as to normalize the kinds of personalization that people take for granted in consumer apps. Such personalization of alert content could greatly improve the ability to reach diverse recipients with trustworthy and actionable information. It is easy to imagine, for instance, a smartphone setting in which individuals could select a language preference and receive wireless emergency alerts in a language of their choice and automatically receive subsequent messages tailored to their needs. Personalization of some sort is even more essential when we consider that not all alert recipients are equally able to take requested actions due to poverty, disability, or community structures. This is most obvious perhaps when considering how evacuation orders routinely fail to offer significant instructions or resources for people who rely on assistive technologies or healthcare equipment that requires uninterrupted power or cannot easily be moved.[77] That such steps have not been taken indicates an ongoing official address of emergency publics as dominantly English-speaking, nondisabled, and, inferentially, white.

Third-party alerting platforms often incorporate such features but introduce problems of self-selected audiences and unclear uses of the vast quantity of surveillant data that such systems hold. For-profit alerting technologies perpetuate hierarchical arrangements of authority, but often shift the authority at least partially away from professional or state authorities to the technology itself. Automated alerts, "easy button" prewritten messages, and similar features attempt to standardize alerting, but can also lead to impersonal and inappropriate alerts being issued. These technologies further obscure the processes of decision-making, not to mention the political economy of funding, data, and operations. To the degree that the production of emergency by an alert is a matter of trust, there are potentially good reasons for people not to trust alerting technologies that they know to be proprietary (such as campus safety apps) and to question the technological provenance of alerts that they receive from official sources.

Finally, it is worth considering to what degree horizontal and peer-to-peer alerts can provide an alternative to broadcast forms of emergency alerting. Phone trees never really went away. In fact, they have had a notable resurgence since the onset of the COVID-19 pandemic precisely due to the benefits of distant intimacy and shared goals identified in historical phone trees. Iowa reverend Amy Wiles explained to a local newspaper that "it's another way to connect—people can call each other regularly. That's especially important to those who don't have internet access at home or aren't as familiar with technology. . . . We haven't abandoned each other."[78] Such forms of communal outreach point away from the dominance of emergency—which relies on a preexisting, and soon-to-be-reestablished, form of normalcy—and toward forms of responsibility and support that are grounded in vulnerability, ongoing engagement, and mutual effort.

4

What Is Your Emergency?

Reports and Responses

Early one morning in 2016—so early it was still night—Laura Levis walked to a hospital in her Boston area neighborhood in the midst of an asthma attack. When she arrived at the emergency room entrance, she saw two doors, neither clearly labeled. She picked one, only to find it locked. She began walking toward the other and collapsed. Increasingly weak, gasping for air, Levis called 9-1-1: "I'm at Somerville Hospital . . . I'm having an asthma attack. I'm dying." In the ten minutes that followed, as the 9-1-1 call-taker attempted to send help, Levis suffered a cardiac arrest and died, her body found only when it was too late.[1]

Two years later, Levis's husband, Peter DeMarco, wrote about the incident in the *Boston Globe* as "the story of how our entire emergency-response system can completely fail us."[2] As a result of Levis's death, the Massachusetts Senate passed "Laura's Law" in 2020, which requires clear indoor and outdoor signage, increased lighting, and monitoring of all entrances to emergency rooms.[3] While Laura's Law focuses its reforms on hospitals, her tragic death was also partially the result of the labyrinthine technological and labor processes that characterize even the simplest 9-1-1 call. Why, after all, couldn't 9-1-1 find a woman calling from her cellphone on the literal doorstep of a hospital? If, as discussed in chapter 2, Apple can Find My Phone and Find My Friends, why couldn't 9-1-1 find Laura Levis?

DeMarco described some of the hurdles. The regional 9-1-1 call-taker had to connect to Somerville police before they could dispatch an officer, taking extra time and requiring Levis to repeat herself to a new person on the phone. As the process dragged on, the original call-taker left the call and Levis apparently lost consciousness, leaving her unable to clarify her location. The dispatcher lacked GPS information to find Levis; 9-1-1 generally receives the location of the cell tower from which a call pinged, which locates the originating call with a several-mile radius. Thus, 9-1-1 professionals often rely on additional information such as local landmarks—in this case, they worked from the street address of the hospital, which did not correspond to the location of the emergency room doors. The police dispatcher contacted an ambulance center and the fire station located nearest the hospital. Both took off with their own ideas about where in the hospital complex Levis might have been. The dispatcher finally called the hospital, where the security guard was inexplicably away from his post near the doors and the nurse who received the call failed to spot Levis in the darkness outside the doors.[4]

In the years since Levis's death and DeMarco's article, national 9-1-1 operations have seen some changes. Some wireless providers now send a cellphone's GPS coordinates to 9-1-1 automatically, though this is still imprecise in indoor locations. Next Generation 9-1-1, an upgrade process initiated by the FCC, is being implemented gradually across the country, enabling text messages and even video calls to some public safety answering points (PSAPs).

Yet 9-1-1 remains a largely piecemeal system of local operations held together by a shared telephone number. During a one-hour highway drive across a single state, you might pass through three or four jurisdictions that have completely different technological capabilities, different oversight and levels of funding, and differently trained and supported 9-1-1 professionals. Without your knowledge, the support offered by 9-1-1 would shift dramatically. If you called to report an emergency, what would happen and why?

Reporting to Authority

This chapter considers emergency "reports," particularly those reports made by people to institutions or authorities that provide assistance, such as 9-1-1 calls. A report of emergency is a crucial site of mediation at which naturalized meanings of emergency are enforced through technologies and labor practices that ultimately determine what is (and is not) an emergency worthy of response.

I use "report" in its noun form, particularly in reference to its primary definition as an "account of a situation, event, etc., brought by one person to another."[5] In case of emergencies, we are often encouraged or inclined to make some kind of report to an appropriate authority, such as the police, medical authorities, or institutional offices. These authorities are empowered to respond to emergencies, and as such, are set up to receive and evaluate people's emergency claims.[6] In this chapter, I focus specifically on "official" reports by individuals seeking aid from public institutions through a detailed analysis of 9-1-1 operations.

The etymology of "report" is instructive in framing this emphasis on reporting to an authority. There is a thread of authority running through its histories and definitions, dating back to the sixteenth century use of the French *rapport* in reference to written accounts of cases heard in court. From this point, definitions of "report" in the *Oxford English Dictionary* repeatedly emphasize investigation or evaluation by authoritative bodies: a report as information brought by an "official investigator"; an account of legislative proceedings; accounts produced by those "required to do so"; an assessment of students' work; material prepared for publication; or "a written statement in which an accusation is made to a superior authority against a person" in military and law enforcement contexts.[7] To make a report—a police report, a report in court, a summary of events for the public—is to submit a narrative of events to an authority for evaluation. This sense of reporting as submitting to authority is further captured in a secondary definition of the verb "report" as "to tell someone in authority that something has happened, especially an accident or crime."[8] Accidents, crimes, and other emergencies are the stuff of reports, and reports are often made through mediated channels.

Insofar as reports are made to authority in hopes of assistance, they function as a form of what political theorist Jennifer Rubenstein calls "emergency claims." These are claims "that a particular (kind of) situation is an emergency, made by particular actors against particular background conditions to particular audiences, which in turn accept, ignore, or reject" them.[9] This task is fundamentally communicative and intensely normative, with many claims failing because of the difficulty (or impossibility) of presenting chronically bad situations of poverty, abuse, disability, or environmental risk as emergencies that can be remedied.

Rubenstein's work on emergency claims illustrates the hierarchical and conservative dimensions of reports as emergency media. If we understand reports as submitting a claim to an authority, making a report entails subjecting oneself to judgement by that authority, establishing and extending power dynamics that figure the person in emergency as a supplicant to the decision-making authorities that give (or withhold) assistance. To be recognized as a "competent judge of what counts as an emergency"[10] and thus increase the odds of having an emergency claim accepted, one must invoke forms of legitimacy such as proximity and also present oneself in alignment with the expectations of the reporting system ideologically, linguistically, and culturally.[11] Those who cannot do so risk having their claims rejected or themselves becoming the target of risk-reduction efforts and overzealous policing, including violence. These risks of reporting are unevenly distributed: people of color, disabled people, and non-English speakers are particularly likely to find that reporting a situation to police or authorities may worsen circumstances, rather than improve them.[12] Just as the people who were initially entrusted with police and fire callboxes were dominantly white men, those most likely to be believed when they make reports are those who most closely resemble (or mimic) the authorities to which they appeal.

The authoritative component of reporting is particularly crucial when emergency reports are understood as parts of an information order that enables assistance. Reports turn emergency experiences into texts, and texts into legitimate action. For instance, insurance companies might require evidence that a police report of theft was made before fulfilling a claim for the value of goods stolen. The authority of the police, in this case, is needed as a proof of the incident; if it was not reported, the insurance company does not believe it to have occurred. Similar informational authority is at work in rape kits and autopsy reports. An individual's emergency claim—someone was robbed, raped, killed—is only sufficient when it has been transformed into a report through interaction with authorities. Thus, when authorities fail to make a report or accept an emergency claim, they deny the informational authority that enables redress.

As a genre of emergency media, reports are omnipresent. Media technologies and industries have given emergency reports special status, allowing people to make a free 9-1-1 call from a public pay phone, or to contact 9-1-1 without unlocking a smart phone or incurring usual charges on a text message. Many of the examples discussed in earlier chapters incorporate emergency reporting as a secondary feature: activating a fire alarm often initializes a report to the fire department; COVID-19 trackers ask users to self-report symptoms to the app or the health department; PERS buttons and personal safety apps use various triggers, including a lack of response, to initiate reports to personal contacts or local emergency authorities.

The blue light emergency phones discussed in chapter 2 were explicitly offered as a means of reporting. Yet, these and related technologies also illuminate the pitfalls of emergency reports as technologies of normalization and accompanying criminalization. In the case of the University of Colorado Boulder, blue light phones were installed as a way for students to report the following:

1. Crimes in progress
2. Suspicious persons
3. Medical emergencies
4. Concerns about your safety[13]

This short list conveys a wealth of information about what kinds of emergencies were understood as deserving of reports and thus assistance. It also, however, reflects a vagueness that has often resulted in students reporting as "emergencies" simple mistakes such as forgotten keys or the mere presence of homeless or Black people.[14] Not all reports claiming emergency, then, *should* be accepted; reports are subject to bias and can be wielded as tools of violence in a society in which police encounters are often themselves the stuff of emergency. Reports are a crucial means by which emergency is established and are thus an important site at which to contest its normalizing power.

In this chapter, I use 9-1-1 as my primary focus, drawing on interviews with 9-1-1 professionals, observations at two PSAPs, and analysis of public online forums for 9-1-1 professionals, materials from the National Emergency Number Association and International Academies of Emergency Dispatch, and federal messaging about 9-1-1's technological upgrades. I consider 9-1-1 in terms of its bureaucratic and technological infrastructures, the infrastructure of feeling it perpetuates, and the emergency media work of 9-1-1 professionals in producing emergency. 9-1-1 is an uneven infrastructure with divergent relationships to public visibility; it is simultaneously invisible and hypervisible, allowing the service to be taken for granted by most people. Calling 9-1-1 is one of the most obvious forms of mediating emergency in the United States, but few people know details about its operation. This works to the advantage of common sensical understandings of emergency that prioritize a white, masculine, nondisabled, and middle-class form of normalcy.

9-1-1, Where Is Your Infrastructure?

A 2018 episode of the FOX drama *9-1-1* (season 2, episode 6) opened with a visual of red sound waves as a 9-1-1 dispatcher answered a call, asking "9-1-1, what is your emergency?" The dispatcher (played by Jennifer Love Hewitt) becomes frustrated as she tries to get needed information from a caller in crisis, and later exclaims that the job is tough because "it's not like we're set up for FaceTime!" Later in the episode, an older, experienced 9-1-1 dispatcher is revealed to have hung up on a caller because she did not understand his Vietnamese accent. In the episode's climax, the now-disgraced dispatcher calls 9-1-1 to harass Hewitt's character for turning her in, only to end up in a car accident. Hewitt dispatches an ambulance and stays on the line providing comfort and, metatextually, assuring audiences that there are "good" dispatchers.

9-1-1 is just one of many cultural representations of 9-1-1, all of which produce a powerful infrastructure of feeling that characterizes 9-1-1 as a positive, inevitable, and central feature of emergency response in the United States. Television programs, films, podcasts, and countless educational campaigns, and even the printing of "9-1-1" on the side of police cars, remind us that 9-1-1 is available and attempt to encourage its use. As laid out in chapter 2, an "infrastructure of feeling" attempts to capture and solidify ideologies within infrastructure, potentially working against the emergence of new ways of being in the world.

A strong infrastructure of feeling produces a tension between hypervisibility and invisibility, offering an affective safety that overshadows real conditions of risk, inequality, and fragility. 9-1-1's very cultural visibility—and the automaticity it is intended to produce—stands in contrast to how little public attention 9-1-1 operations receive in terms of news, funding, or governmental support. What we think we know about 9-1-1 from popular culture informs understandings of emergency and sets expectations—even and perhaps especially when those understandings and expectations are incorrect. For instance, unlike on 9-1-1, most emergency call-takers now begin by asking *where* not *what* the caller's emergency may be.

Approached with an infrastructural imagination, however, 9-1-1 and similar cultural artifacts can help us to ask questions about the formation, limitations, control, and function of media infrastructures.[15] Why was the initial conversation so frustrating? Why aren't they set up for FaceTime? What safeguards are there against racist or malicious reactions to emergency reports?

9-1-1 is best understood as an uneven and relationally formed infrastructure. It is a layering of federal and state laws, business interests, public safety organizations, technologies, labor practices, and caller expectations. The reports that move through 9-1-1 are shaped by this infrastructure, which enables and delimits possibilities of reports and subsequent emergency response. To echo Susan Leigh Star and Karen Ruhleder's famous question, we might ask not only "when is infrastructure" but "where is infrastructure" in a system characterized by national awareness and hyperlocal variability.[16]

9-1-1 is fundamentally a telephone number, not a coherent institution. Though the first 9-1-1 call was made in Alabama in 1968, "9-1-1" was only designated the sole national emergency number by the Wireless Communications and Public Safety Act of 1999. Prior to this, many areas had their own emergency telephone numbers, which they operated fully independently. 9-1-1 is an intermediary, a site of articulation through which emergency claims are made via media to a public authority, are evaluated and acted on, and subsequent encounters with police, fire, emergency medical services, or other emergency services are initiated.

So how does 9-1-1 work? When a call is made to the 9-1-1 emergency number, it is routed to the closest of the nearly 6,500 PSAPs registered with the FCC,[17] based on the presumed originating location of the call (which, as in the case of Laura Levis, might be incorrect). PSAPs may be located within sheriff, police, or fire departments, with other civic services, in regional centers serving multiple jurisdictions, or in dedicated emergency communications centers (occasionally colocated with emergency management functions). The decisions about funding and oversight of 9-1-1 are made at the state or local levels, resulting in variable financial support. Most funding for 9-1-1 comes from state-level

9-1-1 taxes that are appended to telephone bills, though state 9-1-1 funds are routinely diverted to other state programs, to the tune of over *$1 billion* between 2012 and 2018.[18]

Though the number is standardized, 9-1-1 lacks centralized government standards and financial support, which has resulted in a system woefully out of step with what consumers expect of digital and locative technologies. At its core, 9-1-1 relies on the "installed base"[19] of landline telephone operations in the United States. Elements of older telephonic infrastructures of technology and labor persist, and new elements have been tacked on over time. As with governmental alerts, people often expect 9-1-1 to live up to the technological capabilities of consumer devices, but the public sector has not provided sufficient funding or finesse to implement on a national basis taken-for-granted features such as text messaging or video capabilities.[20] As former FCC chair Tom Wheeler stated in a 2015 *New York Times* editorial, "Our emergency response system faces an emergency of its own in the form of outdated technology."[21]

The federal government's attempts at modernizing 9-1-1 infrastructure have had the disadvantage of relying on states for implementation and offering little centralized funding. The result has been the outsourcing of technological systems to a host of third parties (many of them for-profit companies) and uneven or incomplete upgrades. For instance, the EN-HANCE 9-1-1 Act of 2004 introduced requirements for "E9-1-1," which enabled PSAPs to gather location data from callers to use in routing calls and dispatching vehicles. Implementation of E9-1-1 in Texas involved outside contractors who built a "locational surveillance infrastructure,"[22] which was opaque to citizens and activist groups while usable by state and police authorities and potentially salable to other interests. Similarly, in 2012, the Next Generation 9-1-1 Advancement Act required PSAPs to move toward implementing digital or IP-based systems for call handling, which would allow for new services, such as text messaging. The Act did not, however, provide funding for this, and many jurisdictions continue to operate on legacy technologies, even choosing stopgap measures such as sending and receiving text messages via old TTY devices previously used to communicate with d/Deaf 9-1-1 callers.[23]

Once a 9-1-1 call has found its destination, it is answered by workers variously called "call-takers" (who only answer calls), "dispatchers" (who dispatch emergency services and may also answer calls), "telecommunicators" (used to describe both work functions), or "9-1-1 professionals" (which encompasses all of these and other PSAP support functions). These workers can have greatly varied levels of training and experience; some states require specialized training prior to beginning work in 9-1-1, some local agencies advocate for ongoing training, and many PSAPs continue to rely primarily on on-the-job training by existing staff members.

The 9-1-1 professional who answers a call likely sits at a workstation, known as a console, that might include multiple computer monitors, a multiline telephone, a radio unit (often with foot-pedal control), as well as keyboard, mouse, paper, and pen. From this post, they may engage in multiple simultaneous activities: looking for available emergency vehicles while talking to a caller; listening for important background noise that could indicate severity of a call, or specifics about location; navigating emergency medical protocols to provide guidance in a health emergency; attempting to pinpoint the location of a call by contacting service providers; and so on. The mental and physical labor of the 9-1-1 professional "knit[s] disparate communications networks together."[24] This is similar to what media scholar Elinor Carmi describes as "processed listening," which "describes the way media workers selectively tune into different sources through the media apparatus, by using several tools (which can be automatic or manual), in different temporalities, to produce different kinds of knowledge for various purposes."[25] Through integrated use of multiple technologies, 9-1-1 professionals turn information into knowledge, experience into emergency.

Next, the 9-1-1 professional must decide on a course of action and "translate it into one single CAD code—robbery, electric odor, man down"[26]—in order to dispatch the best available response. This is cultural labor, interpretative and agential, in which the dispatcher's work produces the emergency for action, enacting logistical gatekeeping by evaluating and acting upon a caller's emergency claim. In short, 9-1-1 professionals are engaged in *emergency media work*, through which they construct knowledge of a situation as an emergency, and then determine an appropriate response.

Producing Emergency through 9-1-1's Media Work

The emergency media work of 9-1-1 professionals is crucial to the production of emergency. Emergency reports are not neutral but are co-produced through an infrastructure that includes multiple media technologies glued together through the intellectual and physical labor of 9-1-1 professionals. Digging into this labor involves attention to the "assemblage, the delicate, complex weaving together of desktop resources, organizational routines, running memory . . . and all manner or articulation work performed invisibly"[27] by 9-1-1 professionals so as to produce infrastructure that is ready on demand for members of the public. As Tony, an IT specialist in an East Coast 9-1-1 center, explains, answering a call is a "nexus of emergency communications."[28]

That nexus is a moment of articulation between the "messy reality" of the everyday world and the official protocols and codes of law enforcement and other emergency response organizations.[29] 9-1-1 professionals are tasked with calmly getting necessary information from callers who are often scared, sad, in pain, and encountering an unfamiliar bureaucratic system, and then with converting that information into a service code and using a separate system to transmit that code and dispatch responders. In this process, they operate multiple media systems—telephones, radios, online maps, computer software such as Computer Aided Dispatch (CAD) systems, multimedia interfaces, and so on—to receive, interpret, and produce mediated messages. The dispatcher is the central node in making 9-1-1 *happen*, through their embodied use of multiple media technologies. The emergency media work of 9-1-1 is a form of interpersonal and informational labor that involves the use, interpretation, and creation of media systems in order to produce infrastructure for the public's use.

Studying dispatch as media work is an interventionist choice, countering the outsized focus on the production of media texts within studies of media industries. Apart from the industrial cultures of film and television,[30] or the participatory cultures of amateur production,[31] there are a host of understudied workers whose labor relies on the use and interpretation of media systems or content. As cultural theorist Melissa Gregg observes, "media scholarship has been surprisingly reticent in investigating the use of online platforms and devices for work purposes"[32] given the centrality of communications media to facilitating pervasive cultures of work. We might think about these as paraindustries, where work depends on the use of media content and technology but does not result in the provision of media content to a public.

Framing this labor as media work focuses attention on how the professionalized interpretation of media is a meaningful activity, to which workers bring their own values and through which they make decisions that refract back onto the construction of ideologies and practices within a larger society. This is one of the central theoretical contributions of critical media industry studies—that workers are themselves culturally shaped and bring that to bear on their subsequent creation of cultural artifacts.[33] In the case of emergency media work, this influence occurs through the production of actionable knowledge and interpretations born out of both mainstream and localized cultural values and narratives. In short, studying the work and culture of 9-1-1 professionals enables us to understand how they extend and produce this logistical infrastructure and attendant meanings of emergency itself.

The media work of 9-1-1 begins with an individual caller's emergency claim, which 9-1-1 professionals must understand, evaluate, and act on (or not). Thus, much research on 9-1-1 professionals has focused on interactional communication and the possibility of breakdowns in the communicative exchange between a caller and a call-taker.[34] After all, the ability to make a report—to have an emergency claim accepted— requires crafting an emergency narrative that will be accepted by the call-taker, who is granted such authority on behalf of larger public safety apparatus.

This means that 9-1-1 professionals can be understood as gatekeepers, seeking information and assurance of a valid emergency. Sociologists John Heritage and Steven Clayman studied 9-1-1 calls as a form of "institutional talk," in which both caller and call-taker adopt discrete communicative roles.[35] They observe that call-takers direct the conversation, asking questions "about the problem itself (the type of problem, degree of urgency, etc.), its location (the street address, type of dwelling, how to gain access, etc.), and sometimes other details such as the caller's identity, involvement, and basis for believing that the problem is genuine" in order to evaluate a request for help.[36] In return, the caller provides information that justifies their request by clearly indicating the genuineness (is there really a problem?) and relevance (can available services solve the problem?) of the situation.[37] Call-takers then assess whether "the caller is reliable and his or her account genuine" based on signs such as proximity to the problem and its urgency.[38]

Michelle, a longtime 9-1-1 professional in the southeastern United States, describes such an evaluation as follows:

> But you also have to be able to listen, really listen, because you're not just listening to what they're saying, you're listening to how they're saying it and any other kind of little clues, what background noise you're hearing . . .
>
> Because you might have somebody say, "Oh, I'm fine. I don't need the police." And you hear something in the background, you know . . . I've had a feeling that she said everything was fine, but I think somebody needs to go over there and check on her. She just kept saying she didn't need help, she said it a little too much.
>
> Let somebody go over there and just check, and come to find out, yeah, there was a domestic situation.

The interactional communication of making and evaluating a request is thus only part of what goes on in Michelle's interpretation of calls. Michelle performs empathetic processed listening, alert to signs that a caller's account might be incomplete or compromised. A retracted report—"Oh, I'm fine"—becomes actionable through the intervention of the 9-1-1 professional as a *coproducer* of the report and emergency response.

Gatekeeping via conversation and audio cues differentiates 9-1-1 as a public service from common experiences with customer service, where the customer may always be right.[39] In customer service contexts such as technical support lines, operators are tasked with the emotional labor of producing a "compliant customer who will stay on the phone line and work with the agent to fix his or her technological failure themself."[40] Similar emotional labor occurs in 9-1-1 calls, as 9-1-1 professionals must soothe the anger or terror of a caller while managing their own emotions.[41] However, 9-1-1 professionals may have fewer options for such emotional management, as they are also tasked with evaluating urgency and triaging response.

Cathy, who has worked in rural midwestern PSAPs for over thirty years, recalled one such instance of mismatched expectations. The caller, a woman, had been in a small car accident and she and the other party had managed to move their cars from the road to a Taco Bell parking lot. No one was injured, but they needed police to document the incident. For Cathy, this was a low-urgency call. She put the incident in the CAD system but did not immediately dispatch police. Instead, it would have appeared in an incident queue for officers in the area. For the caller, however, this delay was infuriating—she called back multiple times in the next hour, yelling and cursing about the delay in what she was treating as an on-demand service.

At the core of the tension between Cathy and her caller was what communication scholar Karen Tracy identified as a conflict between public service and customer service expectations,[42] which persists in contemporary 9-1-1 operations.[43] Yet it's hard to blame callers for approaching 9-1-1 with a customer service frame. While protocols and training have enabled 9-1-1 professionals to develop a strong set of routines and expectations for how a call "ought" to progress, the public is often encountering a bureaucratic system for the first time and under duress.[44] For the caller, in Tony's words, "it's the worst moment of your life, you're calling, you have no idea really what someone is going to ask you or do beyond what you've seen on TV." The infrastructure of feeling around 9-1-1, in this case, does little to prepare people for direct encounters with the system, which has its own routines and interests.

For 9-1-1 professionals, emergency is everyday, and the workflow of 9-1-1 professionals operates to define "emergency" in terms of urgency and available resources. This is the "master narrative" of 9-1-1 infrastructure;[45] all of the tasks—from call-taking to dispatching, providing support to victims or responders, inputting data, and so on—are centered on logistical distribution of resources to those judged to need them. To do this distributive labor, 9-1-1 professionals engage in the evaluation of emergency, which is "shaped by what is taken as routine and normal" by the professionals themselves.[46] They perform cultural work as they make these decisions, hewing to cultural narratives and previous experience to judge what does or does not require immediate response. This can result in quick or misguided judgements, the dismissal of what appear to be non-emergencies, or a brusqueness in interacting with the public. Callers expect a level of service that prioritizes their needs and expectations, but 9-1-1 professionals are seeking specific information to allocate often scarce resources from the larger public safety apparatus.

9-1-1 professionals are a link between public safety agencies and the public. Caroline Burau, a former 9-1-1 professional, describes this tension in her memoir: "We are the middlemen between the cops and the "customers"—the public. It's hard not to get trampled when you're standing between people in crisis and cops who just want to go home at the end of the day."[47]

Although many 9-1-1 professionals have experience or family connections in emergency medical services, police, or fire departments, 9-1-1 was often described to me as the "black sheep" of emergency response. Often deprioritized in terms of funding or training (particularly when under the auspices of law enforcement), 9-1-1 operations both are and are not part of these other public safety systems. As ethnographer Phoebe Wang writes, dispatchers may feel that their difficult work is nonetheless "regarded by certain people [they] work with [implying public safety colleagues] as easy, safe, and even dispensable."[48] This imbalance is evident in efforts to recognize 9-1-1 professionals as first responders; they have historically been ineligible for these workplace protections, classed instead as clerical staff. Undoubtedly, this is also related to the long-standing feminization of 9-1-1 work through connections to telephone operators, secretaries, or customer service fields.[49] 9-1-1 professionals are not only or always cops; they occupy a liminal occupational and communicative role, and as such individual 9-1-1 professionals have some power to shape the operations of emergency. New technologies can either foster such reshapings or prevent them, handing over the labor of 9-1-1 professionals to opaque algorithmic systems.

New Technology, New Problems

9-1-1 professionals' media work produces emergency not only through interpersonal labor but by forging technological linkages between multiple technical systems, enabling emergency response. Considering current shifts in the technological environment of 9-1-1 allows us to see both the complexity and limitations of how "emergency" is produced and how it might be produced differently.

Increasingly, the technologies that support 9-1-1 professionals attempt to integrate multiple systems and workflows as they update PSAPs to NG9-1-1 standards, enabling greater digital capabilities. In doing so, these technologies often replicate older ways of doing things, illustrating the intransigence of infrastructure. In Indiana, for instance, a public-private partnership with a company called INdigital enabled the entire state to adopt text-to-9-1-1 in 2014. INdigital built a platform—Textty—which allowed 9-1-1 professionals to send and receive text messages. Like many systems, Textty offered the ability to load prewritten messages, such as "Where is your emergency?" The choice to preload this question about location in an NG9-1-1 system—in which, presumably, the phone's location could be sent by the carrier—reflects the persistence of older routines in the institutional talk of call-taking. Textty and similar platforms also initially disallowed images and emoji, due to anxieties about new communication formats.[50] Capt. Dave Bursten of the Indiana State Police, for instance, warned that "autocorrect can change 'my house is on fire' to 'my horse is on fire.'"[51] Modeling new systems on old procedures resulted in prioritizing known ways of doing things over the possibilities and expectations supported by consumer technologies.

Instead of launching text-to-9-1-1 as an exciting and useful tool for the general population, Indiana and many other states have heavily emphasized its role as an accessibility technology for d/Deaf, hard-of-hearing, and communicatively disabled people and discouraging "frivolous" uses of the technology. As I have argued elsewhere, the rollout of text-to-9-1-1 capabilities across the country can be understood to be deploying disability as an excuse for the larger failure to update both technologies and operations, justifying the limitations of the service by casting it as "only" an assistive technology for d/Deaf, hard-of-hearing, and communicatively disabled people.[52] But as of June 2019, the FCC had 1,478 PSAPs registered as capable of accepting text messages, out of the more than 6,000 PSAPs in the United States overall.[53] As a result, most of the country cannot text 9-1-1 regardless of their disability status.

In contrast to the slow infrastructural adjustments brought by text-to-9-1-1, private CAD technologies and related dispatching software are rapidly transforming the work of dispatch. While there has been a great deal of recent research on the rise of big data and predictive algorithms within policing, there has been comparatively little research focused on the information technologies that have been implemented in dispatch. In fact, emergency call-taking and dispatch are invisibilized in some of this work. Legal scholar Brian Ferguson opens *The Rise of Big Data Policing* with an example from the Los Angeles Police Department's Real-Time Analysis Critical Response Division (RACR), which operates in partnership with a private tech company called Palantir: "A 9-1-1 call. A possible gang fight in progress. RACR Command directs patrol units to the scene all the while monitoring their real-time progress. Data about the fight is pushed officers on their mobile phones."[54] The people who answered the call, dispatched police cars, and initiated data pushes are replaced by predictive technology in Ferguson's telling. Assuming that these people were 9-1-1 professionals—and not, say, police chiefs—this oversight suggests a continuation of telecommunications histories in which predominantly female workforces were conceived of as "part of the communication channel,"[55] unseen and ignorable.

Yet just as policing has been transformed by datafication and the rising value in "informational capital" for technology firms,[56] so have technology companies found 9-1-1 operations rich territories for growth. These systems are transformative not only in their technological capabilities, but in terms of the working conditions, data privacy, and public service offered by 9-1-1.

Motorola's VESTA Command Center Software presents itself as a technical solution for PSAPs, centralizing information, consolidating desktop tools, and offloading some tasks while promising better information than could be received by relying on the caller alone.[57] In a 2018 promotional video, VESTA further promises to integrate "additional information from external data sources" with the mapped location of a call and the locations of emergency vehicles; this is illustrated in the promotional video with an indication that a caller was Spanish-speaking and had a history of seizures (see figure 4.1). This is a clear example of unclear extraction and recombination of data from government, commercial, or other sources. While the video presents data about language (or ethnicity) and disability as useful for ensuring the safety of the individual—a form of safety surveillance—it is also clearly being offered in order to inform police responses to unknown situations and people. As legal scholar Andrew Ferguson warns, one of the biggest threats of such "black data" is that it can be wrong, resulting in predictive policing

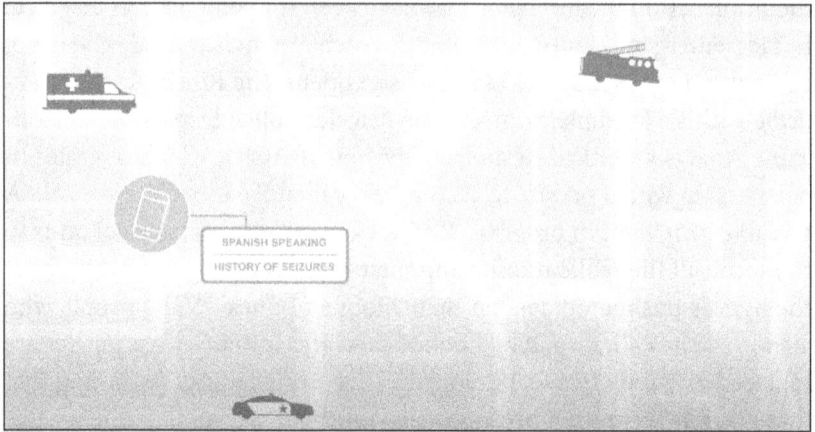

Figure 4.1. Author's screenshot of 2018 VESTA promotional video, showing a street map with the locations of fire, police, and medical vehicles as well as a green dot indicating caller's location and personal details.

maneuvers that put people and communities at greater risk.[58] VESTA enables incorrect data to guide response from the moment of an emergency response, replacing the interpretive work of the 9-1-1 professional with an algorithmic decision.

Integrating call-taking, text message interfaces, and CAD data input, the VESTA Command Center is promoted as a streamlined solution for PSAPs looking to modernize their technology and increase efficiency. The tagline on the 2018 promotional video—"Save Clicks. Save Seconds. Save Lives"—draws a straight line between technology, time, and safety. VESTA's public-facing materials offer little concrete information about either pricing or data practices, with the website prompting users to "schedule a demo" in order to learn more (implying that only potential clients would be granted such a demo).

In many ways, VESTA presents itself identically to a competitor, a CAD called RapidDeploy. A recent analysis of RapidDeploy argues that it represents the datafication of emergency response, extracting public data with little public transparency regarding its subsequent storage, use, or ownership.[59] As such, it is a form of extractive surveillance capitalism,[60] profiting from the data generated by 9-1-1 calls and undermining the strength of public governance and public values within public safety. RapidDeploy is an opaque infrastructure to members of the public and researchers, deliberately rendering its workings invisible and thus nearly impervious to public comment or critique.

Private technologies like VESTA and RapidDeploy have filled the void left by insufficient public awareness and investment in 9-1-1 operations. Often, they do so with little public awareness, as agencies contract with companies in closed-door negotiations that are covered through repurposed press releases. This means that these companies now have a growing role in shaping how emergency reports are made and received; the close and procedural listening that has characterized the emergency media work of 9-1-1 professionals is being devalued and replaced by algorithmic representations of risk and reliability. If interpersonal 9-1-1 exchanges broke down over mismatched expectations relating to the logistical mandates of evaluating and coordinating emergency response, algorithmic evaluations are even more likely to operate in the interests of institutions and at the expense of the caller.

This is the core of the lawsuit filed by Bre and Kali Lasley, Utah sisters who faced an intruder armed with a knife in 2019. The sisters attempted to fight him off while making four calls to 9-1-1; however, no one was ever dispatched.[61] The Lasleys alleged that the "rigid" series of questions and answers required by Priority Dispatch—the software system used by Salt Lake City, and owner of the International Academies of Emergency Dispatch—were impossible to answer in the moment and resulted in them being denied needed help.[62] While protocols have value in standardizing operations and gathering needed information, they have long provoked caller frustration because of the sense that scripted questions ignored important context.[63] As digitized and datafied systems come to characterize more 9-1-1 systems, potentially preventing professionals from deviating from scripted questions and decisions, standardization may result in further constriction of what emergency reports can be made, accepted, and acted upon.

Racist Reports, Fabricated Emergencies

While much of this chapter has proceeded as if reports are made only *after* or *in a response to* a situation believed to be an emergency, the media infrastructure of reporting can also be (mis)used to *create* emergencies. This is particularly evident in the racist deputization of 9-1-1 and emergency response institutions—most often the police—to address situations involving Black people and other people of color, disabled people, ethnic and linguistic minorities, and impoverished or homeless people.

On Memorial Day, 2020—just before the eruption of nationwide protests over the police killing of George Floyd—a Black man named Christian Cooper went bird-watching in Central Park. He encountered a white woman, Amy Cooper (no relation), walking her dog off-leash, a violation of park rules. He asked her to leash it and an argument ensued. He began to record the interaction on his phone and in response, she called 9-1-1, saying "There is a man, African-American, he has a bicycle helmet and he is recording me and threatening me and my dog."[64] After the initial call, a 9-1-1 operator called back, and Cooper claimed she was being assaulted. Police responded and found no justification for these claims; Amy Cooper was charged with filing a false police report. In the words of New York senior prosecutor Joan Iluzzi, Cooper "used the police in a way that was 'both racially offensive and designed to intimidate.'"[65]

Here, the report to 9-1-1 transforms a situation into an emergency, creates an official response, and becomes a site of possible danger for those being reported (and not, usually, for callers themselves). In a host of cases, only a handful of which receive news coverage, privileged people (usually white, often women) call 9-1-1 to report people for minor infractions or inconveniences. Doing this in a culture in which it is known that inviting police intervention brings attendant risks of escalation, violence, or death amounts to a weaponization of reports and the concept of emergency.

Amy Cooper was far from the first white woman to treat 9-1-1 as her personal security force. Throughout 2018 and 2019, similar situations gained traction online and in the media through the Twitter hashtag #LivingWhileBlack and through catchy hashtag monikers applied to white informants. #LivingWhileBlack originated on Black Twitter[66] to highlight instances of "a black or brown person, doing something innocuous or nothing at all, [prompting] a suspicious white person to call the police."[67] A conflict over a charcoal grill in an Oakland, California, park became a threat of criminalization and police violence to two Black men thanks to #BBQBecky.[68] Other well-publicized incidents included two

Black men confronted in a Philadelphia Starbucks and a Black graduate student at Yale confronted for his use of a student space.[69] Such calls "allow white callers to control public spaces and use the police as an enforcer, intimidation tool, and removal service."[70]

The racist instrumentalization of 9-1-1 to fabricate emergency stems directly from its dominant infrastructure of feeling. An infrastructure of feeling prioritizes the affective security of mainstream or desired audiences—parents, the wealthy, white people, elites—over the needs of those in more vulnerable social positions. Just as emergency blue light phones on college campuses produce a feeling of safety among parents or incoming students while doing nothing to reduce incidents of sexual assault or racial violence, the cultural hypervisibility of 9-1-1 offers many relatively privileged people a sense that any emergency can be reported and addressed (reassuring them of their safety) while continuing to work against the interests of those most marginalized, whose precarious living conditions may not even be recognizable in a claim of emergency.

9-1-1's infrastructure of feeling is established through its cultural ubiquity. 9-1-1 appears on squad cars, publicly posted safety instructions, and has a popular culture footprint evident in television shows including *Rescue 9-1-1* (CBS, 1989–96), *COPS* (FOX, 1989–2013), *9-1-1* (FOX, 2018–present), episodes of crime procedurals, in films, and in the use of 9-1-1 calls as part of true crime podcasts. Additionally, children are a primary audience for 9-1-1 education, with games, mazes, coloring books, and other resources available from various jurisdictions as part of an effort to teach children how and when to call for help. This very cultural prevalence may be what allows 9-1-1 to function in emergency; philosopher Elaine Scarry describes thinking in an emergency as a matter of offloading predetermined, thought-laden processes into routines and infrastructures that become habitual.[71] Rather than deliberating and making conscious decisions, such offloading enables quasi-automatic actions to occur.

Because of its ubiquity and the encouragement of offloading, 9-1-1 is often a first point of call for people looking to report an emergency and receive some kind of assistance. Burau advises "always just to call 9-1-1. Don't call your mom, don't call OnStar, and for God's sake don't call your friend who's a cop in another city ten miles away."[72] And people do call 9-1-1 for a range of situations, as evidenced in the routine human interest stories seen on local news and social media about children who call for homework help, pets rescued, and minor irritations reported as emergencies. Is it any wonder that white people socialized in such a context would turn to 9-1-1 to address their racial discomfort, which they may feel or represent as fear?

Affective rationales are frequently used by 9-1-1 callers when they realize they may be calling about something that is not quite an emergency, such as in calls about "virtual, impending, or not-yet-actualized problems."[73] Expressions of fear are deployed to justify requests for help that might otherwise appear frivolous, and to convince the 9-1-1 professional on the other end of the call to accept the emergency claim. But whose fear is actionable, and whose fear is provoked by racially motivated calls to 9-1-1? And how do 9-1-1 dispatchers accept, reject, or negotiate such fears or possibilities of emergency?

In discussing the affect of fear, Sara Ahmed reminds us that fear is felt when danger is approaching, in anticipation.[74] Thus, it is neither fully rational nor fully located in the present; feeling fear is not equivalent to being in danger. Or, in the case of frivolous, racist claims of emergency, "'feeling' threatened doesn't mean you are."[75] Fear is a privileged affect, most often "spoken from white middle-class, heterosexual male social positions" as if its meanings are self-evident.[76] Fear can also be a "gendered maneuver"[77] in that (white) women are particularly encouraged to represent their feelings and needs in affective language of fear, safety, and presumptive victimization. Thus, for white women to speciously call 9-1-1 on Black or other people of color is to deploy a familiar gendered and racialized script in which their discomfort is a sign of victimization, and in which public safety exists to protect them from such feelings.

While some discussions of racially motivated 9-1-1 calls have suggested that they are microaggressions or expressions of implicit bias,[78] this minimizes the scope of agency in making such a call and the potential severity of its effects. Instead, we should see the deputization of the emergency system as evidence of the entitlement of many white people to government services, an entitlement that enacts a form of racial superiority. Legal scholar Jonathan Kahn describes this entitlement in terms of the "9-1-1 covenant," a use of legal channels to produce and further racist restrictions on public space and life.[79] Drawing on historical housing covenants, which restricted home ownership on the basis of race, Kahn argues that the 9-1-1 covenant "is grounded on the tacit understanding that white people can call 9-1-1 when they are made uncomfortable by the presence of a person of color in a particular space in which they are perceived to be 'out of place.'"[80]

Crucially, this notion of the 9-1-1 covenant allows us to consider racism rather than simply unintended or implicit bias; Kahn makes the point that making and responding to a 9-1-1 call is not an implicit action but requires thought and action that leave multiple chances to make different decisions.[81] While there may be infrastructures of feeling that promote the routinized and racialized use of 9-1-1, there are also many people who can and do make different decisions regardless of circumstances or experiences of fear or discomfort, including 9-1-1 professionals. Kahn's analysis places the 9-1-1 dispatcher at a fulcrum point:

> A white person sees a black person in a coffee shop, sleeping in a college common room, existing an AirBnB, or trying to use a public pool, and they call 9-1-1. The dispatcher does not question their characterizing the situation as a 9-1-1 emergency. This is the first part of the covenant—accept the legitimacy of the call.[82]

By *accepting the legitimacy* of the call, 9-1-1 professionals accept (and create) an emergency report. Kahn acknowledges that 9-1-1 professionals are operating under time and other pressures, and might be constrained by local policies, workflows, and the threat of liability for negligence in not dispatching in response to a call. In many cases, the operating principle ("when in doubt, send it out") favors accepting an emergency claim and sending emergency services, exacerbating racist and otherwise biased calls.[83] However, 9-1-1 professionals do not accept every call as an emergency; they reject prank calls, and sometimes suggest alternative resources for callers with non-emergency issues. There is room for discretion in the production of fabricated emergencies such as racist reports.

Implicitly or explicitly, 9-1-1 professionals can push back on the racist operation of emergency reports. Sociologist Jessica Gillooly describes such pushback as characteristic of a "gatekeeping orientation"[84] seen in 9-1-1 professionals who take an active role in determining the outcome of a call. She gives an example of her own growth in this gatekeeping function, drawing out a caller reporting a black man who "could" have a gun by clarifying that, in fact, no gun was visible. Thus, Gillooly input the call at a lower priority for police response.[85] By contrast, in the case of Tamir Rice, a 9-1-1 caller reported someone, "probably a juvenile," carrying a "probably fake" gun, but the 9-1-1 call-taker did not include this detail and input the case as a top priority, leading to an outsized police response that killed a twelve-year-old boy.[86]

In addition to making choices about the categorization and severity of a report, 9-1-1 professionals may use language to indicate doubt about a racist report. Gillooly gives the example of a call-taker inputting an incident by writing "2 BMs (black males) wearing hoodies are loitering in the area. Caller thinks they live in a nearby apartment complex but thinks it's suspicious because they keep 'looking around.' Caller doesn't want contact."[87] The quotation marks here likely indicate a direct quotation from the caller, but Gillooly argues that they also indicate that the call-taker does not find the claim of emergency credible.

Such negotiated, partial acceptances of emergency claims rely in part on interpersonal context. Former Bay Area call-taker Rachael Herron wrote in the aftermath of #BBQBecky that "I'm guessing that the dispatcher rolled his eyes at this call so hard they almost fell out of his head. Yet another white lady upset over what black people were doing" and that the low priority assigned to the call was "dispatch code" for an irritating, unnecessary, and racist use of emergency resources.[88] Through experience, context, and their familiarity with the system, 9-1-1 professionals can push back on how the infrastructure that their labor produces is used and misused by people whose main understanding of it stems from its partial and ideologically powerful cultural representation.

By recognizing the actual operations of 9-1-1 as infrastructure and emergency media work, we may work towards infrastructural "legibility." Germaine Halegoua and Jessa Lingel define this as "unpacking the stories, processes, and ideologies that shape ways of seeing (and not seeing)" infrastructures ideologically and affectively.[89] By considering the infrastructure of feeling surrounding 9-1-1 in combination with its infrastructural and labor operations, a richer picture of its operations may be found. When an infrastructure of feeling provokes an affective sense of safety, it concretizes particular ideas about fear and stymies radical change. Yet, infrastructures of feeling do not work uniformly; their affective work succeeds best for people for whom the infrastructure might be perceived to be functioning. Those who have encountered the inner workings or failures of an underlying infrastructure are likely to see through the assurances offered by an infrastructure of feeling. Amy Cooper, #LivingWhileBlack, and similar uses of 9-1-1 infrastructure make legible—and politically actionable—what was a taken-for-granted infrastructure of emergency.

In fact, the attention generated by these cases in the past few years has led multiple states to consider ways to penalize people who make racially biased calls. These include San Francisco's CAREN (Caution Against Racially Exploitative Non-Emergencies) Act, which criminalizes making a racially motivated call, and is accompanied by efforts to make such calls hate crimes in California.[90] New York is similarly working to add false reporting to a list of possible hate crimes, while Michigan considered making racially motivated false reports a felony, and Oregon has considered legislation to "authorize the victims of racially motivated 9-1-1 calls to bring civil litigation against the caller."[91] Such interventions indicate a greater attention to 9-1-1 operations than is usually granted, illustrating that as popular coverage of racial bias challenged the infrastructure of feeling around 9-1-1, its actual operations became understandable and actionable in ways that have not historically been available.

Conclusion

9-1-1 is not the only means of reporting an emergency; reports made to non-emergency police telephone lines, medical reports, reports to neighborhood watches and other local groups, reports to corporate or educational authorities, and other forms of reports may be made in cases of accidents, health scares, crime, violence, and other emergencies. However, 9-1-1 is unique in that it is often the gate through which many of these (and other) reports of emergency are routed. As a "universal emergency number" with high cultural visibility, 9-1-1 is many people's first (or only) option. This media infrastructure is the primary channel for individual emergency claims, and its technological and labor operations are therefore key to understanding how "emergency" is understood and acted on by those with the power to do so.

The emergency media work of 9-1-1 professionals is central to making this system work; they link together multiple systems, technologies, institutions, and people to produce emergency response. In so doing, these workers also participate in the construction of emergency through the evaluation and even coproduction of reports. Their agency—evident in their conversational practices, their listening, their decisions about specific callers or events—enables them to function as gatekeepers. Their structural position as representatives of the state's authority to give or withhold assistance grants them a great deal of power in determining the course of events in a given emergency, even as their position within the larger infrastructures of public safety is routinely devalued.

9-1-1 professionals have done this work with constantly changing technological tools over the past thirty years. Now, as 9-1-1 operations attempt to modernize in line with caller's expectations of consumer technologies, integrating text, multimedia, and automatic location data, 9-1-1 professionals are facing technologies that automate some of this labor. Preloaded responses, rigid question protocols embedded in software systems that require an answer before allowing a user to move forward to enter a code or initiate dispatch, and opaque systems that operate as data brokers to provide "context" to a call will all transform the nature of 9-1-1 work. In so doing, they will change what it means to make a report and have it accepted; what kinds of emergency claims will such systems recognize, or dismiss?

The infrastructure of feeling promoted by 9-1-1—a ubiquity, reliability, and affective safety for desired audiences—has long overshadowed the decidedly unglamorous work and tools of 9-1-1 operations. Yet if we rely on children's books, television dramas, or intense calls featured on *Tapes from the Darkside* or other true crime podcasts, 9-1-1 remains illegible and its operations unavailable for intervention. The reassurance offered by an infrastructure of feeling renders 9-1-1 precarious in its status as a public service; the infrastructures of feeling allow for the practical elements of safety technologies to become forgotten, unfunded, and outdated or to be replaced by commercial technologies that are opaque, extractive, and dubiously helpful in producing emergency aid. People who cannot see the gaps in emergency media are not empowered to create the forms of protection that they want and deserve; we must look beneath the intentionally comfortable affective dimensions of emergency media to explore how these media could better serve the diverse populations to whom they are, ostensibly, accountable.

5

Help!

Social Media Testimony and Emergency Bids

In the previous chapter, I argued that when Amy Cooper called 9-1-1 to retaliate against Christian Cooper, a Black man who requested she leash her dog in the park, she made a racist, fraudulent emergency report. But while she was using her phone, so was Christian Cooper. As she reported, he recorded. This video, circulated online by his sister, was viewed over forty-five million times,[1] drawing attention to the frivolous police reports that subject Black people's everyday lives to carceral oversight. In the aftermath of George Floyd's death, this media testimony highlighted the ongoing emergency of racist police action.

Publishing this video, viewing it (or choosing not to), recirculating it, discussing it, and bringing it to the attention of national media allowed a collective reinterpretation of this moment as evidence of structural racism as an emergency. The very impact of such videos over the past five years has been to argue that the normalcy of racist and violent policing is, in fact, an emergency that demands a response. Videos and other user-generated evidence of experiences of danger, trauma, or death serve as *testimonies* and *emergency bids* that can challenge the default meaning of emergency as deviation from normalcy.[2]

This chapter considers *testimony* as a form of emergency mediation through which people share experiences and make a *bid* that those experiences be recognized as emergencies. I use "testimony" to describe media artifacts that share individual experiences to highlight structural emergencies and demand response. People address their testimonial emergency media not to authorities or institutions but to varied audiences of peers or publics who may accept this evidence of structural emergency by engaging, responding, or further circulating testimony. In doing so, these audiences grant the bid emergency status: this happened, this requires response. Because of the flexibility in both the creation and uptake of testimony as emergency media, it represents a prime means through which people may rearticulate the meanings of emergency, re-envision emergency response, and wrestle with safety surveillance, infrastructures of feeling, and emergency media work.

After a brief theorization of testimony and emergency bids, this chapter moves through several cases through which to tease out testimony's possibilities and limitations in relation to previously discussed dynamics of emergency media. First, I consider historical examples of testimony that called attention to systemic injustices, usually couched within alternative or activist media environments. This leads into discussion of contemporary online networks that circulate #BlackLivesMatter content, focusing on the examples of Philando Castile and Breonna Taylor. These testimonies make a bid for people to recognize the structural racism that entrenches police brutality as an emergency that demands response. By bringing attention to these realities, they break down the infrastructures of feeling around 9-1-1 or emergency response (discussed in chapter 4). The power of such peer testimony is such that many major platforms have incorporated emergency and disaster response features, restricting the scope of user testimony and subsuming testimony to logics of safety surveillance. Finally, I consider the widespread use of online media to organize mutual aid groups where people routinely make bids to have their needs recognized as emergencies—and addressed—by their communities. This requires mutual aid volunteers to engage in many of the same communicative and evaluative practices that characterize other forms of emergency media work. Highlighting testimony's unique capabilities and its relationship to previously explored logics of emergency media helps to see where it offers provocative possibilities for reimagining emergency and its mediation.

Testimony and Emergency Bids

Testimony works quite differently from alarms, maps, alerts, or reports. Those media are variously linked to authoritative sources of information, aid, or response, as when a fire alarm is set off in a commercial building and the fire department is automatically notified, when an alert is issued by a local government agency, or when a report is made to the police via 9-1-1. I use "testimony," by contrast, to capture the informal ways that people use familiar and available forms of consumer media technologies—cellphone videos, social media posts, crowdfunding platforms, and sharing economy apps[3]—to share their experience, express their needs, and generate attention from a broader public in the interest of addressing emergencies caused by structural social problems. This public may include family, friends, social media networks, and even the mainstream media, but it is not a guaranteed audience and the audience does not necessarily formulate a response. In doing so, people often challenge mainstream understandings of "emergency" by drawing attention to events that are "normal" but nonetheless deplorable, such as ongoing police brutality and racism.

Testimony, according to literary critic Shoshana Feldman and psychologist Dori Laub, is a performative discursive practice that creates events or interpretations as it recounts them.[4] In many contexts, such as a court of law, "testimony is used to establish what happened."[5] By offering testimony, one attempts to create truth and have that truth accepted by others. The power of testimony as emergency media comes from those occasions on which it is accepted by an audience, when people recognize others' experiences as emergencies that require action. When a cell phone video enables millions of people to see the racism of overzealous policing and reporting, it allows people to see racist policing as an emergency worthy of action rather than a normalized part of everyday life.

In moments like this, a media artifact like the smartphone video functions as a "witnessing text" that can use forms of perspective and address to facilitate intimacy with viewers and lead them to adopt witnessing as a form of reception and subsequent action.[6] People around the world produce such witnessing texts to share what media scholar Kari Andén-Papadopoulos refers to as "graphic testimony in a bid to produce feelings of political solidarity."[7] In the contexts of protests, elections, acts of violence, interpersonal conflicts, or moments of celebration, these media allow people to imagine themselves within (or even filming) the scenes at hand, bringing them closer to the events recorded and perspective espoused.[8]

The normalization of such sharing has changed the way that people behave in crises or emergency, turning to smartphones to "make their eyewitness experience more evidential."[9] The impulse to produce tes-

timony is particularly relevant in moments of obvious violence or oppression, and on behalf of those whose perspectives are often subject
to doubt including people facing varied forms of social marginalization, oppression, or violence. In these moments, testimony is offered to
encourage its audience "to identify an injustice, a harm or a wrong."[10]
When Christian Cooper held his phone in front of his face, recording a
malicious 9-1-1 call, he enabled people to formally take up the position
of a Black man being unjustly targeted. Such mediated witnessing may
be powerfully affective and productive of further action, as in the experiences of many Black Americans viewing instances of police violence.[11]

Yet, media theorist John Durham Peters writes that "testimony always
has a twilight status between certainty and doubt,"[12] indicating that not
all forms of testimony may be accepted by their audiences (for a variety
of reasons). This uncertainty may be one reason that mediated forms of
witnessing are not always productive of action.

Thus, testimony functions as a tentative emergency claim—what we
might think of as an "emergency bid"—offered to uncertain audiences
with uncertain outcomes. To make a bid is to make "an attempt to win or
secure something,"[13] in this case, recognition that a situation is an emergency, that some action is required, and that the people to whom this
bid is made have a moral (rather than official) responsibility to facilitate
that response.[14] This differs from the framing of "emergency claims,"
which often involve people asserting their rights within a governmental
or political framework.[15] Testimonial emergency bids are offered to the
judgement of one's peers, and as such they incorporate a wide range of
requests, conceptions of emergency, and possible outcomes. Often, these
bids may not even include the word "emergency," even as they indicate a
variety of needs, emotional distress, violence, danger, or injury. Importantly, bids rarely emphasize a previous, "normal" state of affairs from
which people have fallen; the testimony offered in emergency bids often
concerns ongoing struggles, making it a site of important challenges to
the normalizing mainstream ideology of emergency.

Conceptualizing testimony in terms of a witnessing text, rather than
a single speaking individual, is particularly important to understanding
how testimonial emergency bids are made and accepted. Following the
initial sharing of testimony, via text, video, or image, its circulation on
social media networks is central to how it may (or may not) gain vis-

ibility and foster further action. This circulation is completed through the accumulation of people's choices to watch, talk about, and share the content,[16] a "going viral" that cannot always be predicted or achieved. Through networks of activists, the use of hashtags on social media, and the growing influence of social media content on mainstream news coverage, testimony may gain widespread attention and acceptance of its emergency bid.[17]

In the following sections, I consider how emergency bids are made via testimony in a range of circumstances. In each case, I consider not only how testimony enables people to push back on and expand the meanings of emergency, but how previously discussed logics of emergency media may themselves be challenged or replicated through testimonial forms of emergency media.

Testimony, Activism, and Alternative Media

Much of this chapter addresses testimony as a form of emergency media located on and around social media platforms. However, testimony and attendant challenges to the normalizing frame of emergency obviously predate and surpass social media contexts. It has been particularly important in the cultural and political activism of oppressed groups, who often called on others to see, to recognize, to act. As such, histories of activist and alternative media are powerful sites at which testimony has been offered and taken up, shifting the ground of what normal life could or should be.

Activist and niche media outlets have historically been prime sites for the sharing of information and building of community and culture, and at times they have also functioned as outlets for testimony and emergency bids. The gay press in the early years of the AIDS crisis, for instance, was a crucial site for expanding awareness of HIV/AIDS. As early as 1982, the gay press recognized a growing crisis and objected to the Centers for Disease Control's hesitancy in labeling HIV/AIDS a public health emergency.[18] In the absence of such recognition, activists and media creators took it upon themselves to produce and distribute material about the nature of AIDS, preventative and care measures, and personal experiences. Writer and activist Simon Watney wrote in 1993 that "the gay press is the only institution which is able to reach significant numbers of gay men and lesbians with reliable, up to date information."[19] Thus, he understood there to be a responsibility to inform, to counter mainstream media narratives that were false or prejudicial, and to engage in activism when needed. Similarly, scholar-activist Alexandra Juhasz describes producing alternative AIDS television as "a political act that allows people who need to scream with pain or anger, who want to say 'I'm here, I count,' who have internalized sorrow and despair, who have vital information to share about drug protocols, coping strategies, or government inaction, to make their opinions public and to join with others in this act of resistance."[20] Whether in print, video, online, or in other formats, these alternative media outlets enabled people to share knowledge and experiences for the benefit of others, fostering a recognition of the scope and severity of HIV/AIDS.[21]

Watney writes that "activism is a politics of emergencies," what happens when the usual channels do not produce results.[22] When there is no official response in the face of personal or localized emergencies, activism becomes a way of soliciting attention and demanding action through strategies of visibility. Such strategies are visible in the alternative forms of cultural production seen in anti-rape activism, including zines and graffiti. Understood as part of a "fighting spirit" in anti-rape feminist activism, strategies like publishing abusers' names or addresses in zines or newsletters, writing them on a bathroom wall, and naming them at public events such as Take Back the Night marches were explicitly a form of testimony made powerful through their aggregation.[23] While one account is an anecdote, an outpouring of accounts reframes pervasive sexual violence as an emergency requiring action.

The emergency bids made by alternative and activist media testimony are powerful, but they do not necessarily attempt to address an audience beyond the communities that they build through the sharing of experiences and oppressions. To understand what is gained—and what is lost—when testimony is offered to a broader audience, we might consider two moments in Black and media history.

The murder of Emmett Till in 1955 precipitated a widespread media witnessing of racist violence. Emmett's mother, Mamie Till, invited a photographer from *Jet* magazine to the funeral, who photographed Till's open (glass-covered) casket, publishing the graphic images nationwide.[24] *Jet*, a magazine aimed at the Black community, had a reputation as "the most authoritative outlet for black witnessing"[25] in the mid-twentieth century, enabling it to function as a niche publication with a national footprint. Mamie Till famously stated, "I wanted the world to see what they did to my baby," demonstrating a desire to share with a public, to inform, and to outrage through testimony. Young people who saw the photograph and heard Till's story grew into "the Emmett Till generation," participating in the sit-ins, church and community organizations, unions, and protests that together formed the substance of the civil rights movement. The ability of testimony to make an emergency bid and spawn action is evident in the long influence of Till's short life.

Over thirty years later, another instance of racist violence was captured on video and nationally televised. In 1991, Rodney King was beaten by four white Los Angeles police officers while a bystander, George Holliday, recorded the incident on VHS. The "King video" was shared on television and used in the officers' trial, fundamentally shaping understandings of what happened, what was at stake, and what might be an emergency.

Cultural theorist John Fiske referred to the King *videos*, plural, because of how the original, low-tech video was recontextualized through computer augmentations and adjusted speeds in the courtroom, and variably recontextualized on television.[26] Fiske argued that these different permutations resulted in different perceptions of relative authenticity and meaning; a low-tech recording conveyed a kind of authenticity, while a manipulation or enhancement of that video produced distance from the on-screen events and enabled alternate readings. For instance, a brief clip of King moving in slow motion allowed the jury to perceive him moving toward officers, where the same motion in context appears an uncontrolled physical response to being struck. What would seem to be obvious evidence—a live video—was cast into doubt through manipulation and appeals to racist stereotypes of Black men as large, dangerous, and wild.

If we understand the King video to have made an emergency bid through its testimony, highlighting an abuse of police power, that bid was not accepted in court. Three of the four officers were acquitted, and a verdict could not be reached on the fourth. However, there was quick awareness that another emergency might emerge; the Los Angeles County Emergency Operations Center went into operation prior to the announcement of the verdict in anticipation of public outcry. That outcry came, and sparked the 1992 LA Riots, which themselves were quickly understood as an emergency. The Emergency Broadcast System was activated to announce a curfew throughout the city and surrounding areas, with at least one television station accompanying the audio message with what appeared to be live aerial footage of burning buildings.[27] As in the protests surrounding more recent police killings of Black Americans, understandings of racism and injustice as emergencies conflicted with official attempts to declare emergency and impose control. In some sense the public itself *was* the emergency, and this top-down declaration of emergency served not to protect them but to protect property and propriety.

Both the Till and King cases involve the failures of justice, institutional racism, and public outcry. Both revolved around testimonial media. Where they differed was in audience. The mass audience and courtroom (racist) readings of the video in King's case meant that Black Americans' recognition of a crisis of police brutality was undermined by an official (white) framing of the subsequent outrage as an emergency (rioting). What, then, happens when both niche and mainstream audiences are hailed by testimonial emergency bids? To answer this question, we can move forward nearly thirty years to consider the use of social media to produce testimony and make emergency bids in the Movement for Black Lives. Social media allows testimony to find larger audiences, enhancing searchability and findability of activist and niche media, and using links and networks to make nearly instant connections between media content, communities, and action. Simultaneously, social media threatens the potential of testimony to transform the nature of emergency by aggressively incorporating these functions under the auspices of technology companies and opaque platform policies.

Racial Justice Versus Infrastructures of Feeling

One of the most powerful examples of testimony in recent years has been the use of videos and images circulated on social media to draw attention to the Movement for Black Lives. From the 2014 police killing of Michael Brown in Ferguson, Missouri, to the deaths of Sandra Bland,

Eric Garner, Philando Castile, George Floyd, Ahmaud Arbery, Breonna Taylor, and others, testimonial media has circulated alongside hashtags that organize and magnify this content, driving awareness online and in mainstream media and political conversations. Repeatedly, this content has been described as illuminating "racism as an emergency," or as "replacing 9-1-1." I take up these claims through the deaths of Philando Castile and Breonna Taylor to see how the circulation of testimony about racist police violence comes to disrupt the very infrastructure of feeling that has supported emergency media and response. These incidents show that the system is not working—or is working only to oppress—and in so doing, make an emergency bid regarding the state of race and policing in the United States. Racist police are an emergency; emergency systems need to be addressed.

In July 2016, Philando Castile was driving through Forest Heights, Minnesota, with his girlfriend Diamond Reynolds and her four-year-old daughter Dae'Anna. A police officer, Jeronimo Yanez, pulled him over for a traffic stop. Castile, a beloved elementary school cafeteria worker, told Yanez that there was a registered firearm in the car. Yanez, flustered, told Castile to get his identification and to put his hands up; when Castile reached for his identification, Yanez shot him seven times. As Castile lay dying, Reynolds began streaming to Facebook Live from her phone. The video chronicled Reynolds's eerily calm explanation of events and her attempts to reason with Yanez. Reynolds continued filming and speaking to the officer until she was handcuffed and escorted—along with her daughter—to a waiting police car. Media scholar Allissa Richardson describes Reynolds as "the first person to capture police brutality in near real time."[28]

The filming of Castile's death can be understood as an act of what surveillance scholar Simone Browne calls "dark sousveillance," a form of critique that "centers black epistemologies of contending with surveillance."[29] Following a traffic stop, itself likely a result of racist surveillance, Castile is dead and Reynolds "understands that the only way to assert that Castile is human whose black life did, indeed, matter is to document and film his death."[30] Though the video briefly disappeared from Facebook and was later restored with a content warning,[31] it had already been saved and copied, making the leap to Twitter where it continued to circulate and was viewed nearly three million times.[32]

The day after Castile's death, several news publications drew a parallel between Reynolds's use of Facebook and 9-1-1. Online magazine *Inc.* ran the headline "How Facebook Live Is Becoming the Social 911 for People Who Can't Trust the Police," and *Wired* ran "For Philando Castile, Social Media Was the Only 911." The former asserted that Reynolds used Facebook Live "as her own 911,"[33] suggesting an equivalence in the two infrastructures but also recognizing that Reynolds (and others like her) are not "owners" of existing emergency systems. Thus, testimony replaces the report. Journalist Issie Lapowsky powerfully situated Reynolds's testimony as "not just a documentation of what happened, it was also a real-time cry for help. Unable to call the authorities as she watched her loved one slip away, Reynolds instead called on the public."[34]

This, then, was testimony in the mode of both emergency bid and black witnessing. Media scholar Allissa Richardson theorizes the Movement for Black Lives' powerful use of social media in terms of "black witnessing."[35] Richardson argues that black witnessing is reflexive and reflective, marked by a desire to do something about what is seen and to make connections to what has happened before.[36] She writes:

> Black witnessing: (1) assumes an investigative editorial stance to advocate for African American civil rights; (2) co-opts racialized online spaces to serve as its ad-hoc news distribution service; and (3) relies on interlocking black public spheres, which are endowed with varying levels of political agency, to engage diverse audiences.[37]

Not all black witnessing functions as an emergency bid, or vice versa, but at times these frames overlap. There is a similarity in the structure of emergency bids that I have described and the activist practice of black witnessing, both of which call on one or more publics to recognize and act.

With no ability to report Castile's injuries and receive aid from authorities—because those authorities caused his ultimate death—Reynolds's video asks others to recognize the emergency in this moment. Yet the emergency bid that Reynolds's video makes is not for aid in the moment; by the time we watch it, he has already died. *The emergency that demands recognition is police violence itself.* The video is intended to rupture easy assumptions about the role of the police as protectors or community servants; for those who watch it, it should disrupt any lingering sense of safety that police and emergency response organizations have long cultivated. Reynolds's comments cement this understanding: "I wanted to put it on Facebook to go viral, so that the people could see . . . I wanted the people to determine who was right and who was wrong. I want the people to be the testimony here."[38]

Testimony, then, is not simply located in Reynolds's video of the lived moment, but also in the viewing, sharing, and assessments by the people to whom Reynolds made her bid. Many researchers have argued that videos such as this are most powerful when they are placed in conversation with ongoing social justice movements, such as the Movement for Black Lives. Connection to activist networks gives the testimony context and aids its spread across interrelated social media networks.[39] In *#Hashtag Activism*, Sarah J. Jackson, Moya Bailey, and Brooke Foucault Welles argue that activist hashtags on Twitter enable "historically disenfranchised populations to advance counternarratives and advocate for social change."[40] They find that "overlapping social media infrastructures and networks" were used to build attention and outrage around #PhilandoCastile,[41] particularly as that hashtag was often combined with #BlackLivesMatter. Such combinations make the historical connections that Richardson identifies as key to black witnessing, telling "complicated and difficult stories that members of counterpublics are more than familiar with and allies are encouraged to learn."[42] Emergency bids made via testimony work at multiple levels, prompting recognition in some audiences and shock in others, and potentially enabling those who encounter testimony to shift their thinking about what is taken for granted in the "normal" state of affairs.

The ability of testimony to circulate and produce emergency bids that resonate differently for different social media audiences means that even seemingly less-direct forms of evidence can be powerful sources of emergency bids about structural racism. Thus, I turn to the case of Breonna Taylor, whose death was not recorded but whose name, story, and image became important means of drawing attention to racial justice and police brutality.

Four years after Philando Castile's death, twenty-six-year-old emergency room technician Breonna Taylor was shot and killed by police in her own home in Louisville, Kentucky. Shortly after midnight one night in March 2020, officers arrived to serve a "no-knock warrant," which did not require them to announce their presence. Police were looking for a suspect who did not live at that address and was, in fact, already in custody. Taylor and her boyfriend got up from bed as police battered down the door; thinking it was a break-in, her boyfriend fired a single gunshot toward the door, hitting one of the officers in the leg. The police fired into the home in response, hitting Taylor eight times. Police recalled an ambulance to the apartment, but Taylor received no medical attention during this time. She died on the scene. Taylor's boyfriend made a call to 9-1-1, but there are no images or video testimony of this incident. Instead, Breonna Taylor's death functioned as another emergency bid in the Movement for Black Lives and protests of police brutality through the circulation of her image and story on social media.

Images of Taylor emphasized her life rather than her death: her graduation, wearing work clothes, all dressed up for a night out. Initially photographs were circulated by her mother and sister, but soon illustrators began to create portraits of Taylor. Artist Shirien Damra filled her Instagram account with brightly colored portraits of Black victims of police violence, often accented with floral borders, throughout 2020. Her portrait of Taylor featured an abstracted portrait of Taylor in a flattering dress on a purple background, with a garland of pink and yellow roses and the words "Justice for Breonna." Damra described her motivation for this and other social justice portraits in terms of wanting "to raise awareness of what happened . . . without sharing the triggering video."[43] As the repeated sharing and viewing of videos of Black death can be overwhelming or traumatic, particularly for Black Americans,[44] the production of beautiful portraits like Damra's offers social media users an alternative means to circulate content and raise awareness. Damra's and other illustrations were massively reused on Instagram posts and stories, on Twitter, and in protest organizing around the country. Twitter and Instagram users replaced their avatars with illustrations of Taylor, often with her name or the phrase "say her name" superimposed.

The circulation of testimony concerning Taylor, often tagged with #BreonnaTaylor or #JusticeforBreonnaTaylor and #BlackLivesMatter, built on and recirculated the activist hashtag #SayHerName. First used in 2015, #SayHerName both eulogizes women who died as a result of state violence, valuing their lives, and demands change.[45] Jackson, Bailey, and Welles argue that "#SayHerName began by focusing on the extrajudicial murders of Black women by police but evolved to shed light on all state and communal violence faced by Black women."[46] By naming these incidents and building activist opposition, #SayHerName is a form of resistance to what gender and race theorist Moya Bailey terms "misogynoir," the unique anti-Black racist misogyny perpetuated in media, medicine, and other realms of U.S. culture.[47] The reappearance of this hashtag for Taylor links these incidents, offering evidence that these are not isolated but pervasive, and this pervasive, normalized state of affairs is the true emergency that demands action.

As in earlier uses of #SayHerName, the testimonial impact of Breonna Taylor demonstrated "the integration of an online and offline activist network in which the hashtag is used both to insist on the value of Black women's lives and to drive attention to activist organizations, protests, academic and policy research, and particular political and civil interventions."[48] Protests in Taylor's name took place across the country, and those in Louisville were met by aggressive city responses including additional violence and a preemptive curfew on the day that the grand jury released its decision minimally sanctioning the police officers involved.[49]

The rallying cry "arrest the cops who killed Breonna Taylor" solidified into a demand, and the demand became a meme. A meme is a recirculating and adaptable form of online communication that may have many meanings simultaneously and over time. Memes have been used for humor and politics, harassment and activism.[50] The widespread use of the phrase generated attention, particularly in June when the Birthday for Breonna campaign used what would have been her twenty-seventh birthday as a time of remembrance and action.[51] But such visibility was not entirely welcome, as the memes mutated in ways that seemed to minimize Taylor's life or misunderstand the issue.

The initially straightforward call to arrest the cops who killed Breonna Taylor began to be incorporated at the end of lengthy or misleading social media posts, such as one by (white) actress Lili Reinhart that featured a nude but not revealing photo and the caption "Now that my side boob has gotten your attention, Breonna Taylor's murderers haven't been arrested. Demand justice."[52] While Reinhart quickly apologized for what seemed to be insensitivity or poor taste, similar takes on the phrase recirculated for months, even appearing on the long-running game show *Wheel of Fortune*.[53] In these forms, the meme became disconnected from larger activist contexts and practices of black witnessing, serving as a not-always-sincere indicator that someone was "woke" or politically (and culturally) aware.

While some objected to this shift in social media usage, others saw something both familiar and important.[54] Richardson attributed the circulation of illustrations and the memeing of the phrase as indications of a sophisticated attempt to gain visibility by breaking through social media algorithms.[55] Meredith Clark, a leading scholar of Black Twitter, described the memes as a form of communication that could reach people who were less aware, offering a gateway into the topic and larger issues.[56] As such, these scholars understood the Taylor memes as *both* important and frivolous, a means of garnering mainstream attention through sophisticated uses of popular media to build momentum among supporters and welcome in people newer to the cause.

As a form of testimony, the memeification of Breonna Taylor illustrates how an emergency bid may be made primarily through users' circulation and adaptation of material, rather than through a single "witnessing text" like Reynolds's livestream. Each user who made their own version—even those, like Reinhart, who perhaps made poor choices—engaged and to a degree accepted the emergency bid contained in the phrasing. *Action must be taken.* Implicitly—something has happened, is happening—police violence and structural racism are an emergency.

The examples of Philando Castile and Breonna Taylor are just two of many such circulating testimonies regarding racism, police brutality, and structural oppression within and beyond the Movement for Black Lives. They are powerful illustrations of how testimony and emergency bids may undermine existing infrastructures of feeling by highlighting their failures. These media highlight the failures of police to protect Americans, and the hollowness of claims that government serves us all equally. Circulating again and again, they may begin to form and strengthen a counternarrative that can compete with the mainstream ubiquity of pro-police messaging.

The very power of social media testimony has led to increasing attempts to capture and direct these forms of expression. In the next section, I explore how social media platforms have recognized the value of testimony and attempted to secure that value for themselves.

Social Media, Testimony, and Safety Surveillance

One of the most well-known uses of emergency bids is the use of social media during weather disasters. During hurricanes, tsunamis, blizzards, and other moments of extreme weather, people increasingly turn to digital and social technologies to share their observations, experiences, and request help. For instance, Annie Swinford, a member of a Facebook Group called "Hurricane Harvey 2017—We're In This Together," called 9-1-1 on behalf of others, explaining that "when you see that somebody has posted that they're on their roof with their one-, three- and four-year-olds and the water's up to the roof line, you have to be willing to make that phone call for them."[57] The testimony posted to the group functioned as an emergency bid that was accepted by Swinford, a bystander who took action that led to eventual assistance from the authorities.

Over the past decade, social media has become a routine part of the official and unofficial responses to emergencies and disasters, with people using social media to request aid, share experiences, find friends and family, and connect with institutions from the news media to local relief groups. While some of these uses originally stemmed from users who used available and popular technologies to connect to one another in moments of crisis, these are increasingly integrated into the largest social media platforms. Integrating emergency features into these platforms—and integrating these platforms into official forms of emergency response—can be understood as a form of incorporation that neutralizes the oppositional understandings of emergency, responsibility, and normalcy that testimony can offer. The success of the example above was, undoubtedly, due to how closely circumstances matched a standard emergency narrative and response. The visibility of emergency testimonies on social media has been used to justify increasing safety surveillance measures on social media platforms that ultimately uphold normalizing visions of emergency, materially benefit platforms themselves, and come to shape official forms of disaster response.[58]

The best-known example of the integration of emergency features and social media is Facebook's Safety Check. Launched in 2014, Safety Check enabled people in areas known to be experiencing upheaval or disaster to use a checkbox to easily publicize their safety to their friends on the platform. At the 2017 International Association of Emergency Managers conference, a Facebook representative described the origins of Safety Check as based on "things we've seen" previously. In other words, it seems that Safety Check literally incorporated developed this feature to capture and capitalize on the forms of testimony users offered via the interface.

Cultural studies scholars often use "incorporation" or "containment" to describe how corporations or governments adopt some elements of oppositional groups' style or ideology in order to neutralize those groups' threats to the center of power. Incorporation of user behaviors into a media technology "attempts to rob them of any oppositional meaning"[59] while demonstrating that the tech company in question is attentive, adaptable, and ultimately benevolent. Furthermore, by incorporating emergency bids (and their opposite, assurances), Facebook had the opportunity to "control, circumscribe, and manage"[60] users' unexpected emergency uses of the platform through interface design.

As seen in figure 5.1, Safety Check prompts users to choose "I'm Safe" by default, with the other option being "Doesn't apply to me." There is, notably, not an option to easily indicate that you are *not* safe, or what you might need. Safety Check does not allow users to activate their community for aid or even sympathy, reflecting a common side effect of safety surveillance: the disempowerment of the individual ostensibly in need of protection in order to provide reassurance for others.

Once users' emergency behavior could be funneled through Safety Check, Facebook could justify ongoing and expanded surveillance, in Mark Zuckerberg's words, as "helping to keep you safe."[61] In its reliance on location and posting trends to define areas in which to activate Safety Check, Facebook entrenches ongoing data and locative surveillance. This safety surveillance, as is often the case, primarily serves people other than those at the center of an emergency, by offering assurance of safety rather than allowing users to communicate about their experiences of emergency.

Facebook quickly drew criticism for its decisions regarding when and where to offer Safety Check, as it seemed initially limited to locations

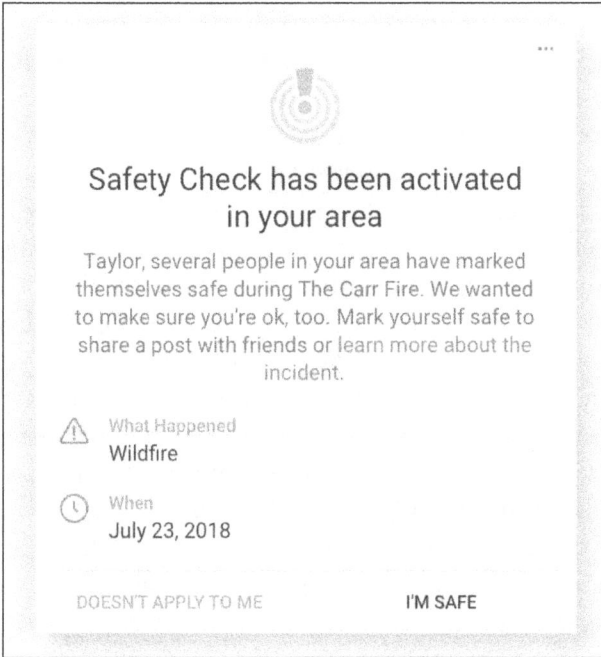

Figure 5.1. Author's screenshot of the Safety Check image used on Facebook's Crisis Center, which shows no option to indicate that the user is not safe.

in the Global North and discrete circumstances such as weather disasters or terrorist attacks.[62] In this usage, Facebook literally encoded the dominant ideology of emergency as a negative deviation from normalcy, excluding places that face regular conditions of risk and uncertainty from this feature. Now, Facebook claims to use a variety of algorithmic and human intelligence to identify areas experiencing crisis and roll out Safety Check features.[63] Its geographical and discrete conception of emergency (or disaster, used interchangeably) remains grounded in the notion of normalcy and its hoped-for restoration.

Since 2017, Safety Check has been part of a larger Facebook Crisis Center that also encompasses fundraising features and Community Help, which centralizes opportunities to help in response to a disaster.[64] Recent critiques of these features have noted that they hew to a limited ideology of corporate responsibility. Information scholar Megan Finn points out that the dynamically constructed algorithmic publics that are shown information on a social network may not reflect those who most need to know.[65] Yet such effectiveness is hard to demand. Technology critic Siva Vaidhyanathan writes that there is no meaningful oversight of Safety Check or other Facebook programs "for social good" because "after all, it's free. And it's better than nothing."[66] In the absence of robust public information infrastructures for emergency, commercial tools both serve a purpose and narrow the possibilities to those that serve their bottom line.

This tension was evident when I attended the 2017 International Association of Emergency Managers conference. Multiple speakers called on their audiences to stop building or searching for new, perfect apps that would force the public to behave in optimal ways. Instead, attendees were reminded that people "use what they use," especially in an emergency; familiar and regularly used technologies are always more reliable than asking people to use a novel system while under stress. In practical terms, this meant that many representatives of government response agencies were being taught how to best use Facebook pages ("Keep your content fresh to increase emergency preparedness!"), Twitter ("If you're not on Twitter, I can't help you on Twitter"), and other popular platforms.

Many in emergency management and related fields have already fully embraced corporate forms of emergency testimony and the limitations they impose. Social media management is part of the media work done by many people in emergency management and response, both monitoring and producing content, as discussed in chapter 3. For instance, Finn explains that the earthquake disaster plans for San Francisco and the state of California position social media sites as central forms of information distribution and knowledge gathering.[67] She writes that "the city of San Francisco encourages people to use Facebook. This reinforces the idea that Facebook is a place where people should register their status and cements the company at the center" of people's emergency experience.[68]

Just as Facebook becomes incorporated into disaster response because it offers services that the government does not, so have Uber and

Airbnb emerged as resources for transportation and housing in the wake of varied disasters and as options for people facing personal emergencies. In addition to a dedicated staff using "state-of-the-art tools and advanced technology to detect emergencies," Uber offers "resources set aside for free rides to shelters, meals for first responders, transportation for volunteers, logistics facilitation, and support to local non-profit organizations."[69] The vagueness of Uber's monitoring would be humorous if it were not so crucial; the definition of emergency is left deliberately broad, while the description of response clearly indicates a disaster-oriented response. Airbnb's Open Homes Disaster Relief feature relies entirely on the generosity of "hosts" who open their spaces to relief volunteers and displaced individuals as needed and without compensation.[70] Unsurprisingly, it too falls back on a top-down understanding of emergency or disaster and builds in vetting by authoritative groups to ensure that people using Open Homes are, in fact, displaced. For these companies, the state of emergency legitimizes the use of their resources for public purposes, even as their usual operations undermine public transit and housing markets.[71]

Testimonial forms of emergency media seem, at first, as if they might facilitate redefinitions of emergency within a peer-to-peer system in which people can, together, decide to accept or reject emergency bids. While this is true to a degree, as there are forms of horizontal information exchange on social media that exhibit alternative framings of emergency and normalcy, it is also true that these uses of social media are increasingly contained and redirected by social media platforms themselves. Again and again, the infrastructural choices of major tech companies fall back on a dominant ideology of emergency that upholds normalcy and re-entrenches the logic of safety surveillance even as they ostensibly work with people and governmental agencies for the common good. To see how people might work with and around the affordances of social media platforms such as Facebook, I turn next to the many, multiply mediated forms of mutual aid that arose in 2020.

Mutual Aid as/and Emergency Media Work

The use of testimony to highlight structural emergencies and the incorporation of social media testimony into regimes of safety surveillance demonstrate the conflicting possibilities of social media as a means of offering testimony and making emergency bids that may redefine what "counts" as emergency. While these tools can expand the reach of testimony and activist communities, they can also restrict the possibilities for emergency communication and aid. But not all emergency or disaster-related emergency bids are as easily assimilated by platforms and institutions as those related to disasters. The "beautiful flowering of mutual aid"[72] during the COVID-19 pandemic provided an outlet for emergency bids related to personal circumstances, structural conditions, and other atypical emergencies.

Legal scholar Dean Spade defines mutual aid as "collective coordination to meet each other's needs, usually from an awareness that the systems we have in place are not going to meet them."[73] Mutual aid has a long history in social movements, as in the operations of the Black Panther Party, which included free breakfast and free ambulance programs. Crucially, beyond simply providing financial or material assistance, mutual aid can be a form of political engagement that can shift participants' understandings of social change and dissent, a goal evident in the common mutual aid slogan of "solidarity, not charity."[74]

Because mutual aid groups are not part of the state or private sector dedicated to disaster response, they have operational flexibility to accept emergency bids that do not clearly align with mainstream ideologies of emergency and normalcy. Being short on rent money, needing a specific kind of kitchen gadget, and looking for assistance for a homeless acquaintance are all valid reasons to post in many of these groups; the normalcy of poverty does not prevent mutual aid groups from recognizing these needs as valid. As a result, mutual aid groups—whatever their means of local or online organization—are home to a wide range of emergency bids that must be either accepted, negotiated, or rejected. The work of mutual aid is also emergency media work: interpreting members' messages, decision-making around urgency and emergency, and communicating with members.

In 2020, when traditional in-person means of mutual aid such as distribution centers were made impractical by a pandemic, mutual aid organizing increasingly happened online. In place of physical organizing, media technologies became infrastructures of emergency care and connection. Groups use Google Docs or Sheets to arrange work shifts or track donations. Google Forms, in conjunction with Sheets, are often used to collect both requests for and offers of help. GoFundMe, Venmo, PayPal, Cash App, and other forms of social payment are used to redistribute funds.[75] Individual and group text messages are used to work out the logistics of a drop-off. Facebook Groups host exchanges of material goods and information, as well as ongoing conversations between community members as relationships build over time. Slack is used to organize among and between groups of volunteers. Privacy-oriented organizers rely on Signal and Keybase to communicate outside of the extractive algorithms of major technology and media companies. In all cases, media bridge the distance between people who need help and those who can provide it, even (or especially) during times of social distancing.

The reliance on consumer technologies and social media may also impede access, of course. Cost, ownership, accessibility, and other barriers to entry to these systems may prevent some of the most impacted members of a community from receiving aid or volunteering in mutual aid groups.[76] Organizers are often aware of these drawbacks, as a group conducted primarily via Facebook may find that it does well at reaching people between twenty-five and sixty-five, but fails to connect with those younger or older who may need aid. Thus, many groups provide alternatives to social media technologies, including hotlines (often in multiple languages), phone trees, text messaging, static websites, and paper flyers through which people can gain access.

Whether via social media or other channels, the testimonial emergency bids made in mutual aid groups engender emergency media work. Like dispatchers or emergency managers, mutual aid volunteers may take up a position at the "nexus" of a larger articulation of emergency media, infrastructure, and response. Volunteers create spreadsheets of needs and offerings, donations and expenditures, enacting what information historian Cait McKinney describes as "information activism" in the construction of information infrastructures that support social transformation.[77] They also engage in back-and-forth exchanges, clarifying requests, explaining group policies, and teaching people about the goals of mutual aid as opposed to charity; and defining what is or is not an "emergency," recalling the emotional labor and definitional work seen in emergency dispatch.

Many requests received by mutual aid groups come from people in distress, who explicitly frame their needs as "emergencies." As midwestern organizer Abby Ang recounted, members' emergency bids range from escaping situations of domestic violence, to needing a new washing machine, to needing chili powder. What should be prioritized and what can wait? What can the mutual aid peer-to-peer support provide, and what requires other social services, such as connection to a local domestic violence shelter? Claims of emergency are made and potentially rejected by the mutual aid volunteers doing the media work of emergency, a particularly difficult task that involves the navigation of social, ethical, and practical concerns within organizations that strive to be egalitarian.

For instance, the emergency bid for chili powder may not be accepted. In this case, volunteers would have to initiate a conversation in which they further educate community members about the purpose and capacity of the group. These are conversations (via email, social media, or telephone) that require significant time and emotional management. Unlike social media companies, which achieve this through interface design, mutual aid groups achieve this through delicate acts of communication.

These conversations may not end well; like 9-1-1 professionals, mutual aid volunteers may find themselves the target of anger or harassment when they explain that some things are outside of their scope. As in the work of emergency dispatch, community support is important;[78] Mutual Aid Philly, for instance, has found value in putting volunteers on shared FaceTime or Zoom calls while they work through requests, to provide companionship, coordination, and emotional support.[79] This is important for dealing not only with definitional work and aggressive callers, but with the sheer constancy of emergency bids and the difficult circumstances in which people find themselves. Relying on the work of unpaid volunteers requires mechanisms for building in breaks, preventing burnout, and enabling volunteers to maintain their own well-being as well as that of the community.

One of the major differences between emergency bids made in mutual aid contexts and those made to authorities is that mutual aid can support ongoing needs. The legacies of disability justice work in many mutual aid groups reveal strategies for providing ongoing physical and material support to community members. Disability activists, for instance, have long been invested in "collective access" and "care webs" through which they organize, together, to give and receive the forms of aid, care, and accessibility that were needed.[80] Disability justice writer Leah Lakshmi Piepzna-Samarasinha describes these efforts in contrast to the "emergency-response care webs" that are seen when someone who is not disabled becomes injured or disabled; the emergency-response care webs leap into action and then collapse, exhausted by the unaccustomed constancy of needs. COVID-era mutual aid groups could be seen as similar bursts of activity from people not accustomed to collective organizing. In both cases, Piepzna-Samarasinha suggests that people could benefit from looking to disability communities,

For one thing, disability communities may live in closer connection to emergency or disaster. Disability activist Stacey Park Milbern, a queer Korean American disability activist who cofounded the Bay Area mutual aid group known as the Disability Justice Culture Club (DJCC), reflected in 2019 that many "people aren't used to thinking about what they need in emergencies,"[81] but that disabled people are often more aware of their needs and how they might lose the access and support that they have. Crip knowledge becomes valuable in an emergency;[82] as Milbern explained prior to her untimely death, "We know how infections spread and how to properly wear a mask and wash your hands."[83]

Disability communities had experience building relationships of mutual care and ongoing collective action that incorporate pleasure as well as work. These are important ways of building community such that people can and will continue to show up for one another's needs when there is not an evident emergency. Thus, mutual aid organizers may also engage in lighter forms of emergency media work. Use of current memes and other images, as seen in the Monroe County Mutual Aid group of Indiana, can increase the algorithmic visibility of request posts and foster community engagement with the page and between members through comments on- and offline. Some groups even offer social and mental health support, combatting isolation through events such as the Bay Area "Justice Brunches" hosted online each week to provide a chance for people to gather.[84]

Finally, some mutual aid groups engage in the media work of fostering connections between members and other organizations, arranging phone calls, sending emails, and otherwise interpreting and producing mediated messages in order to respond to the community's emergency bids. As volunteer groups, however, many mutual aid groups cannot sustain "providing what's basically around-the-clock emergency assistance"[85] because, as one mutual aid organizer explains, "we're not always prepared for an emergency" that requires immediate intervention. Media studies scholar Nathan Schneider argues that building long-term mutual support networks requires establishing some division of labor and setting of expectations in order to persist beyond periods of crisis, translating enthusiasm into organization.[86] One way of doing this is by not trying to "reinvent the wheel" but to be aware of the limitations of volunteer-led mutual aid projects and the benefits of established community resources including emergency services and nonprofit organizations and other forms of community aid.

Mutual aid, in providing physical and digital spaces dedicated to alternative infrastructures for crises, builds emergent understandings of what aid—and emergency—could be. Mutual aid groups provide a space for emergency bids that don't fit the usual narrative but can nonetheless be accepted by the community. The media labor of organizers is particularly central to making the connections that transform these emergency bids into a response that may not only restore someone to their "normal" state of being, but offer what Jimmy, a volunteer with Mutual Aid Disaster Relief, describes as "a sense of connection, a heightened sense of what's possible." Mutual aid is emergency as consciousness-raising, a space for testimonies that do not fit official or corporate templates but can nonetheless be treated as worthy of response by a community invested in supporting one another in a variety of vulnerabilities.

Conclusion

Testimony is a powerful site for rearticulating the meanings of emergency; as such, it is also a site at which companies and organizations may attempt to constrain these possibilities for their own interests. Such containment is only partially successful, however. The emergency bids described in this chapter are made by people using the tools available to them and addressing the audiences they can reach in forms that resonate culturally. They are instances of a more popular or participatory engagement with the boundaries of "emergency," where rejected emergency claims may become emergency bids that communities accept and respond to.

In Rubenstein's work on emergency claims, she argues that "no matter how bad a situation is in absolute terms or compared to how things are elsewhere, it is unlikely to be socially recognized as an emergency if it has persisted unchanged for a long time."[87] Thus, Rubenstein argues that emergency claims are often deeply regressive and conservative in their protection of the interests of the powerful through limited interpretations of "emergency" that cannot address many problems faced by marginalized populations. If their claims of emergency are routinely rejected, it may be seen that their situation—and lives—lack value.[88] Emergency claims about racist policing have largely failed when made to existing authorities, producing a sense that Black lives do not matter. To use social media to assert that Black Lives Matter, then, is to speak back to the lack of value communicated by the repeated failure of U.S. authorities to accept ongoing conditions of racial inequality and violence as an emergency in need of redress. Black Lives Matter functions as an emergency bid where claims have fallen short, and the circulation of testimony has been crucial to making this bid legible to multiple audiences.

This chapter has explored several historical and contemporary examples of testimony used to make emergency bids to particular publics, with a range of outcomes. The legacies of dominant forms of emergency media are visible in the varied structures that recognize testimonial emergency bids. Yet, it is clear that testimony can be powerful in its ability to galvanize a community and produce action around "long emergencies," persistent, structural conditions of danger and marginalization. It is equally clear that testimony can be co-opted and channeled by powerful institutional actors, such as social media platforms and disaster response organizations. I do not pin all hopes for the transformation of emergency media and emergency itself on testimony, but insofar as testimony *can* be different, those differences reveal that the taken-for-granted structures of other emergency media may themselves be available for intervention and change.

Conclusion

From Emergency to Engagement

This book has been guided by two questions: what is emergency, and how do we understand it through mediation? Emergency is affectively produced in time and space. Emergency is a threat that justifies safety surveillance in the name of reassurance and in the interests of power. Emergency may be declared by state and other authorities' use of media or individuals may make emergency claims and bids through media systems. Emergency surrounds us in infrastructures of feeling that remind us of risks even as they are designed to reassure us and prevent hard questions about what happens if the worst happens. Emergency is defined—again and again—by not only those in crisis, but by emergency media workers who are themselves embedded in cultural contexts. Emergency and its mediation have served as sites of cultural power that protect some people while criminalizing or minimizing the plights of others. And yet emergency shifts.

As emergency shifts, it can be shifted. This book has demonstrated that emergency media are a site at which the meanings of emergency are articulated to particular technologies and ideologies. As such, emergency media are a site at which these linkages might be intentionally altered. To remake emergency media and begin to re-signify "emergency" itself, perhaps we begin in the realm of speculation.

In the context of Black Lives Matter protests against racist police violence, growing numbers of people endorsed defunding or abolishing the police. The following words circulated (uncredited) on Facebook and possibly beyond in summer 2020, envisioning such a future:

Picture this.
It's 2030.

You're walking down the street. You see a man who is clearly in distress (mental health and/or drugs). He's walking in and out of traffic and doesn't seem to be aware of his surroundings.

You open your Social Services app and request emergency help. You select "mental health / substance abuse emergency care" and your location is sent one-time with your permission.

Four minutes later, an ambulance arrives. Two unarmed but trained specialists get out and talk to the man. The man seems to recognize one of the specialists ("hey Mike!") and the specialist recognizes him ("you doing alright, John? Looks like you may have forgotten your medication. Do you need us to take you back to the group home?"). The specialist radios back that the call is calm and no further backup is needed.

John agrees and gets into the ambulance, unrestrained. He gets back on track with his meds and continues his treatment plan. He's in a trade program and hopes to work as a contractor one day, but his schizophrenia is a major obstacle. He's making it work, though, and only has 6 months left before he has his certifications.

This is what public health and safety looks like. We can have this, y'all. We really can.[1]

This imagined future, with its vision of a publicly supported multipurpose app, is a fantasy of emergency mediation. I mean fantasy not in sense that this is impossible, but in the sense that it is a wished-for outcome, unencumbered by practical considerations. In this short tale, the author reconceives of reporting ("open your Social Security app"), dispatch and interagency cooperation (a centralized point of contact that can dispatch an ambulance carrying mental health specialists to arrive within minutes), and the role and outcome of testimony ("you" witness both the moment and outcome of the emergency). This viral post combines bureaucratic, technological, infrastructural fantasy, and interpersonal fantasies, producing a compelling technosolutionist imaginary in which building the right app integrates resources and solves complicated social problems.[2] There are many hurdles to the implementation of such a system, including city, state, and federal jurisdictional politics and operational infrastructures, the forms of technology available to dispatchers, emergency responders, and the public, and the formation of corps of social workers to act in such moments. In places such as Denver, Colorado, where 9-1-1 can dispatch mental health professionals, two staffers responded to over 350 calls in a less than three-month pilot period; there is much work to do to scale up such programs as envisioned above.[3]

Of course, the feasibility is not the point. The point—and power—of the post comes from *imagining* a different relationship between emergency, mediation, responsibility, and aid. In this imagining, emergency is mediated differently and outcomes are therefore different. The hinge of media communication has been rearticulated, and a new understanding of "emergency" may emerge out of new linkages between consumer-friendly technology, varied forms of response, and abolitionist perspectives on intervention rather than incarceration. In this wished-for future, emergency is not an aberration to be cured and forgotten but is one moment of intervention and care among many. The meaning of emergency shifts along with its means of mediation.

The year 2020 also saw competing fantasies of emergency mediation. A Trump 2020 campaign ad titled "9-1-1 Call" opened with a shot of an abandoned dispatch desk and audio of an ostensible recording answering a call: "You have reached the 9-1-1 police emergency line. Due to defunding of the police department, we're sorry, but no one is here to take your call." The audio then conveys a phone menu ("To report a rape, press one"), and juxtaposes images of the abandoned phone with footage of defund the police protests, buildings on fire, and people smashing store windows. Following a claim that "violent crime has exploded," the ad concludes, "You won't be safe in Joe Biden's America." The ad pandered to the fears of financially comfortable white voters through its association of protests, fire, and property damage (implicitly reminding viewers of the coverage of Black Lives Matter protests against police violence in Minneapolis, Portland, Atlanta, and elsewhere earlier in the year). Like countless prior racist invocations of safety and law and order, it centered white women as potential victims by placing "rape" as the first option for reporting.[4] Ultimately, it represented a "lurid rehash of Trump's 2016 campaign strategy," attempting to scare and thus win over older (white) voters.[5]

Like the Facebook post, this ad was a fantasy (albeit a dystopian one). Trump's campaign threatened a future in which emergency media are weakened or eliminated. To do so, this ad employs signs of emergency media work—the desk, the female voice of the 9-1-1 recording—but mis-

represents them for effect. The recording declares 9-1-1 a "police emergency line," centering policing and downplaying the role that many 9-1-1
centers already play in providing medical, fire, and other forms of community aid. While some 9-1-1 dispatch is done under the auspices of the
police, the ad produces a tighter linkage between the two, imagining a
world in which the *only* form of emergency aid is policing. The dystopian future also aligns 9-1-1 with semi-automated forms of customer
service through the phone menu, recalling the frustrating experiences
viewers may have had with businesses' automated phone menus, canned
responses, and endless waits—emergency dispatch reimagined as a call
to the cable company. Imagining the disappearance of emergency media
also shifts the meaning of emergency, suggesting a world in which there
is no one there to hear claims of emergency or offer aid.

While these fantasies of emergency media may read as opposites—
one progressive, one conservative—both preserve emergency's ideological dependency on normalcy. In the Trump ad, that normalcy is
implicitly represented by white, property-owning Americans who rely
on and support the police and the state. Emergency is figured as that
which disrupts those lives, which must be restored to their previous
comfort. In the Facebook post, however, an emergency is evident when
"mental health and/or drugs" disrupt the normalcy of walking down
the street, and the moment concludes with the removal of "John" from
public space. As estimates indicate that between one-third and one-half
of people killed by police are disabled and/or neurodivergent,[6] this example is both useful and troubling. Disability and mental illness often
appear as excuses for continuing carceral logics of incarceration, separation, and stigmatization, even in progressive or prison-abolitionist
contexts.[7] When disability appears as a deviation from normalcy that
constitutes an emergency to be solved by removing disabled people from
public spaces, the normalizing ideology of emergency is intact.

The anonymous author of the Facebook post that opened this chapter began to wrestle with this normalizing logic in an addendum: "I'd
also like to add that people DESERVE this. Society has been lied to that
people who need extra help are a drain of resources or not a member of
society because they can't contribute like able-bodied people. That's a
lie. Everyone deserves a chance at a good life." Not only do all people—
including disabled people—deserve respectful care and resources in the

face of crisis, but they deserve the opportunity to define what is a good life, a good outcome, and what is or is not an emergency. What might emergency look like decoupled from normalizing imperatives? What kinds of ethical frameworks support such redefinition? And how can we intervene in emergency media systems to move toward such outcomes?

From Emergency to Engagement

The current emergency media ecosystem in the United States—like our medical system, in too many cases—is based around absences of care punctuated by moments of crisis. We delay regular health checkups because of costs and the difficulty of establishing a primary care physician, until serious symptoms drive us to seek care at an emergency room (at great cost). We lack mechanisms to give or receive other forms of aid until we are in crisis, when we turn to 9-1-1, policing, and similar infrastructures invested in the restoration of a normal state of affairs. To rearticulate emergency media and create forms of communication and intervention that promote access, equity, and care requires opening up, acknowledging vulnerability, and engaging in ongoing commitments of care.

Engagement with one another, with government and other institutions, with infrastructures is a particularly useful framework for thinking about alternatives to emergency. Engagement is not a technocratic fix. Engagement is not a single intervention. Rather, we might understand engagement as what abolitionist disability scholar Liat Ben-Moshe calls "an ethical commitment, one that calls on us to embrace vulnerability and uncertainty."[8]

Vulnerability is a potent contrast to normalcy. To theorize from vulnerability means recognizing injury, exhaustion, dependence, debility, oppression, isolation, and more as common and valuable features of life, rather than conditions of exclusion and stigmatization. Sara Ahmed suggests that vulnerability involves a bodily openness to the world, an invitation to the world that is potentially dangerous.[9] To imagine ourselves vulnerable to emergency means being open to the possibility of being injured, violated, harmed; many people understandably resist such vulnerability, proclaiming themselves "no victim" in advance of any possible victimization. Or we may deny our vulnerability through preventative or preemptive actions, stockpiling mountains of toilet paper at the first wave of pandemic shutdowns. In refusing vulnerability, we cling to normalcy and resist substantive change.

Embracing vulnerability and recognizing it not as a flaw, but as a foundational element of human experience "centers our social responsibility toward others, while striving to revitalize state obligations promoting robust human rights and security."[10] As explicated by feminist legal scholar Katie Oliviero, vulnerability methodologies offer us the chance to understand how precarity is unevenly and intersectionally distributed among populations, and how shifting policies and infrastructures can worsen or improve such conditions.[11]

Emergency is not sustainable, and neither is normalcy. To address "emergency" as something other than a departure from a reified, normal state of affairs requires us to think not only about moments, but processes. Shifts in vulnerability and capacity over time and geography, variances in social services and care structures, and forms of intervention and interpersonal connection all inform a politics of vulnerability and care. To move from moments to processes, normalcy to vulnerability, we might look to disability justice movements.

Emerging from the Sins Invalid collective, "disability justice" is an intersectional framework for collective, anti-capitalist access and liberation. Disability justice activists and theorists have long worked to build "models of centering sustainability, slowness, and building for the long haul"[12] rather than succumbing to logics of cure or restoration that seek to restore normalcy. From disability justice, we can learn that responding to emergency does not have to mean restoring normalcy. Instead, emergency can be situated as one engagement among many that constitute ongoing commitments of care within a society.

Political theorist Mara Marin theorizes "commitment" as a pattern of connection between people, formed out of cumulative actions and obligations that we have to other people both at a personal and political level.[13] Commitments, she argues, arise out of patterns of actions and expectations, and form bonds that require us to "stand by" our relationships and responsibilities to one another through how we choose to engage and act in relationships. Commitments are a means of forming our location within social structures and norms and, importantly, of shifting those norms through the ways in which we act on our commitments to one another. This theorization of commitment through action resonates with philosopher Eva Feder Kittay's understanding of an ethics of care, in which care "is a disposition manifested in caring behavior (the labor and attitude)."[14] Care is not only a feeling, but an action—a commitment. This commitment may be uneven, with some individuals more or less likely to be the cared for or the carer; both parties, though, are entitled to experience relations of care and dependency within "a dignified, flourishing life."[15]

Ongoing commitments of care can not only structure our relationships with other people but can form the basis of social and technological infrastructures. In the recently published *Care Manifesto*, the authors argue that care is "a social capacity and activity" of nurturing and interdependence.[16] The *Manifesto* calls for a "queer–feminist–anti-racist–eco-socialist political vision of 'universal care'"[17] in which care is prioritized in the private, public, and economic sectors of society. Calling for a revitalization of the public good and the demarketization of care infrastructures, the *Manifesto* offers a model of what a societal commitment to care might look like in practice: "collectively owned, socialized forms of provision, space and infrastructure."[18] Our emergency media could follow a similar model, serving as ongoing commitments of care for ourselves, one another, and the larger public good.

To enact commitments of care—establishing emergency as a need for engagement—we should also recognize and extend the care, maintenance, and oversight given to our emergency media systems, which have often been ignored by the public and policymakers alike. As technology scholar Steven J. Jackson argues in the context of technological repair, "care" can describe the continual labor of maintaining media technologies and affirming that we "bear and affirm a moral relation to [them]."[19] Infrastructural media activism is care; maintenance and gradual change are care; political action is care.

What Next?

Much of this book has engaged in historicizing and critiquing different forms of emergency media, in part because these media have not often been studied as artifacts of cultural power. There are many more stories to tell about emergency media systems, their operations, and their relation to individuals and cultural change. This book, then, is in part a call to academic action.

Yet, given the powerful effects of emergency media in constructing moments of crisis as moments to be "fixed" and rendered normal—at the expense of people for whom "normal" has often been unattainable—I also offer a practical call to action. What follows are seven tactical interventions that individuals, activists, policymakers, and other parties can use to reshape emergency in their local contexts.

1. Observe and Act on Local Infrastructures of Feeling

Homes, neighborhoods, cities, campuses, workplaces, businesses, and public spaces all feature media technologies dedicated to the creation of feelings of "safety." These features—such as security cameras—act as infrastructures of feeling designed to make some people feel safe, while ensuring that others know that they are being watched, criminalized, and targeted. When confronted with the emergency media systems that permeate daily life, we must follow the words of Angela Davis in recognizing and resisting "what makes people *feel* safer, rather than what actually makes people be safer."[20]

The protests against "smart streetlights" in San Diego, California, offer one example of such pushback on infrastructures of feeling. Streetlights, perhaps assumed to be a benign and helpful city infrastructure, have been retooled with technology that captures live video and audio. Ostensibly, this recording is being used by the San Diego police to address traffic and other crimes; activists (including technology researcher Lily Irani) contend that this is an instance of "data creep" in which much more material is being captured and used than can be justified by its stated purpose.[21] Like blue light emergency phones, these systems attempt to conjure a feeling of safety while failing to address underlying concern. Smart streetlights, furthermore, capture data that enabled increased criminalization of behavior and bodies that might otherwise have gone unnoticed, making the city distinctly less safe for homeless people, among others.

Interrogating infrastructures of feeling means noticing changes such as the datafication of streetlights and asking tough questions. How are safety and risk constructed by these systems, and for whose benefit?

What new risks are created, and for whom? Asking these questions regularly, and making decisions about what technologies we employ, accept, and deputize in pursuit of safety for ourselves, our loved ones, and our communities can enable us to recognize systems of safety surveillance and ideologies of emergency and normalcy.

2. Learn Context, Demand Transparency

Throughout this book, I have demonstrated that the functioning of emergency media systems is often a matter of piecemeal technologies and workflows loosely connected to one another and to the publics they serve. Thus, a first step must be to learn the full context of operations in a given area rather than assuming that we know how emergency media works.

The operations of 9-1-1 are a powerful example of the importance of knowing such context in order to act accordingly. As abolitionist activist Ejeris Dixon cautions, "we must acknowledge that we have yet to build an alternative to 911"[22] for quickly accessing multiple forms of assistance in an emergency. This means that many people contact 9-1-1 despite the risks or their political stance on policing because they "have no idea what to do instead."[23] Domestic violence, health and mental health crises, accidents, and other circumstances may require the kind of immediate intervention most available through 9-1-1.

Therefore, many activist groups focus on harm reduction that begins by "find[ing] out more about how your local government addresses 9-1-1 dispatch . . . map[ping] your local resources, relationships, and needs."[24] For instance, in New York City, all dispatch routes through the police department; this requires different strategies for securing nonpolice aid than in a municipality where a PSAP dispatches multiple forms of response without direct police oversight. When we know who is answering the phones—and the source of their funding—as well as what kinds of responders can be sent, to where, and in what conditions, we are better prepared both for individual interactions with emergency reporting and for political intervention. Learning about local emergency media operations—and related resources, such as hotlines, aid groups, and other nonpolice interventions—allows us to go beyond the intellectual arguments for defunding police or pursuing transformative justice by focusing on "the nitty-gritty work needed to create an alternative to policing"[25] and alternative forms of emergency response. When context is known, we can demand transparency regarding the operation, funding, and data practices of local and consumer emergency media systems.

3. Value and Interrogate Emergency Media Work

Part of understanding the context of emergency media involves recognizing the workers who facilitate its operation. This book has argued that people who produce and participate in emergency media—dispatchers, emergency managers, campus staff, app designers, and mutual aid volunteers—are involved in a kind of cultural labor through which they can both exert agency and replicate structures of existing emergency response institutions. To work toward a version of emergency grounded in caring engagement rather than technosolutionism, it is imperative to learn about how this work is currently done, and how it might be done differently.

On a practical level, this means noticing both the demands of emergency media workers themselves and changes to their working environments. For instance, the past five years have seen growing national activism around the recategorization of the work of 9-1-1 telecommunicators as a "protective service occupation" rather than "office and administrative support" in the Bureau of Labor Statistics' Standard Occupational Classification system. Such a shift would recognize the changes in 9-1-1 work in recent decades,[26] which include more complex technological skills and more direct assistance to callers through the provision of medical protocols. In some states, such as Texas and West Virginia, reclassification has already begun, enabling 9-1-1 professionals to be recognized as "first responders" in emergency situations, and granting them improved access to overtime pay, mental health support, and other benefits. Members of the public can support such efforts, ensuring that emergency media work remains a viable and attractive career.

Similarly, when new software packages are purchased and emergency media work becomes more datafied or automated, it is important not simply to accept press releases about these systems.[27] We can ask about the data collected, the labor required, and the decisions that may be built in to such systems, and we can attend to what dispatchers are saying about the work they do and the tools they use. Most dispatchers, for instance, are profoundly hesitant about receiving video, which is likely to dramatically increase the trauma of their work. Technological suites that tout video as a benefit, then, should be subject to close consideration as their benefits come at a cost for these media workers.

Emergency media workers know their work; for them, it is not infrastructural but everyday. We cannot take them or their work for granted, nor can we assume it to be neutral. The cultural meanings of emergency circulate with the aid of these workers, and they have (limited) agency with which to begin to rearticulate those meanings.

4. Separate Emergency Media from Law Enforcement

While policy changes won't solve all problems with emergency media, it may be possible to at least start by pushing for some official separation between emergency media systems and law enforcement, including policing. At the top level in the United States, this would mean restoring FEMA to a cabinet-level agency, outside the scope of the Department of Homeland Security (DHS). Since FEMA's integration to DHS, its staff and funding have been reduced and its weakened decision-making power has led to worse responsiveness to disasters.[28] At state and local levels, it also means moving local emergency management and 9-1-1 dispatch outside of the physical, funding, and personnel oversight of police or sheriff's departments. Emergency management and dispatch centers might better function under the auspices of local governments, directly, enabling them to make decisions about defining and responding to emergency outside of a carceral context. A greater degree of worker and public oversight of these systems could result in new procedures and draw on the input of workers, experts, and academics who have deep understandings of the functions, flaws, and potential of these fields.

5. Consider Emergency Media as Part of a Total Media Environment

This book has attempted to tease out different forms of emergency media for the sake of analysis; realistically, they are often bound up in one another and in other media technologies that are part of daily life.

Thus, we should pay attention to where emergency media systems have become integrated with other platforms and uses of media.

In chapter 3, I highlighted the overlaps between emergency alerts and myriad other, mundane forms of smartphone alerts. These systems inform one another and our use of them. While there is a strong desire on the part of those sending messages via the federal system not to inconvenience or alienate their audience by sending too many alerts, the more likely scenario is that emergency alerts are just one of many kinds of notifications on the average person's mobile device—text messages, emails, app notifications, game pings, news articles, calendar reminders, and more appear nearly identical to emergency alerts. Constant notifications blur together, with the result that alerts are normal. This makes them profoundly challenging as a means of communicating emergency (understood as that which is not normal). In such a total media context, it becomes clear that emergency alerts must differentiate themselves in order to be effective. Regular testing of the system, for instance, might enable emergency alerts to be more effective in conveying information without causing confusion.

Alternately, we might look to how commercial platforms have integrated emergency features to see what is, or is not, improved. Uber, for example, integrated a host of safety features in 2018, including the ability to activate an escort feature allowing trusted contacts to watch a ride and the initiation of 9-1-1 calls.[29] In 2019, Uber partnered with RapidSOS, an emergency communications platform, to transmit location data to emergency services.[30] And in 2020, in response to ongoing issues with assault and mistaken identities, Uber announced plans to integrate a text-to-9-1-1 interface, PIN systems to confirm a driver-rider match, and facial recognition for drivers.[31]

At the surface, these features may seem like steps closer to the fantasy of a total app that offers multiple forms of integrated protection. Looked at more closely, these features function as safety surveillance, in which the app is deputized to care for the rider and the rider's use of the system is recorded for unknown uses. Furthermore, in-app 9-1-1 systems are inefficient, inserting multiple technological steps between the user and the PSAP and sometimes not enabling 9-1-1 professionals to get necessary information from the caller because messages may be automated. In a context in which text-to-9-1-1 is available in a minority of PSAP jurisdictions, such features may offer a false sense of security as they promise emergency media capabilities that may not match the infrastructure on the ground.

Emergency media is a growing area of interest and monetization for a range of technology companies, through social platforms, home security systems, smart home technologies, health monitors, fitness devices, and more. As these systems proliferate, it is worthwhile to ask what emergency media functions they purport to integrate, and to what degree those functions are well justified and supported.

6. Cultivate Uses of Emergency Media That Foster Commitments of Care

In the crush of emergency media systems, apps, wearables, and other technologies, we can choose to use (or make!) those that foster commitments of care rather than imposing safety surveillance. Rather than tracking our family members through an app like Life360—which constantly monitors locations and sets up some users with surveillant control over others—we can look for technological solutions that foster mutual accountability and protect users' data and privacy.

This might look like Circle of 6, described in chapter 3, which enabled users to set up a group of people to learn and support one another regarding personal safety and sexual assault. Alternately, it might look like the unexpected uses of Facebook and Google Drive employed by mutual aid groups and care circles. MealTrains, social financial platforms, specialized apps such as CircleOf (an organizational platform for long-term caregiving), and social media platforms are all ripe for usage as means of establishing commitments of care to those around us (even when such usage is not intended). Use of apps like Signal, which use end-to-end encryption on text, audio, and video communications, can further protect us from the extractive practices of safety surveillance. Attention to privacy settings, turning apps on and off as needed, and communicating with friends, family, and others about what constitutes support and what oversteps into surveillance can all reinforce our agency in making the repeated choices that constitute commitment.

This recommendation calls for consumer or lifestyle activism, not as a single solution, but as a means of putting into practice the commitments of care that can shift the meaning of emergency from a deviation from normalcy to a form of shared, vulnerable engagement. To care for one another means to engage with—not only monitor—one another. To the extent that consumer technologies can foster such interactions, they can participate in the "webs of care" that we form for ourselves and our communities.

7. Participate in Outreach and Education

Finally, we can foster commitments of care and the redefinition of emergency by educating others about the use and functions of emergency media. Share what you learn about your local context, challenge the infrastructures of feeling that construct safety for some at the expense of others, point out when forms of safety surveillance slip from care to control, and help others in your life to manage settings such as opting in or out of federal emergency alerts or transmitting location data. Just as people had to be taught the operation and meanings of fire alarms, we will need to learn about mainstream and alternative forms of mediating emergency in order to use, reject, or reform them.

Outreach and education may be individual and social or more organized. One example of more organized educational activism around emergency media can be seen in the creation of resources for "what to do instead of calling the cops." Standing Up for Racial Justice in Washington, DC, for instance, has created and distributed a free decision tree for calling 9-1-1 (figure c.1). Regardless of one's answers and path through the chart, it never explicitly advises calling the police or 9-1-1, instead asking the user to consider whether they "understand how involving the police could impact me and the other person."[32] In addition to such just-in-time resources, the DC group uses online tools to distribute information about community groups offering resources for homelessness, sexual assault, and other circumstances that may result in calls to 9-1-1, and lists of resources for trainings and other forms of preparation that people can pursue to feel better prepared to handle emergencies without police assistance.

Educational materials and outreach efforts are particularly important to reframing emergency, its mediation, and what we do in emergency. If emergencies are matters of action in which habituation takes over, as suggested by Elaine Scarry, we need exposure and practice to coun-

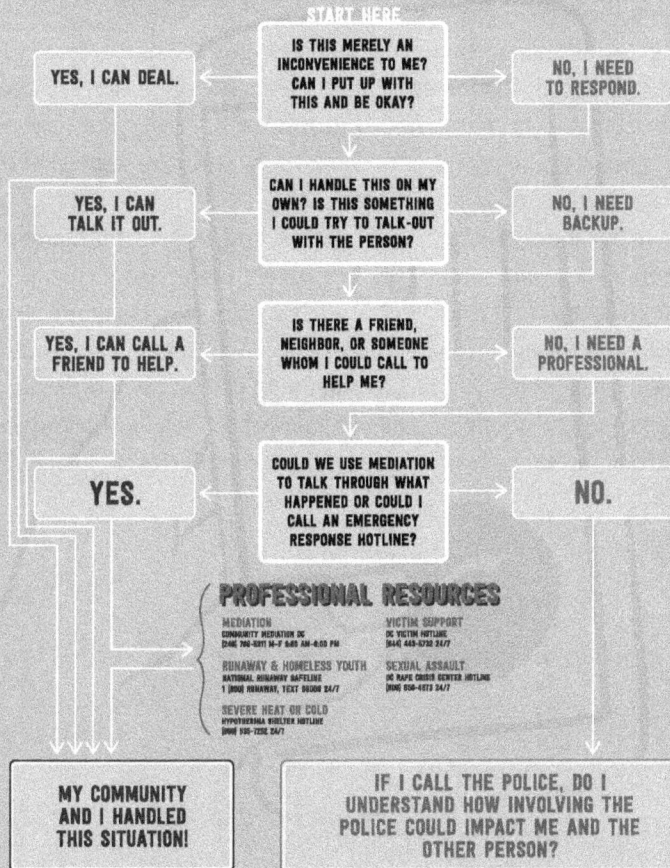

Figure C.1. Flow chart to guide decisions about calling the police while reducing harm. Courtesy of Standing Up for Racial Justice, Washington, DC.

teract the institutions and infrastructures of feeling already in place.[33] Resource banks, decision trees, preparedness exercises, drills, testing, and other forms of exposure to alternative ways of linking emergency, experience, mediation, and response can help to transform what happens when the worst happens.

Too often, emergency media are taken for granted or forgotten in their ubiquity or silence. To challenge and change the operations of normalizing power that have characterized most forms of emergency media, we have to draw attention to them. Make them strange—remarkable—so that we can notice and act on them.

What is our emergency? It is an ossified and exclusive understanding of emergency and normalcy that ultimately maintains the status quo, discriminates and oppresses, and prioritizes efficiency over understanding. Media have long upheld this ideology of emergency, but it may be that they are uniquely well placed to begin to dismantle it, building commitments of care and ongoing engagement that serve and recognize the ever-present and unevenly experienced vulnerabilities of human life.

ACKNOWLEDGMENTS

While no book is truly a solo endeavor, this book is particularly indebted to the collaborations and conversations that have taken it from idea to completion. My deepest thanks go to my research collaborators and assistants. At the University of Virginia, I worked with Rose Buckelew, Christopher Gist, and Sophie Trawalter to develop and carry out research funded by the Office of the Vice President for Research through the "Three Cavaliers" initiative for interdisciplinary research. We turned the group of three into four, and I can't overstate how much your expertise and support enabled the completion of this book. I must also thank our research assistants: Patrice Wright, Parker Bach, Angel Martinez, and Ty'leik Cleveland conducted outreach, facilitated focus groups, and ensured that we stayed in touch with the actual media practices of current college students. Special thanks to Parker for doing a gut check on my analyses of this data in the book.

I have worked with other research assistants as well. Particular thanks go to Alexander Rudenshiold, who handled much of the citational and formatting work on this manuscript, and also offered his insights, questions, and corrections. I am grateful for the time and thought that he has dedicated to this project. Other research assistants included Lauren Savit, who conducted research in the Indiana University archives, and Emily Zou and Delaney Liskey, who scanned documents, compiled news archives, and sorted countless Instagram photos.

This project was wide-ranging, and I am eternally grateful to the archives, organizations, and individuals that welcomed me and my questions. Archival research was done at the special collections of the University of Virginia; at the special collections of my alma mater, Georgetown University; at George Washington University; and at the University of Colorado Boulder. I am also indebted to the online archives of the University of Pennsylvania, the Five Colleges of Ohio

(Denison University, Kenyon College, Oberlin College, Ohio Wesleyan University, and the College of Wooster), and the Indiana Historical Society.

I attended and observed the International Association of Emergency Managers conference in 2017, through which I connected with many of my interview participants in emergency management fields. I visited several emergency communications centers in the course of research on 9-1-1, speaking with 9-1-1 professionals including dispatchers, managers, and technologists. These observations, interviews, and discussions of initial research results strengthened my understanding of this field immeasurably. I have a new respect for the work they do, along with a certainty that I would be terrible at it. Additionally, I am grateful to the representatives of the Annals of Emergency Dispatch Research, who spoke to me and connected me to others in 9-1-1-related fields.

I feel lucky to have a department full of supportive colleagues, many of whom provided direct feedback on this project and manuscript. My thanks go out to current and former Media Studies faculty at the University of Virginia, and particularly to Hector Amaya, Camilla Fojas, Jack Hamilton, Aswin Punathambekar, Lana Swartz, and Siva Vaidhyanathan for their feedback on this project in its several stages. To Meredith Clark and Aynne Kokas, my Friday writing buddies, my deepest thanks for giving me the accountability and support that enabled me to move from thinking to writing. My thanks also go to my students who, over the past few years, have tolerated my many examples and questions drawn from this research and offered me their own understandings of emergency media.

This research has been several years in the making, and my thanks go out to all of the conference organizers and attendees, anonymous peer reviewers, and colleagues who have offered feedback on earlier versions of this work and improved it through their generosity and brilliance. Included in this group are Meryl Alper, Hamilton Bean, Shira Chess, Nora Draper, Julie Passanante Elman, Megan Finn, James N. Gilmore and Blake Hallinan, Elizabeth Guffey and Bess Williamson, Aimi Hamraie, Amy Hasinoff, Bill Kirkpatrick, Lisa Parks, Carrie Rentschler, Jennifer Rubenstein, Sami Schalk, and Jonathan Sterne, among countless others.

My thanks to my editors at New York University Press, who showed interest in this project in its earliest stages and ultimately shepherded it to completion, and to Laura Portwood-Stacer for thoughtful editorial feedback at several stages of this project.

I do not recommend completing a book during a global pandemic. This could not have happened without the support of my family. My parents provided more than six weeks of childcare when we otherwise had none, taking health precautions and traveling across the country to give us their time and support. My children adapted to a sudden shift in my work life, learning to give me time and space even when I was at home (at least sometimes). Their happiness at spending extra time together made the sacrifices of social distancing far more tolerable.

Most of all, I thank my husband, Sean. He provided endless support in the form of meals cooked, children watched, breakdowns weathered, errands run, and soothing television watched. When I needed "writing retreats" at a local hotel, he picked up the slack. When I needed to vent, he listened. When I pushed myself too far, he pulled me back. As soon as possible, he deserves a vacation.

Earlier versions of portions of this book appeared in the following publications:

Ellcessor, Elizabeth. "Blue-Light Emergency Phones on Campus: Media Infrastructures of Feeling." *International Journal of Cultural Studies* 22, no. 4 (July 2019): 499–518. https://doi.org/10.1177/1367877918820336.

Ellcessor, Elizabeth. "Call If You Can, Text If You Can't: A Dismediation of U.S. Emergency Communication Infrastructure." *International Journal of Communication* 13 (September 2019): 4487–4506, https://ijoc.org.

Ellcessor, Elizabeth. "The Care and Feeding of 9-1-1 Infrastructure: Dispatcher Culture as Media Work and Infrastructural Transformation." *Cultural Studies*, 2021, https://doi.org/10.1080/09502386.2021.1895249.

NOTES

INTRODUCTION

1 Ariana Eunjung Cha, "Quadriplegic Man's Death from COVID-19 Spotlights Questions of Disability, Race and Family," *Washington Post*, July 5, 2020, www.washingtonpost.com.

2 Due to a conflict between Hickson's wife and sister regarding his medical guardianship, a third-party guardian (Family Eldercare) ultimately approved the removal of life-continuing measures.

3 Emily Ladau, "As a Disabled Person, I'm Afraid I May Not Be Deemed Worth Saving from the Coronavirus," *HuffPost*, March 25, 2020, www.huffpost.com.

4 Minyvonne Burke, "Florida Child's Mother Shot and Killed during Online Zoom Class as Teacher Watches," *NBC News*, August 12, 2020, www.nbcnews.com.

5 Judith Butler, *Frames of War: When Is Life Grievable?* (2009; repr., New York: Verso, 2010).

6 Stuart Hall, "On Postmodernism and Articulation: An Interview with Stuart Hall," *Journal of Communication Inquiry* 10, no. 2 (1986): 45–60, https://doi.org/10.1177/019685998601000204; Jennifer Daryl Slack and J. MacGregor Wise, "Cultural Studies and Technology," in *Handbook of New Media: Social Shaping and Consequences of ICTs*, ed. Leah A. Lievrouw and Sonia Livingstone (Thousand Oaks, CA: SAGE Publications, 2002), 485–98; Julie D'Acci, "Cultural Studies, Television Studies, and the Crisis in the Humanities," in *Television after TV: Essays on a Medium in Transition*, ed. Lynn Spigel and Jan Olsson, Console-ing Passions: Television and Cultural Power (Durham, NC: Duke University Press, 2004), 418–45; Lawrence Grossberg, *Cultural Studies in the Future Tense* (Durham, NC: Duke University Press, 2010).

7 *In Case of Emergency* focuses on the landscape of emergency media in the United States between 2006 and 2020. This period is bracketed on one side by the commencement of the Wireless Emergency Alert—a federal recognition of the need to reach Americans on mobile phones in moments of disaster—and on the other by the growth and mismanagement of the COVID-19 pandemic, which drove people to work and live in new relationships to media technologies and ongoing emergencies. These years represent a specific conjunction in which mediated communication, cultural practices, and dynamics of social power may be observed and untangled in the interest of remaking these relationships along new lines.

8 Sarah Sharma, *In the Meantime, Temporality and Cultural Politics* (Durham, NC: Duke University Press, 2014), 485.

9 Marshall McLuhan, *Understanding Media: The Extensions of Man* (New York: McGraw Hill, 1964), 1.

10 Many scholars of new media have found mediation a useful bridge between technologically and-socially focused traditions of communication scholarship. See Leah A. Lievrouw, "New Media, Mediation, and Communication Study," *Information, Communication and Society* 12, no. 3 (April 2009): 303–25, https://doi.org/10.1080/13691180802660651; Sonia Livingstone, "On the Mediation of Everything: ICA Presidential Address 2008," *Journal of Communication* 59, no. 1 (2009): 1–18; Sarah Kember and Joanna Zylinska, *Life after New Media: Mediation as a Vital Process* (2012; repr., Cambridge: The MIT Press, 2014); and Richard A. Grusin, "Premediation," *Criticism* 46, no. 1 (July 2004): 17–39.

11 Michael Hardt and Antonio Negri, *Multitude: War and Democracy in the Age of Empire* (New York: Penguin Press, 2004), 9.

12 Hardt and Negri, 7.

13 The continuation of post-9/11 airport security measures comes to mind as an example. For discussion of other expansions of power that come in the wake of disaster, see Naomi Klein, *The Shock Doctrine: The Rise of Disaster Capitalism* (London: Picador, 2008).

14 For historical examples of this normalcy-based distribution of aid, see Megan Finn, *Documenting Aftermath: Information Infrastructures in the Wake of Disasters* (Cambridge, MA: MIT Press, 2018).

15 Jennifer C. Rubenstein, "Emergency Claims and Democratic Action," *Social Philosophy and Policy* 32, no. 1 (2015): 102, https://doi.org/10.1017/S0265052515000096.

16 Rubenstein, 103.

17 Rubenstein, 114.

18 Eli Clare, *Brilliant Imperfection: Grappling with Cure* (Durham, NC: Duke University Press, 2017); Jaipreet Virdi, *Hearing Happiness: Deafness Cures in History* (Chicago: University of Chicago Press, 2020).

19 Rosemarie Garland-Thomson, "Integrating Disability, Transforming Feminist Theory," *NWSA Journal* 14, no. 3 (2002): 14.

20 Rosemarie Garland-Thomson, *Extraordinary Bodies: Figuring Physical Disability in American Culture and Literature* (New York: Columbia University Press, 1997); Rachel Adams, *Sideshow U.S.A.: Freaks and the American Cultural Imagination* (Chicago: University of Chicago Press, 2001).

21 Lennard J. Davis, *Enforcing Normalcy: Disability, Deafness, and the Body* (New York: Verso, 1995), 39.

22 Julie Avril Minich, "Enabling Whom? Critical Disability Studies Now," *Lateral* 5, no. 1 (June 1, 2016), https://doi.org/10.25158/L5.1.9.

23 Tobin Siebers, *Disability Theory*, Corporealities (Ann Arbor: University of Michigan Press, 2008); Garland-Thomson, "Integrating Disability, Transforming Feminist Theory"; Robert McRuer, *Crip Theory: Cultural Signs of Queerness*

and Disability (New York: NYU Press, 2006); Alison Kafer, *Feminist, Queer, Crip* (Bloomington: Indiana University Press, 2013); Sami Schalk and Jina B. Kim, "Integrating Race, Transforming Feminist Disability Studies," *Signs: Journal of Women in Culture and Society* 46, no. 1 (September 2020): 31–55, https://doi.org/10.1086/709213.

24 Historically, disability studies has been critiqued for its inattention to race, though this is changing. See N. Erevelles, *Disability and Difference in Global Contexts: Enabling a Transformative Body Politic* (New York: Palgrave Macmillan, 2016); Chris Bell, "Is Disability Studies Actually White Disability Studies?," in *The Disability Studies Reader*, ed. Lennard J. Davis, 3rd ed. (New York: Routledge, 2010), 374–82; Schalk and Kim, "Integrating Race, Transforming Feminist Disability Studies"; Minich, "Enabling Whom?"

25 Schalk and Kim, "Integrating Race, Transforming Feminist Disability Studies," 38. Schalk and Kim are clear that feminist-of-color disability studies scholarship is not an identity, but an orientation and citational practice; to fully interrogate the normalizing ideologies of emergency, I align myself with this practice.

26 Rubenstein, "Emergency Claims and Democratic Action."

27 David M. Perry and Lawrence Carter-Long, "The Ruderman White Paper on Media Coverage of Law Enforcement Use of Force and Disability" (white paper, Ruderman Foundation, March 2016), https://rudermanfoundation.org; Talila Lewis, "Honoring Arnaldo Rios Soto and Charles Kinsey: Achieving Liberation through Disability Solidarity," *Harvard Kennedy School Journal of African American Public Policy*, Spring 2017, 73–78.

28 Erevelles, *Disability and Difference in Global Contexts*, 98.

29 Schalk and Kim, "Integrating Race, Transforming Feminist Disability Studies," 43.

30 Feliks Garcia, "Mother Posts Huge Sign on House to 'Protect Autistic Son from Police,'" *Independent*, September 2, 2016, www.independent.co.uk.

31 Greg Siegel, "Radiating Emergency: The Perils and Promise of the Broadcast Signal in the Atomic Age," *Communication and Critical/Cultural Studies* 8, no. 3 (September 2011): 286–306, https://doi.org/10.1080/14791420.2011.594069; Elizabeth Ellcessor, "Is There a Sign for That? Media, American Sign Language Interpretation, and the Paradox of Visibility," *Perspectives* 23, no. 4 (October 2015): 586–98, https://doi.org/10.1080/0907676X.2015.1056814.

32 Ilan Kelman and Laura M. Stough, eds., *Disability and Disaster: Explorations and Exchanges* (New York: Palgrave Macmillan, 2015).

33 Elizabeth Ellcessor, *Restricted Access: Media, Disability, and the Politics of Participation*, Postmillennial Pop (New York: NYU Press, 2016).

34 Aimi Hamraie, *Building Access: Universal Design and the Politics of Disability* (Minneapolis: University of Minnesota Press, 2017), 13.

35 Bess Williamson, "Access," in *Keywords for Disability Studies*, ed. Rachel Adams, Benjamin Reiss, and David Serlin (New York: NYU Press, 2015), 16–17.

36 Alice Wong, "'Normal' Was Actually Not Great for a Lot of People," *Esquire*, June 15, 2020, www.esquire.com.

37 Scott Gabriel Knowles, *The Disaster Experts: Mastering Risk in Modern America* (Philadelphia: University of Pennsylvania Press, 2013), 222.

38 Ronald W. Perry and E. L. Quarantelli, *What Is a Disaster? New Answers to Old Questions* (La Vergne, TN: Xlibris, 2005), 6.

39 Perry and Quarantelli, 9.

40 Tracy C. Davis, *Stages of Emergency: Cold War Nuclear Civil Defense* (Durham, NC Duke University Press Books, 2007), 21.

41 Knowles, *Disaster Experts*, 233.

42 Perry and Quarantelli, *What Is a Disaster?*, 10.

43 See Sara Ahmed, *The Cultural Politics of Emotion* (New York: Routledge, 2004); and Berlant as quoted in Wendy Hui Kyong Chun, *Updating to Remain the Same: Habitual New Media*, illustrated ed. (Cambridge, MA: MIT Press, 2016), 3.

44 Brian Massumi, *Ontopower: War, Powers, and the State of Perception* (Durham, NC: Duke University Press, 2015), 15.

45 Massumi, 190.

46 Greg Siegel, *Forensic Media: Reconstructing Accidents in Accelerated Modernity* (Durham, NC: Duke University Press, 2014), 15.

47 Paul Virilio, "Speed and Information: Cyberspace Alarm!," trans. Patrice Riemens, *Le Monde diplomatique*, August 1995; Steven Shaviro, *No Speed Limit: Three Essays on Accelerationism* (Minneapolis: University of Minnesota Press, 2015).

48 Virilio, "Speed and Information."

49 Shaviro, *No Speed Limit*, 9.

50 Siegel, *Forensic Media*, 24.

51 Rubenstein, "Emergency Claims and Democratic Action," 105.

52 Rubenstein, 108.

53 Rubenstein, 106.

54 Elaine Scarry, *Thinking in an Emergency* (2010; repr., New York: W. W. Norton, 2012), 7.

55 Accessibility of Programming Providing Emergency Information, 47 U.S.C. § 79.2 (2015).

56 Siegel, "Radiating Emergency," 302.

57 Siegel, 288.

58 Knowles, *Disaster Experts*; Finn, *Documenting Aftermath*.

59 Bean's detailed analysis of the Wireless Emergency Alert system is a notable exception.

60 Lisa Parks and Janet Walker, "Disaster Media: Bending the Curve of Ecological Disruption and Moving Toward Social Justice," *Media+Environment* 2, no. 1 (2020), https://mediaenviron.org.

61 Susan Leigh Star and Karen Ruhleder, "Steps Toward an Ecology of Infrastructure: Design and Access for Large Information Spaces," *Information Systems Research* 7, no. 1 (March 1996): 112, https://doi.org/10.1287/isre.7.1.111.

62 The study of infrastructure in science and technology studies, media studies, and related fields has dramatically expanded in recent years. See, for reference, Lisa

Parks and Nicole Starosielski, eds., *Signal Traffic: Critical Studies of Media Infra-structures* (Urbana: University of Illinois Press, 2015); John Durham Peters, *The Marvelous Clouds: Toward a Philosophy of Elemental Media* (Chicago: University of Chicago Press, 2016); Star and Ruhleder, "Steps Toward an Ecology of Infra-structure"; Keller Easterling, *Extrastatecraft: The Power of Infrastructure Space* (New York: Verso, 2014); and Ara Wilson, "The Infrastructure of Intimacy," *Signs: Journal of Women in Culture and Society* 41, no. 2 (2016): 247–80, https://doi.org/10.1086/682919.

63 Alice Emily Marwick, *Status Update: Celebrity, Publicity, and Branding in the Social Media Age* (New Haven, CT: Yale University Press, 2013); Chun, *Updating to Remain the Same*; Lee Vinsel and Andrew L. Russell, *The Innovation Delusion: How Our Obsession with the New Has Disrupted the Work That Matters Most* (New York: Currency, 2020).

64 Matthew Fuller and Andrew Goffey, *Evil Media* (Cambridge, MA: MIT Press, 2012).

65 Erika Rawes, "Can Alexa Call 9-1-1? How to Set Up Alexa for Emergencies," *Digital Trends*, October 25, 2020, www.digitaltrends.com.

66 *Adventures of Sonic the Hedgehog*, "Super Special Sonic Search and Smash Squad," written by Bruce Shelly and Reed Shelly, aired October 6, 1993, on USA Network.

67 Patricia T. Clough, "The Affective Turn: Political Economy, Biomedia and Bodies," *Theory, Culture and Society* 25, no. 1 (January 2008): 1–22, https://doi.org/10.1177/0263276407085156; Melissa Gregg and Gregory J. Seigworth, eds., *The Affect Theory Reader*, illustrated ed. (Durham, NC: Duke University Press, 2010).

68 Gregory J. Downey, *Telegraph Messenger Boys: Labor, Communication and Tech-nology, 1850–1950* (New York: Routledge, 2002); Elinor Carmi, "Sonic Publics | The Hidden Listeners: Regulating the Line from Telephone Operators to Content Moderators," *International Journal of Communication* 13 (January 2019): 440–58, https://ijoc.org; Sarah T. Roberts, *Behind the Screen: Content Moderation in the Shadows of Social Media* (New Haven, CT: Yale University Press, 2019).

69 Jennifer Daryl Slack, "Technology," in *Keywords for Media Studies*, ed. Laurie Ouellette and Jonathan Gray (New York: NYU Press, 2017), 191.

70 Hamraie, *Building Access*; Bess Williamson, *Accessible America* (New York: NYU Press, 2020); Kafer, *Feminist, Queer, Crip*; Ellcessor, *Restricted Access*; Tanya Titch-kosky, *The Question of Access: Disability, Space, Meaning* (Toronto: University of Toronto Press, 2011).

71 National Academies of Sciences, Engineering, and Medicine, *Emergency Alert and Warning Systems: Current Knowledge and Future Research Directions* (Washing-ton, DC: National Academies Press, 2018), https://doi.org/10.17226/24935.

1. ALARM!

1 Michael Perchick, "Raleigh Family Escapes Fire Tragedy Thanks to 4-Year-Old Child's Quick Thinking," *ABC11 Raleigh-Durham*, October 9, 2020, https://abc11.com.

2 Tama Leaver, "Intimate Surveillance: Normalizing Parental Monitoring and Mediation of Infants Online," *Social Media + Society* 3, no. 2 (April 2017): 1–10, https://doi.org/10.1177/2056305117707192.

3 Keller Easterling, *Extrastatecraft: The Power of Infrastructure Space* (New York: Verso, 2014).

4 Marshall McLuhan, *Understanding Media: The Extensions of Man* (New York: McGraw Hill, 1964), 2.

5 Jussi Parikka, *A Geology of Media* (Minneapolis: University of Minnesota Press, 2015), 1.

6 Silvan Tomkins, *Affect Imagery Consciousness, Volume II: The Negative Affects* (New York: Springer Publishing, 1963).

7 *Emergency Signaling* (New York: Gamewell Fire Alarm Telegraph Co., 1916), https://catalog.hathitrust.org.

8 Rachel Plotnick, *Power Button: A History of Pleasure, Panic, and the Politics of Pushing* (Cambridge, MA: MIT Press, 2018), 17–18 and 176.

9 Joshua Reeves, *Citizen Spies: The Long Rise of America's Surveillance Society* (New York: NYU Press, 2017), 60.

10 Plotnick, *Power Button*.

11 Reeves, *Citizen Spies*, 58.

12 Charles S. Peirce, *The Essential Peirce, Volume 2: Selected Philosophical Writings, 1893–1913*, Peirce Edition Project (Bloomington: Indiana University Press, 1998).

13 Peirce, 5. Cited in Brian Massumi, *Ontopower: War, Powers, and the State of Perception* (Durham, NC: Duke University Press, 2015), 202.

14 Peirce, 69.

15 V. N. Volosinov, *Marxism and the Philosophy of Language*, trans. Ladislav Matejka and I. R. Titunik (Cambridge, MA: Harvard University Press, 1986), 68.

16 Volosinov, 68.

17 Stuart Hall, "Encoding/Decoding," in *Media and Cultural Studies: Keyworks*, ed. Meenakshi Gigi Durham and Douglas Kellner (Malden, MA: Blackwell, 2001), 167.

18 Ryan Douglas Nestor, "This Is Not a Drill: The Siren as a Symbol and Musical Instrument" (PhD diss., UC San Diego, 2018), https://escholarship.org.

19 McLuhan, *Understanding Media*, 8–9.

20 Rachel Plotnick, "Panic Button: Thinking Historically about Danger, Interfaces, and Control-at-a-Distance," in *Communication and Control: Tools, Systems, and New Dimensions*, ed. Robert MacDougall (Lanham, MD: Lexington Books, 2015), 45–58.

21 Elyse Graham, "This Might Make You Feel Differently about Your Morning Alarm: The Origins of 'Alarm,'" *OxfordWords* (blog), April 23, 2018, https://blog.oxforddictionaries.com.

22 Åsun Øien Josefsen, "Don't Let Me Burn!," in *Disability and Disaster: Explorations and Exchanges*, ed. Ilan Kelman and Laura M. Stough, trans. Ilan Kelman (New York: Palgrave Macmillan, 2015), 95–96.

23 Andrew Valente, "The ADA's Impact on Fire Alarm Systems," *Journal of Property Management* 64, no. 1 (February 1999): 46; Heidi M. Berven and Peter David Blanck, "Assistive Technology Patenting Trends and the Americans with Disabilities Act," *Behavioral Sciences and the Law* 17, no. 1 (1999): 47–71.

24 Valente, "ADA's Impact on Fire Alarm Systems."

25 Emily Ladau, "As A Disabled Person, I'm Afraid I May Not Be Deemed Worth Saving from the Coronavirus," *HuffPost*, March 25, 2020, www.huffpost.com.

26 "Emergency public" draws on Finn's formulation of "earthquake publics." See Megan Finn, *Documenting Aftermath: Information Infrastructures in the Wake of Disasters* (Cambridge, MA: MIT Press, 2018), 5.

27 Peters, *Marvelous Clouds*, 37.

28 Ned Rossiter, *Software, Infrastructure, Labor: A Media Theory of Logistical Nightmares* (New York: Routledge, 2016), 56.

29 Peters, *Marvelous Clouds*, 38.

30 Dan Hassoun and James N. Gilmore, "Drowsing: Toward a Concept of Sleepy Screen Engagement," *Communication and Critical/Cultural Studies* 14, no. 2 (April 2017): 103–19, https://doi.org/10.1080/14791420.2016.1276611.

31 Sylviane Agacinski, *Time Passing*, trans. Jody Gladding, illustrated ed. (New York: Columbia University Press, 2003).

32 Paddy Scannell, *Television and the Meaning of "Live": An Enquiry into the Human Situation* (Cambridge: Polity, 2014), 45.

33 Dylan Mulvin, "Media Prophylaxis: Night Modes and the Politics of Preventing Harm," *Information and Culture* 53, no. 2 (April 2018): 175–202, https://doi.org/10.7560/IC53203; Matthew Fuller, *How to Sleep: The Art, Biology and Culture of Unconsciousness* (New York: Bloomsbury Academic, 2018); Hassoun and Gilmore, "Drowsing."

34 Christopher O'Neill and Bjorn Nansen, "Sleep Mode: Mobile Apps and the Optimisation of Sleep-Wake Rhythms," *First Monday*, June 1, 2019, https://doi.org/10.5210/fm.v24i6.9574.

35 Nestor, "This Is Not a Drill," 37.

36 Massumi, *Ontopower*, 191.

37 Massumi, 202.

38 Patricia T. Clough, "The Affective Turn: Political Economy, Biomedia and Bodies," *Theory, Culture and Society* 25, no. 1 (January 2008): 2, https://doi.org/10.1177/0263276407085156.

39 Sara Ahmed, *The Cultural Politics of Emotion* (New York: Routledge, 2004), 10.

40 Tomkins, *Affect Imagery Consciousness*, 95.

41 Tomkins, 10.

42 Anna Gibbs, "Panic! Affect Contagion, Mimesis and Suggestion in the Social Field," *Cultural Studies Review* 14, no. 2 (2008): 130–45, https://doi.org/10.5130/csr.v14i2.2076.

43 Ahmed, *Cultural Politics of Emotion*, 65.

44 Scannell, *Television and the Meaning of "Live."*

45 Virilio, "Speed and Information."
46 Peters, *Marvelous Clouds*, 228.
47 Timothy A. Coleman et al., "The History (and Future) of Tornado Warning Dissemination in the United States," *Bulletin of the American Meteorological Society* 92, no. 5 (May 2011): 577, https://doi.org/10.1175/2010BAMS3062.1; Scott Gabriel Knowles, *The Disaster Experts: Mastering Risk in Modern America* (Philadelphia: University of Pennsylvania Press, 2013).
48 Coleman et al., "History (and Future) of Tornado Warning Dissemination," 567.
49 Coleman et al., 578.
50 Ahmed, *Cultural Politics of Emotion*, 68.
51 Ahmed, 69.
52 Sarah Sharma, *In the Meantime*, Temporality and Cultural Politics (Durham, NC: Duke University Press, 2014), 9.
53 Anders Ekström, "Media Times | When Is the Now? Monitoring Disaster in the Expansion of Time," *International Journal of Communication* 10 (October 2016): 20, https://ijoc.org; Rubenstein, "Emergency Claims and Democratic Action"; Didier Fassin and Mariella Pandolfi, eds., *Contemporary States of Emergency: The Politics of Military and Humanitarian Interventions* (New York: Zone Books, 2010); Giorgio Agamben, *State of Exception*, trans. Kevin Attell (Chicago: University of Chicago Press, 2005).
54 Grusin, "Premediation."
55 Ekström, "Media Times | When Is the Now?," 20.
56 Massumi, *Ontopower*, 2015.
57 Rebecca Coleman, "The Presents of the Present: Mindfulness, Time and Structures of Feeling," *Distinktion: Journal of Social Theory*, September 11, 2020, https://doi.org/10.1080/1600910X.2020.1810730.
58 Sharma, "Taxis as Media," 458.
59 Sharma, *In the Meantime*, 9.
60 Leah Lakshmi Piepzna-Samarasinha, *Care Work: Dreaming Disability Justice* (Vancouver, BC: Arsenal Pulp Press, 2018).
61 Alison Kafer, "Un/Safe Disclosures," *Journal of Literary and Cultural Disability Studies* 10, no. 1 (February 2016): 27, https://doi.org/10.3828/jlcds.2016.1.
62 Ellen Samuels, "Six Ways of Looking at Crip Time," *Disability Studies Quarterly* 37, no. 3 (August 2017), https://doi.org/10.18061/dsq.v37i3.5824.
63 Peters, *Marvelous Clouds*, 239.
64 Ahmed, *Cultural Politics of Emotion*; Sara Ahmed, *What's the Use? On the Uses of Use* (Durham, NC: Duke University Press, 2019).
65 Charles R. Acland and Haidee Wasson, "Introduction: Utility and Cinema," in *Useful Cinema*, Charles R. Acland and Haidee Wasson (Durham, NC: Duke University Press, 2011), 6.
66 Ahmed, *What's the Use?*, 65.
67 Ahmed, 45.
68 Ahmed, 27.

69 Jason Farman, *Delayed Response: The Art of Waiting from the Ancient to the Instant World* (New Haven, CT: Yale University Press, 2018).

70 Massumi, *Ontopower*, 202.

71 Sally Wyatt, "Non-Users Also Matter: The Construction of Users and Non-Users of the Internet," in *Now Users Matter: The Co-Construction of Users and Technology*, ed. Nelly Oudshoorn and Trevor Pinch (Cambridge, MA: MIT Press, 2003), 67–79; Laura Portwood-Stacer, "Media Refusal and Conspicuous Non-Consumption: The Performative and Political Dimensions of Facebook Abstention," *New Media and Society*, December 5, 2012, https://doi.org/10.1177/1461444812465139.

72 Sally Wyatt, Graham Thomas, and Tiziana Terranova, "They Came, They Surfed, They Went Back to the Beach: Conceptualizing Use and Non-Use of the Internet," in *Virtual Society? Get Real! Technology, Cyberbole, Reality*, ed. Steve Woolgar (New York: Oxford University Press, 2002), 36.

73 Wyatt, "Non-Users Also Matter," 69.

74 Timothy A. Coleman and Kevin J. Pence, "The Proposed 1883 Holden Tornado Warning System: Its Genius and Its Applications Today," *Bulletin of the American Meteorological Society* 90, no. 12 (December 2009): 1791, https://doi.org/10.1175/2009BAMS2886.1.

75 Coleman and Pence, 1791.

76 Coleman and Pence.

77 Coleman and Pence.

78 "Apple Watch Series 3," Apple, accessed April 16, 2018, www.apple.com.

79 Tim Hardwick, "Apple Watch Patent Turns Device into Urgent Care Alert System," *MacRumors*, March 10, 2016, www.macrumors.com.

80 Elizabeth Ellcessor, "Designing Emergency Access: Lifeline and LifeCall," in *Making Disability Modern: Design Histories*, ed. Bess Williamson and Elizabeth Guffey (London: Bloomsbury Visual Arts, 2020), 193–208.

81 Andrew S. Dibner, Closed-Loop Emergency Alarm and Response System, U.S. Patent 4064368A, filed June 7, 1976, and issued December 20, 1977.

82 Andrew S. Dibner, Automatic Telephone Alarm System, U.S. Patent 3989900A, filed November 4, 1974, and issued November 2, 1976.

83 Dibner, automatic telephone alarm system patent, 5.

84 *Statistical Abstract of the United States* (Washington, DC: Bureau of the Census, 1999), www.census.gov.

85 Dibner, automatic telephone alarm system patent, 1.

86 Xing Tan et al., Detecting Falls Using a Mobile Device, U.S. Patent US20190103007A1, filed September 11, 2018, and issued April 4, 2019.

87 L. Dennis Shapiro, Personal Alarm System , U.S. Patent 4524243A, filed July 7, 1983, and issued June 18, 1985.

88 Patrick Verel, "Calling for Help Devices Help Seniors, Disabled in Case of an Emergency," *Augusta Chronicle*, January 11, 2005.

89 Ellcessor, "Designing Emergency Access."

90 David Lyon, *Surveillance after September 11* (Malden, MA: Polity, 2003), 7.

91 Lyon, 7.

92 Leaver, "Intimate Surveillance," 2.

93 Leaver, 4.

94 Rachel E. Dubrofsky and Shoshana Amielle Magnet, eds., *Feminist Surveillance Studies*, Edition Unstated (Durham, NC: Duke University Press, 2015).

95 Jose van Dijck, "Datafication, Dataism and Dataveillance: Big Data between Scientific Paradigm and Ideology," *Surveillance and Society* 12, no. 2 (May 2014): 197–208, https://doi.org/10.24908/ss.v12i2.4776.

96 Jennifer Pattison Tuohy, "The Smart Home Device Every Home Needs," *New York Times*, September 18, 2020, www.nytimes.com.

97 "Caught in the Spotlight," *Urban Omnibus*, January 9, 2020, https://urbanomnibus.net.

98 Gilbert Caluya, "Pride and Paranoia: Race and the Emergence of Home Security in Cold War America," *Continuum: Journal of Media and Cultural Studies* 28, no. 6 (December 2014): 815, https://doi.org/10.1080/10304312.2014.966406.

99 Kari Paul, "Amazon's Doorbell Camera Ring Is Working with Police—and Controlling What They Say," *The Guardian*, August 30, 2019, www.theguardian.com.

100 Lauren Bridges, "Infrastructural Obfuscation: Unpacking the Carceral Logics of the Ring Surveillant Assemblage." *Information, Communication and Society* 24, no. 6 (April 2021): 830–49, https://doi.org/10.1080/1369118X.2021.1909097.

2. MAPS AND THE AFFECTIVE SURVEILLANCE OF "SAFETY"

1 Stacy R. Stewart and Robbie Berg, *National Hurricane Center Tropical Cyclone Report: Hurricane Florence* (University Park, FL: National Hurricane Center, 2019), www.nhc.noaa.gov/.

2 Jordan Frith, *Smartphones as Locative Media*, Digital Media and Society (Malden, MA: Polity, 2015).

3 Johanna Drucker, *Graphesis: Visual Forms of Knowledge Production* (Cambridge, MA: Harvard University Press, 2014), 32.

4 Aimi Hamraie, "Mapping Access: Digital Humanities, Disability Justice, and Sociospatial Practice," *American Quarterly* 70, no. 3 (September 2018): 455–82, https://doi.org/10.1353/aq.2018.0031.

5 Germaine R. Halegoua, *The Digital City: Media and the Social Production of Place*, illustrated ed. (New York: NYU Press, 2020), 147.

6 "iCloud—Find My," Apple, accessed November 18, 2020, www.apple.com.

7 Focus groups were primarily organized through student organizations, enabling discussion of common identities and experiences along lines of race, gender, disability, and religion.

8 Most often, and perhaps due to the sampling, people invoked threats of sexual assault, abduction, or racial violence.

9 "Ella" is a pseudonym chosen by a participant.

10 Halegoua, *Digital City*, 134.

11 For more on the "spatial self," see Raz Schwartz and Germaine R Halegoua, "The Spatial Self: Location-Based Identity Performance on Social Media," *New Media and Society* 17, no. 10 (November 2015): 1643–60, https://doi.org/10.1177/1461444814531364.

12 Tama Leaver, "Intimate Surveillance: Normalizing Parental Monitoring and Mediation of Infants Online," *Social Media + Society* 3, no. 2 (April 2017): 8, https://doi.org/10.1177/2056305117707192.

13 Nellie Bowles, "Thermostats, Locks and Lights: Digital Tools of Domestic Abuse," *New York Times*, June 23, 2018, www.nytimes.com.

14 More about these platforms, which often offer alerting features, is covered in chapter 3.

15 My attendance at promotional events, conversations with company representatives, and interviews with campus emergency managers inform this and related conclusions about these platforms.

16 Elizabeth Ellcessor, "Companion: Mobile Personal Safety," in *Appified: Culture in the Age of Apps*, ed. Jeremy Wade Morris and Sarah Murray (Ann Arbor: University of Michigan Press, 2018), 156–68.

17 Ellcessor.

18 Jason Farman, *Mobile Interface Theory: Embodied Space and Locative Media* (New York: Routledge, 2012), 54.

19 Natasha Singer, "The War on Campus Sexual Assault Goes Digital," *New York Times*, November 13, 2015, www.nytimes.com.

20 Elizabeth Ellcessor, "Blue-Light Emergency Phones on Campus: Media Infrastructures of Feeling," *International Journal of Cultural Studies* 22, no. 4 (July 2019): 499–518, https://doi.org/10.1177/1367877918820336.

21 University of Colorado Boulder Chancellor's Office records, COU:2347, box 317, folder 1, Special Collections and Archives, University of Colorado Boulder Libraries.

22 Ellcessor, "Blue-Light Emergency Phones on Campus."

23 Other institutions studied included George Washington University, Georgetown University, Indiana University, the University of Pennsylvania, the University of Virginia, and the Five Colleges of Ohio (the College of Wooster, Denison University, Kenyon College, Oberlin College, Ohio Wesleyan University). News coverage of other institutions, including Syracuse University, Howard and Gallaudet Universities, and Lehigh University, has also informed this research.

24 George Washington University, Vice-President for Student and Academic Support Records—Communication, 1989–96, RG0006 series 6, box 2 folder 43, University Police Department "Security Blanket" 1994–95, Special Collections and Archives, George Washington University Libraries.

25 Valerie Strauss, "Area Universities Tighten Security," *Washington Post*, May 3, 1997, www.washingtonpost.com.

26 *Annual Report, 1998–1999* (Philadelphia: University of Pennsylvania, 1999), 13.

27 H. Goodman, "Parents' Ivy Dreams Taking Root," *Philadelphia Inquirer*, August 8, 1995.

28 Carrie Rentschler, "Designing Fear: How Environmental Security Protects Property at the Expense of People," in *Foucault, Cultural Studies, and Governmentality*, ed. Jack Z. Bratich, Jeremy Packer, and Cameron McCarthy (Albany: State University of New York Press, 2003), 247.

29 Georgetown University Campus Security records, GTA 000130, box 3, folder 1, "Annual Reports," box 3, folder 11, "Crime Awareness and Campus Security 1992 Annual Report," Special Collections, Georgetown University Libraries.

30 Ellcessor, "Blue-Light Emergency Phones on Campus."

31 Raymond Williams, The Long Revolution (1961; repr., Cardigan: Parthian Books, 2013), 68.

32 Ara Wilson, "The Infrastructure of Intimacy," *Signs: Journal of Women in Culture and Society* 41, no. 2 (2016): 249, https://doi.org/10.1086/682919.

33 Wilson, 262.

34 Patricia T. Clough, "The Affective Turn: Political Economy, Biomedia and Bodies," *Theory, Culture and Society* 25, no. 1 (January 2008): 1–22, https://doi.org/10.1177/0263276407085156; Melissa Gregg and Gregory J. Seigworth, eds., *The Affect Theory Reader*, illustrated ed. (Durham, NC: Duke University Press, 2010).

35 Harold A. Innis, *Empire and Communications* (Toronto: Dundurn, 2007).

36 Drucker, *Graphesis*.

37 Julia Leyda and Diane Negra, "Introduction: Extreme Weather and Global Media," *Extreme Weather and Global Media*, ed. Julia Leyda and Diane Negra (New York: Routledge, 2015), 3.

38 Frances Bonner, *Ordinary Television: Analyzing Popular TV* (London: SAGE Publications, 2003).

39 Leyda and Negra, *Extreme Weather and Global Media*.

40 Minh D. Phan et al., "Weather on the Go: An Assessment of Smartphone Mobile Weather Application Use among College Students," *Bulletin of the American Meteorological Society* 99, no. 11 (November 2018): 2245–57, https://doi.org/10.1175/BAMS-D-18-0020.1.

41 Phan et al.

42 Morris and Murray, *Appified*, 12.

43 Wendy Hui Kyong Chun, *Updating to Remain the Same: Habitual New Media*, illustrated ed. (Cambridge, MA: MIT Press, 2016), 1.

44 Megan Finn, *Documenting Aftermath: Information Infrastructures in the Wake of Disasters* (Cambridge, MA: MIT Press, 2018), 2.

45 David Smith, "Trump Shows Fake Hurricane Map in Apparent Bid to Validate Incorrect Tweet," *The Guardian*, September 4, 2019, www.theguardian.com.

46 This tendency of the Trump administration perhaps culminated in the tragicomic election press conference at Four Seasons Total Landscaping in Philadelphia, PA.

47 Emily Stewart, "Donald Trump's Hurricane Sharpie Map and How the Media Made It Worse—Vox," *Vox*, September 6, 2019, www.vox.com; Toluse Olorunnipa and Josh Dawsey, "'What I Said Was Accurate!': Trump Stays Fixated on His

Alabama Error as Hurricane Pounds the Carolinas," *Washington Post*, September 5, 2019, www.washingtonpost.com.

48 False Weather Reports, 18 U.S.C. § 2074 (1948).

49 Jason Leopold, "wow. These emails underscore how angry NOAA officials were about the Hurricane Dorian tweets by Trump and how NOAA handled and responded to the controversy (and sharpiegate). 'You have no idea how hard I'm fighting to keep politics out of science . . .' #FOIA," Twitter, January 31, 2020, 8:05 p.m., https://twitter.com/JasonLeopold/status/1223457425015001088.

50 Phan et al., "Weather on the Go," 2252.

51 Sarah Underwood, "Can You Locate Your Location Data?," *Communications of the ACM* 62, no. 9 (September 2019): 19–21, https://doi.org/10.1145/3344291; Shoshana Wodlinsky, "Your Weather App Is Selling You Out," *Gizmodo*, September 14, 2020, https://gizmodo.com.

52 Wodlinsky, "Your Weather App Is Selling You Out"; Jennifer Valentino-DeVries and Natasha Singer, "Los Angeles Accuses Weather Channel App of Covertly Mining User Data (Published 2019)," *New York Times*, January 4, 2019, www.nytimes.com.

53 Stefanie Dazio, "Weather Channel App to Change Practices after LA Lawsuit," *Washington Post*, August 19, 2020, www.washingtonpost.com.

54 Phan et al., "Weather on the Go."

55 Shoshana Zuboff, *The Age of Surveillance Capitalism: The Fight for a Human Future at the New Frontier of Power* (New York: PublicAffairs, 2019).

56 Tony D. Sampson and Jussi Parikka, "The Operational Loops of a Pandemic," *Cultural Politics*, August 4, 2020; Drucker, *Graphesis*.

57 Drucker, *Graphesis*, 5.

58 Drucker, 8.

59 Sara Ahmed, *The Cultural Politics of Emotion* (New York: Routledge, 2004).

60 The JHU global, U.S., and state-level maps were published online and updated daily with new data from the Coronavirus COVID-19 Global Cases by the Center for Systems Science and Engineering (CSSE) at Johns Hopkins University, the Red Cross, the Census American Community Survey, and the Bureau of Labor and Statistics. Johns Hopkins University of Medicine, "FAQ—COVID-19 United States Cases by County," Johns Hopkins Coronavirus Resource Center, accessed November 21, 2020, https://coronavirus.jhu.edu.

61 Johns Hopkins University of Medicine, "FAQ."

62 Caity Weaver, "The Unmitigated Chaos of America's Attempt at Color-Coded COVID Guidance," *New York Times*, April 2, 2021, www.nytimes.com.

63 Johns Hopkins University of Medicine, "FAQ."

64 As of 2010, Benson County had a population of under 7,000.

65 Keith Mayer, "Nursing Homes Inflate Coronavirus Positives and Deaths in Certain ZIP Codes," *Reading Eagle*, May 6, 2020, www.readingeagle.com.

66 Mayer.

67 Liat Ben-Moshe, *Decarcerating Disability: Deinstitutionalization and Prison Abolition* (Minneapolis: University of Minnesota Press, 2020).

68 danah boyd and Kate Crawford, "Critical Questions for Big Data," *Information, Communication & Society* 15, no. 5 (June 2012): 662–79, https://doi.org/10.1080/13 69118X.2012.678878.

69 "OPHAS with Alert Indicators," Ohio Department of Health, 2020, https://public. tableau.com.

70 "OPHAS with Alert Indicators."

71 Emily Bowe, Erin Simmons, and Shannon Mattern, "Learning from Lines: Critical COVID Data Visualizations and the Quarantine Quotidian," *Big Data & Society* 7, no. 2 (July 2020): 22, https://doi.org/10.1177/2053951720939236.

72 Sampson and Parikka, "Operational Loops of a Pandemic," 8.

73 A. T. Chande et al., "Interactive COVID-19 Event Risk Assessment Planning Tool," Georgia Institute of Technology, accessed November 22, 2020, https://covid19risk.biosci.gatech.edu.

74 Jordan Frith and Michael Saker, "It Is All about Location: Smartphones and Tracking the Spread of COVID-19," *Social Media and Society* 6, no. 3 (July 2020): 1–4, https://doi.org/10.1177/2056305120948257; Bowe, Simmons, and Mattern, "Learning from Lines"; Sampson and Parikka, "Operational Loops of a Pandemic"; Andrew Campolo, "Flattening the Curve: Visualization and Pandemic Knowledge," *The Stevanovich Institute on the Formation of Knowledge* (blog), April 1, 2020, https://doi.org/10.1101/2020.03.24.20042291.

75 Campolo, "Flattening the Curve."

76 Bowe, Simmons, and Mattern, "Learning from Lines."

77 Drucker, *Graphesis*; Shannon Mattern, *Deep Mapping the Media City* (Minneapolis: University of Minnesota Press, 2015); Hamraie, "Mapping Access"; Bowe, Simmons, and Mattern, "Learning from Lines."

78 "COVID-19 Housing Protections Map," Anti-Eviction Mapping Project, 2020, https://antievictionmappingproject.github.io/covid-19-map/.

79 Bowe, Simmons, and Mattern, "Learning from Lines," 2.

80 Hamraie, "Mapping Access." 456.

3. ALERT

1 Investigation revealed that the false alarm was caused by an employee at the Hawaiʻi Emergency Management Agency who was participating in an unscheduled drill and believed he had been instructed to issue an alert based on real circumstances. Additionally, the technology in question was criticized for providing easily confused menu options and little additional scrutiny. Amy B. Wang, "Hawaii Missile Alert: How One Employee 'Pushed the Wrong Button' and Caused a Wave of Panic," *Washington Post*, January 14, 2018, www.washingtonpost.com.

2 John Thornton Caldwell, *Production Culture: Industrial Reflexivity and Critical Practice in Film and Television* (Durham, NC: Duke University Press, 2008).

3 Bean uses this definition for "warning," while he conceptualizes "alert" as similar to what I have called an alarm (see chapter 1). This difference is due to the fact that Bean is aligning his definitions to the Integrated Public Alert and Warning System (IPAWS), while I am trying to align descriptions to users' experiences and vocabulary. Hamilton Bean, *Mobile Technology and the Transformation of Public Alert and Warning* (Santa Barbara, CA: Praeger, 2019), 21.

4 Megan Finn, *Documenting Aftermath: Information Infrastructures in the Wake of Disasters* (Cambridge, MA: MIT Press, 2018).

5 National Academies of Sciences, Engineering, and Medicine, *Emergency Alert and Warning Systems: Current Knowledge and Future Research Directions* (Washington, DC: National Academies Press, 2018), 49–50, https://doi.org/10.17226/24935.

6 Elaine Scarry, *Thinking in an Emergency* (2010; repr., W. W. Norton, 2012).

7 Deborah Lupton, *The Quantified Self* (Cambridge: Polity, 2016).

8 Stephanie Madden, "Alerting a Campus Community: Emergency Notification from a Public's Perspective," *Journal of Contingencies and Crisis Management* 23, no. 4 (2015): 184–92, https://doi.org/10.1111/1468-5973.12074.

9 There is a general paucity of critical theorization of smartphone alerts or notifications. Though the phenomenon is routinely mentioned as part of mobile media infrastructures, the alert itself is far too often taken for granted as self-explanatory and devoid of specific meaning.

10 Wendy Hui Kyong Chun, *Updating to Remain the Same: Habitual New Media*, illustrated ed. (Cambridge, MA: MIT Press, 2016).

11 David Parisi and Jason Farman, "Tactile Temporalities: The Impossible Promise of Increasing Efficiency and Eliminating Delay through Haptic Media," *Convergence*, December 9, 2018, 55, https://doi.org/10.1177/1354856518814681.

12 James N. Gilmore, "From Ticks and Tocks to Budges and Nudges: The Smartwatch and the Haptics of Informatic Culture," *Television & New Media* 18, no. 3 (March 2017): 192, https://doi.org/10.1177/1527476416658962.

13 Bean, *Mobile Technology*, 72.

14 Gregory Asmolov, "Crowdsourcing and the Folksonomy of Emergency Response: The Construction of a Mediated Subject," *Interactions: Studies in Communication & Culture* 6, no. 2 (July 2015): 173, https://doi.org/10.1386/iscc.6.2.155_1.

15 Amy A. Hasinoff and Patrick M. Krueger, "Warning: Notifications about Crime on Campus May Have Unwanted Effects," *International Journal of Communication* 14 (January 2020): 21, https://ijoc.org.

16 S. J. Blumberg and J. V. Luke, *Wireless Substitution: Early Release of Estimates from the National Health Interview Survey, July–December 2017* (Hyattsville, MD: National Center for Health Statistics, June 2018), www.cdc.gov.

17 Bean, *Mobile Technology*.

18 Bean, xviii.

19 Integrated Public Alert and Warning System (IPAWS), Outreach Plan for Communications and Partner Engagement (Washington, DC: Federal Emergency Management Agency, 2013), 43.

20 "Get Alerts, Stay Alive," Federal Emergency Management Agency, 2012, www.fema.gov.

21 Bean, *Mobile Technology*.

22 Bean, 90; Greg Siegel, "Radiating Emergency: The Perils and Promise of the Broadcast Signal in the Atomic Age," *Communication and Critical/Cultural Studies* 8, no. 3 (September 2011): 286–306, https://doi.org/10.1080/14791420.2011.594069.

23 Tracy C. Davis, *Stages of Emergency: Cold War Nuclear Civil Defense* (Durham, NC: Duke University Press, 2007); Siegel, "Radiating Emergency."

24 John MacDonald, "Emergency Broadcast Test to Tone Down Its Warning," *Los Angeles Times*, November 24, 1996, www.latimes.com.

25 Glenn Collins, "The Silence of the Alert System; Experts Urge Overhaul of Plan Unused Even on Sept. 11," *New York Times*, December 21, 2001, www.nytimes.com.

26 Bean, *Mobile Technology*, xviii.

27 The October 2, 2018, test received on cellphones read "THIS IS A TEST of the National Wireless Emergency Alert System. No action is needed."

28 Beth Skwarecki, "How to Keep Presidential Alerts off Your Phone," *Lifehacker*, September 18, 2018, www.lifehacker.com.

29 Ian Bogost, "Trump Is Not Texting You," *The Atlantic*, October 3, 2018, www.theatlantic.com.

30 Bean, *Mobile Technology*, 105.

31 Bean, 100.

32 Caldwell, *Production Culture*; Vicki Mayer, Miranda J. Banks, and John T. Caldwell, eds., *Production Studies: Cultural Studies of Media Industries* (London: Routledge, 2009); Timothy Havens, Amanda D. Lotz, and Serra Tinic, "Critical Media Industry Studies: A Research Approach," *Communication, Culture and Critique* 2, no. 2 (2009): 234–53, https://doi.org/10.1111/j.1753-9137.2009.01037.x.

33 Vicki Mayer, *Below the Line: Producers and Production Studies in the New Television Economy* (Durham, NC: Duke University Press, 2011); Gregory John Downey, "Making Media Work: Time, Space, Identity, and Labor in the Analysis of Information and Communication Infrastructures," in *Media Technologies: Essays on Communication, Materiality, and Society*, ed. Tarleton Gillespie, Pablo J. Boczkowski, and Kirsten A. Foot (Cambridge, MA: MIT Press, 2014), 141–66; Eleanor Patterson, "Maintaining Transmission: DirecTV's Work-at-Home Technical Support, Virtual Surveillance, and the Gendered Domestication of Distributive Labor," *Television and New Media*, June 9, 2020, https://doi.org/10.1177/1527476420928552.

34 Susan Leigh Star and Karen Ruhleder, "Steps Toward an Ecology of Infrastructure: Design and Access for Large Information Spaces," *Information Systems Research* 7, no. 1 (March 1996): 111–34, https://doi.org/10.1287/isre.7.1.111; Elinor Carmi, "Sonic Publics | The Hidden Listeners: Regulating the Line from Telephone Operators to Content Moderators," *International Journal of Communication* 13 (January 2019): 440–58, https://ijoc.org; Cait McKinney, *Information Activism: A Queer History of Lesbian Media Technologies*, annotated ed. (Durham: Duke University Press, 2020).

35 B. Wayne Blanchard, *Principles of Emergency Management Supplement* (Washington, DC: Federal Emergency Management Agency, 2007), 4, www.iaem.org.

36 Andrew Lakoff, *Unprepared: Global Health in a Time of Emergency* (Berkeley: University of California Press, 2017); Finn, *Documenting Aftermath*; "Principles of Emergency Management."

37 Caldwell, *Production Culture.*

38 "The College List—Emergency Management Programs—Bachelor Degrees," Emergency Management Institute, 2020, https://training.fema.gov.

39 Matthew Fuller and Andrew Goffey, *Evil Media* (Cambridge, MA: MIT Press, 2012).

40 James N. Gilmore and McKinley DuRant, "Emergency Infrastructure and Locational Extraction: Problematizing Computer Assisted Dispatch Systems as Public Good," *Surveillance & Society* 19, no. 2 (June 2021): 187–98, https://doi.org/10.24908/ss.v19i2.14116.

41 Bean, *Mobile Technology*, 4.

42 Lakoff, *Unprepared*, 167.

43 Bean, *Mobile Technology*, 44.

44 Hamilton Bean et al., "Do Wireless Emergency Alerts Help Impede the Spread of COVID-19?" (manuscript in preparation, n.d.).

45 Jessica L. Doermann, Erica D. Kuligowski, and James Milke, "From Social Science Research to Engineering Practice: Development of a Short Message Creation Tool for Wildfire Emergencies," *Fire Technology* 57 (2021): 818, https://doi.org/10.1007/s10694-020-01008-7.

46 FEMA, "FEMA Alert System Helps Communities Communicate during Coronavirus Response," press release, April 14, 2020.

47 "Guiding Communities through Emergency Alerts and Warnings," Department of Homeland Security, September 30, 2020, www.dhs.gov.

48 *FEMA's Oversight of the Integrated Public Alert and Warning System (IPAWS)* (Washington, DC: United States Department of Homeland Security, 2018), www.oig.dhs.gov.

49 "Enhanced Wireless Emergency Alerts Available for Coronavirus Pandemic," Federal Communications Commission, April 2, 2020, www.fcc.gov.

50 This information is taken from a spreadsheet that was provided to the author by Hamilton Bean who, in turn, received it from a contact at FEMA. It was made available prior to the OpenGov release of all WEA messages from 2012 through 2020 and contained preidentified COVID-related messages.

51 DeeDee Bennett, Paul M. A. Baker, and Helena Mitchell, "New Media and Accessible Emergency Communications; a United States–Based Meta Analysis," in *Disability and Social Media: Global Perspectives*, ed. Mike Kent and Katie Ellis (London: Routledge, 2016), 119–30.

52 Bean, *Mobile Technology*, 78.

53 This claim is based largely on social media circulation of screenshots, photos, and context surrounding protests on June 1, 2020. I have avoided crediting any par-

ticular social media user, in this case, as their personal information is not relevant to the larger point.

54 Haven Orrechio-Egrestiz, "Kenosha Police Chief Says 3 People Wouldn't Have Been Shot during Protests If They Weren't Illegally Out Past Curfew," *Insider*, August 26, 2020, www.insider.com.

55 Elizabeth Ellcessor, "Blue-Light Emergency Phones on Campus: Media Infrastructures of Feeling," *International Journal of Cultural Studies* 22, no. 4 (July 2019): 499–518, https://doi.org/10.1177/1367877918820336; Rena Bivens and Amy Adele Hasinoff, "Rape: Is There an App for That? An Empirical Analysis of the Features of Anti-Rape Apps," *Information, Communication and Society* 21, no. 8 (August 2018): 1050–67, https://doi.org/10.1080/1369118X.2017.1309444.

56 The term "phone tree" (or "telephone tree") has also been used in mainstream discourse to refer to the automated touch-tone telephone menus implemented by many businesses beginning in the 1990s. Descriptions of how to "skip the phone tree," for instance, are referring to this automated function.

57 McKinney, *Information Activism*; Hannah Zeavin, *The Distance Cure: A History of Teletherapy* (Cambridge MA: MIT Press, 2021); Barbara Keys, "The Telephone and Its Uses in 1980s U.S. Activism," *Journal of Interdisciplinary History* 48, no. 4 (February 2018): 485–509, https://doi.org/10.1162/JINH_a_01196.

58 McKinney, *Information Activism*; Keys, "Telephone and Its Uses in 1980s U.S. Activism."

59 Zeavin, *Distance Cure*.

60 Keys, "Telephone and Its Uses in 1980s U.S. Activism," 22.

61 "After Attack, We Called Loved Ones," *Associated Press*, September 9, 2002; "Battle Strategies for Blizzards," *Hospital Home Health*, January 1, 1999; David Essex, "Sounding the Alarm: Emergency Notification Systems Can Alert the Right People, No Matter Where They Are, in a Variety of Formats," *Government Computer News*, August 6, 2007.

62 "History Repeats Itself: The Evolution of Campus Security," *Daily Lobo: University of New Mexico*, July 25, 2016.

63 Louise Kertesz, "L.A. Firms Brace for the Worst," *Business Insurance*, April 12, 1993.

64 "A Certification Standard Has Not Emerged in Emergency Preparedness Plans, Says Conference Board," *States News Service*, April 30, 2008.

65 Essex, "Sounding the Alarm."

66 Marie Vasari, "Phone Tree for 21st Century: System Sends Messages in Emergencies," *Monterey County Herald*, April 26, 2007.

67 City of Napa, "Winter Storm 'Phone Tree' Discontinued," *US State News*, October 10, 2013.

68 Security Industry Association, "SIA New Member Profile: Catapult EMS," *States News Service*, March 2, 2020.

69 Megan Friedman, "This App Can Help a Friend Virtually 'Walk You Home' Late at Night," *Cosmopolitan*, September 4, 2015, www.cosmopolitan.com.

70 Friedman.

71 Citizen was initially launched in New York City in 2016 under the name Vigilante, and emphasized tracking 9-1-1 calls to enable people to take safety into their own hands. Many objections to the implied violence of the concept resulted in the app being pulled, restructured, and rebranded.

72 Sebastian Herrera, "Local Crime App Citizen Becomes a Key Tool during Protests," *Wall Street Journal*, June 7, 2020, www.wsj.com.

73 Jennifer Valentino-DeVries. "Coronavirus Apps Show Promise but Prove a Tough Sell." *New York Times*, December 7, 2020, www.nytimes.com.

74 Sarah Fearing, "Virginia Launches 'COVIDWISE Express' for 'App-Less' Exposure Notifications," *WAVY*, February 10, 2021, www.wavy.com.

75 Will Knight, "Why Contact-Tracing Apps Haven't Slowed Covid-19 in the US," *Wired*, September 8, 2020, www.wired.com.

76 Hasinoff and Krueger, "Warning."

77 Leah L. Piepzna-Samarasinha, "Nobody Left Behind, but Wanting to Run Like Hell: Disability Justice Survival Strategies for the Current Apocalypse Moment," *Medium*, September 29, 2020, https://medium.com.

78 Melody Parker, "Church Leaders Put Their Faith in Technology to Serve Their Congregations," *Waterloo Cedar Falls Courier*, March 22, 2020, https://wcfcourier.com.

4. WHAT IS YOUR EMERGENCY?

1 Peter DeMarco, "Losing Laura," *Boston Globe*, November 3, 2018, www.bostonglobe.com.

2 DeMarco.

3 The Editorial Board, "Learning from the Tragic Death of Laura Levis," *Boston Globe*, October 31, 2020, www.bostonglobe.com.

4 DeMarco, "Losing Laura."

5 "Report, n.," in *Oxford English Dictionary Online* (Oxford: Oxford University Press, 2009), www.oed.com.

6 Jennifer C. Rubenstein, "Emergency Claims and Democratic Action," *Social Philosophy and Policy* 32, no. 1 (2015): 101–26, https://doi.org/10.1017/S0265052515000096.

7 "Report, n."

8 "Report, v.," in *Cambridge Essential English Dictionary* (Cambridge: Cambridge University Press, 2011), 335.

9 Rubenstein, "Emergency Claims and Democratic Action," 102.

10 Rubenstein, 110.

11 Chase Wesley Raymond, "Negotiating Entitlement to Language: Calling 911 Without English," *Language in Society* 43, no. 1 (February 2014): 33–59, https://doi.org/10.1017/S0047404513000869; John Heritage and Steven Clayman, *Talk in Action: Interactions, Identities, and Institutions* (New York: Wiley, 2010).

12 Noel A. Cazenave, *Killing African Americans: Police and Vigilante Violence as a Racial Control Mechanism* (New York: Routledge, 2018); Victoria Herrington and Katrina Clifford, "Policing Mental Illness: Examining the Police Role in Addressing Mental Ill-Health," in *Policing Vulnerability*, ed. Isabelle Bartkowiak-Théron and Nicole L Asquith (Annandale, NSW: Federation Press, 2012), 117–31; Andrea Ritchie and Angela Y. Davis, *Invisible No More: Police Violence Against Black Women and Women of Color* (Boston: Beacon Press, 2017).

13 University of Colorado Boulder Chancellor's Office records, COU:2347, box 317, folder 1, Special Collections and Archives, University of Colorado Boulder Libraries.

14 Elizabeth Ellcessor, "Companion: Mobile Personal Safety," in *Appified: Culture in the Age of Apps*, ed. Jeremy Wade Morris and Sarah Murray (Ann Arbor: University of Michigan Press, 2018), 156–68.

15 Lisa Parks, "Stuff You Can Kick: Toward a Theory of Media Infrastructures," in *Between Humanities and the Digital*, ed. Patrik Svensson and David Theo Goldberg (Cambridge, MA: MIT Press, 2015), 355–73.

16 Susan Leigh Star and Karen Ruhleder, "Steps Toward an Ecology of Infrastructure: Design and Access for Large Information Spaces," *Information Systems Research* 7, no. 1 (March 1996): 111–34, https://doi.org/10.1287/isre.7.1.111.

17 "911 Master PSAP Registry," Federal Communications Commission, December 23, 2020, www.fcc.gov.

18 *FCC Fact Sheet: 911 Fee Diversion; New and Emerging Technologies 911 Improvement Act of 2008* (Washington, DC: Federal Communications Commission, 2020), www.fcc.gov.

19 Susan Leigh Star, "The Ethnography of Infrastructure," *American Behavioral Scientist* 43, no. 3 (November 1999): 377–91, https://doi.org/10.1177/00027649921955326.

20 Linda K. Moore, "Emergency Communications: Broadband and the Future of 911," *Journal of Communications Research* 2, nos. 2–3 (April 2011): 180.

21 Tom Wheeler, "The 9-1-1 System Isn't Ready for the iPhone Era," *New York Times*, November 23, 2015, www.nytimes.com.

22 David Phillips, "Texas 9-1-1: Emergency Telecommunications and the Genesis of Surveillance Infrastructure," *Telecommunications Policy* 29, no. 11 (December 2005): 843–56, https://doi.org/10.1016/j.telpol.2005.06.007.

23 Elizabeth Ellcessor, "Call If You Can, Text If You Can't: A Dismediation of U.S. Emergency Communication Infrastructure," *International Journal of Communication* 13 (September 2019): 4487–4506, https://ijoc.org.

24 Greg Downey, "Virtual Webs, Physical Technologies, and Hidden Workers: The Spaces of Labor in Information Internetworks," *Technology and Culture* 42, no. 2 (2001): 211, http://dx.doi.org/10.1353/tech.2001.0058.

25 Elinor Carmi, "Sonic Publics | The Hidden Listeners: Regulating the Line from Telephone Operators to Content Moderators," *International Journal of Communication* 13 (January 2019): 444, https://ijoc.org.

26 Phoenix Chi Wang, "Days and Nights in the Dispatch Center: What I Saw as a Scientist, Experienced as a Person, and How It Changed Me," in *The Resilient 9-1-1 Professional: A Comprehensive Guide to Surviving and Thriving Together in the 9-1-1 Center*, ed. Jim Marshall and Tracey Laorenza (Petoskey, MI: South of Heaven Press, 2018), 15–16.

27 Star, "Ethnography of Infrastructure," 386–87.

28 All names of 9-1-1 professionals are pseudonyms. Much of the theorization of 9-1-1 and media work that follows has been adapted from my work in "The Care and Feeding of 9-1-1 Infrastructure: Dispatcher Culture as Media Work and Infrastructural Transformation," *Cultural Studies*, 2021, https://doi.org/10.1080/0950238 6.2021.1895249. This article also provides discussion of research ethics concerning these interviews.

29 Wang, "Days and Nights in the Dispatch Center," 15.

30 John Thornton Caldwell, *Production Culture: Industrial Reflexivity and Critical Practice in Film and Television* (Durham, NC: Duke University Press, 2008); Timothy Havens, Amanda D. Lotz, and Serra Tinic, "Critical Media Industry Studies: A Research Approach," *Communication, Culture and Critique* 2, no. 2 (2009): 234–53, https://doi.org/10.1111/j.1753-9137.2009.01037.x; Jennifer Holt and Alisa Perren, eds., *Media Industries: History, Theory, and Method* (Malden, MA: Wiley-Blackwell, 2009); Vicki Mayer, Miranda J. Banks, and John T. Caldwell, eds., *Production Studies: Cultural Studies of Media Industries* (London: Routledge, 2009).

31 Axel Bruns, *Blogs, Wikipedia, "Second Life," and Beyond: From Production and Produsage* (New York: Peter Lang, 2008); Henry Jenkins, *Convergence Culture: Where Old and New Media Collide* (New York: NYU Press, 2006); Aymar Jean Christian, *Open TV: Innovation Beyond Hollywood and the Rise of Web Television* (New York: NYU Press, 2018).

32 Melissa Gregg, *Work's Intimacy* (Cambridge: Polity, 2011). 167.

33 Havens, Lotz, and Tinic, "Critical Media Industry Studies."

34 Angela Cora Garcia and Penelope Ann Parmer, "Misplaced Mistrust: The Collaborative Construction of Doubt In 9-1-1 Emergency Calls," *Symbolic Interaction* 22, no. 4 (1999): 297–324; Heritage and Clayman, *Talk in Action*; Karen Tracy, "Interactional Trouble in Emergency Service Requests: A Problem of Frames," *Research on Language and Social Interaction* 30, no. 4 (October 1997): 315–43, https://doi.org/10.1207/s15327973rlsi3004_3.

35 Heritage and Clayman, *Talk in Action*, 2010.

36 Heritage and Clayman, 58.

37 Heritage and Clayman, 72.

38 Heritage and Clayman, 73.

39 Heritage and Clayman; Tracy, "Interactional Trouble in Emergency Service Requests."

40 Eleanor Patterson, "Maintaining Transmission: DirecTV's Work-at-Home Technical Support, Virtual Surveillance, and the Gendered Domestication

of Distributive Labor," *Television and New Media*, June 9, 2020, https://doi.org/10.1177/1527476420928552.

41 Sarah J. Tracy and Karen Tracy, "Emotion Labor at 9-1-1: A Case Study and Theoretical Critique," *Journal of Applied Communication Research* 26, no. 4 (November 1998): 390–411, https://doi.org/10.1080/00909889809365516.

42 Tracy, "Interactional Trouble in Emergency Service Requests," 338.

43 Ellcessor, "Care and Feeding of 9-1-1 Infrastructure."

44 Tracy, "Interactional Trouble in Emergency Service Requests," 338; Heritage and Clayman, *Talk in Action*.

45 Star, "Ethnography of Infrastructure," 384.

46 Tracy, "Interactional Trouble in Emergency Service Requests," 64.

47 Caroline Burau, *Answering 911: Life in the Hot Seat* (St. Paul: Borealis Books, 2007), 211.

48 Wang, "Days and Nights in the Dispatch Center," 16.

49 Ellcessor, "Care and Feeding of 9-1-1 Infrastructure."

50 Ellcessor, "Call If You Can, Text If You Can't," 20.

51 Yvonne Man, "State Launches Text-to-9-1-1 Emergency Service," *Fox 59* (blog), May 14, 2014, http://fox59.com.

52 Ellcessor, "Call If You Can, Text If You Can't."

53 "9-1-1 Master PSAP Registry," Federal Communications Commission, December 23, 2020, www.fcc.gov; "Text 9-1-1 Master PSAP Registry," Federal Communications Commission, December 23, 2020, www.fcc.gov.

54 Andrew Guthrie Ferguson, *The Rise of Big Data Policing: Surveillance, Race, and the Future of Law Enforcement* (New York: NYU Press, 2017), 1.

55 Carmi, "Sonic Publics | The Hidden Listeners," 441.

56 Ferguson, *The Rise of Big Data Policing*, 2.

57 Motorola Solutions, "Motorola Solutions Emergency Call Handling Software," YouTube video, 1;49, uploaded August 13, 2018, https://youtu.be/4-CBV4sOJWk.

58 Ferguson, 3.

59 James N. Gilmore and McKinley DuRant, "Emergency Infrastructure and Locational Extraction: Problematizing Computer Assisted Dispatch Systems as Public Good," *Surveillance & Society* 19, no. 2 (June 2021): 187–98, https://doi.org/10.24908/ss.v19i2.14116.

60 Shoshana Zuboff, *The Age of Surveillance Capitalism: The Fight for a Human Future at the New Frontier of Power* (New York: PublicAffairs, 2019).

61 An officer did arrive at the house and interrupted the assault, but his presence in the neighborhood was coincidental.

62 Jessica Miller, "A Utah Woman Called 9-1-1 after Being Stabbed by a Stranger, but Dispatchers Didn't Send a Cop," *Salt Lake Tribune*, October 30, 2019, www.sltrib.com.

63 Tracy, "Interactional Trouble in Emergency Service Requests."

64 Troy Closson, "Amy Cooper's 9-1-1 Call, and What's Happened Since," *New York Times*, July 8, 2020, www.nytimes.com.

65 Troy Closson, "Amy Cooper Falsely Accused Black Bird-Watcher in 2nd 9-1-1 Conversation," *New York Times*, October 14, 2020, www.nytimes.com.

66 André Brock, "From the Blackhand Side: Twitter as a Cultural Conversation," *Journal of Broadcasting and Electronic Media* 56, no. 4 (October 2012): 529–49, https://doi.org/10.1080/08838151.2012.732147; Meredith Clark, "Black Twitter: Building Connection through Cultural Conversation," in *Hashtag Publics: The Power and Politics of Discursive Networks*, ed. Nathan Rambukkana (New York: Peter Lang, 2015), 205–18; Deen Freelon, Charlton D. McIlwain, and Meredith D. Clark, *Beyond the Hashtags: #Ferguson, #Blacklivesmatter, and the Online Struggle for Offline Justice* (Washington, DC: Center for Media and Social Impact, School of Communication, American University, 2016), https://cmsimpact.org.

67 P. R. Lockhart, "Living While Black and the Criminalization of Blackness," *Vox*, August 1, 2018, www.vox.com.

68 Jessica Guyunn, "BBQ Becky, Permit Patty and Why the Internet Is Shaming White People Who Police People 'Simply for Being Black,'" *USA Today*, July 18, 2018, www.usatoday.com.

69 Jaweed Kaleem, "#LivingWhileBlack: New Laws Could Outlaw Racially Motivated 9-1-1 Calls," *Los Angeles Times*, May 27, 2019, www.latimes.com.

70 Chanelle N. Jones, "#LivingWhileBlack: Racially Motivated 911 Calls as a Form of Private Racial Profiling Comments," *Temple Law Review Online* 92 (2020): 69, https://heinonline.org.

71 Elaine Scarry, *Thinking in an Emergency* (2010; repr., New York: W. W. Norton, 2012).

72 Burau, *Answering 9-1-1*, 163.

73 Heritage and Clayman, *Talk in Action*, 81.

74 Sara Ahmed, *The Cultural Politics of Emotion* (New York: Routledge, 2004).

75 Matthew Fleischer, "White Women Are Still Frivolously Calling Police on Black People," *Los Angeles Times*, June 3, 2020, www.latimes.com.

76 Carol A. Stabile and Carrie Rentschler, "States of Insecurity and the Gendered Politics of Fear," *NWSA Journal* 17, no. 3 (2005): xii, www.jstor.org.

77 Stabile and Rentschler, xii.

78 Robert E Gutsche et al., "#DiminishingDiscrimination: The Symbolic Annihilation of Race and Racism in News Hashtags of 'Calling 9-1-1 on Black People,'" *Journalism*, May 9, 2020, https://doi.org/10.1177/1464884920919279; Jones, "#LivingWhileBlack."

79 Jonathan Kahn, "The 911 Covenant: Policing Black Bodies in White Spaces and the Limits of Implicit Bias as a Tool of Racial Justice," *Stanford Journal of Civil Rights and Civil Liberties* 15, no. 1 (2019): 1–41, https://law.stanford.edu.

80 Kahn, 20.

81 Kahn, 20.

82 Kahn, 25.

83 Jessica W. Gillooly, "'9-1-1, Is This an Emergency?': How 9-1-1 Call-Takers Extract, Interpret, and Classify Caller Information" (PhD diss., University of Michigan, 2020), https://deepblue.lib.umich.edu.

84 Gillooly, 128.

85 Gillooly, 139.

86 Jaeah Lee, "Here's How Cleveland Police May Have Botched a 9-1-1 Call Just before Killing Tamir Rice," *Mother Jones*, June 24, 2015, www.motherjones.com.

87 Gillooly, "'9-1-1, Is This an Emergency?,'" 145.

88 Rachael Herron, "I Used to Be a 911 Dispatcher: I Had to Respond to Racist Calls Every Day," *Vox*, May 30, 2018, www.vox.com.

89 Germaine R Halegoua and Jessa Lingel, "Lit Up and Left Dark: Failures of Imagination in Urban Broadband Networks," *New Media & Society* 20, no. 12 (December 2018): 14, https://doi.org/10.1177/1461444818779593.

90 Jake Sheridan, "San Francisco Lawmaker Proposes CAREN Act, Making Racially Biased 9-1-1 Calls Illegal," *Los Angeles Times*, July 8, 2020, www.latimes.com.

91 Jones, "#LivingWhileBlack," 76.

5. HELP!

1 Troy Closson, "Amy Cooper Falsely Accused Black Bird-Watcher in 2nd 911 Conversation," *New York Times*, October 14, 2020, www.nytimes.com.

2 The redefinition of emergency through this testimony is not its only—or even primary—function, in many cases. There are numerous motivations, contextual differences, and alternate interpretations that can shape the interpretations and effectiveness of such videos. I focus on their work as testimony and emergency media but acknowledge that this is only one of several appropriate lenses of analysis.

3 Will Sutherland and Mohammad Hossein Jarrahi, "The Sharing Economy and Digital Platforms: A Review and Research Agenda," *International Journal of Information Management* 43 (December 2018): 328–41, https://doi.org/10.1016/j.ijinfomgt.2018.07.004.

4 Shoshana Feldman and Dori Laub, *Testimony: Crises of Witnessing in Literature, Psychoanalysis, and History* (Oxfordshire, UK: Taylor & Francis, 1992).

5 Sara Ahmed, *Complaint!* (Durham, NC: Duke University Press, 2021).

6 Paul Frosh, "Telling Presences: Witnessing, Mass Media, and the Imagined Lives of Strangers," *Critical Studies in Media Communication* 23, no. 4 (October 2006): 265–84, https://doi.org/10.1080/07393180600933097.

7 Kari Andén-Papadopoulos, "Citizen Camera-Witnessing: Embodied Political Dissent in the Age of 'Mediated Mass Self-Communication,'" *New Media and Society* 16, no. 5 (August 2014): 753, https://doi.org/10.1177/1461444813489863.

8 Andén-Papadopoulos.

9 Andén-Papadopoulos, 754.

10 Ahmed, *Complaint!*

11 Allissa V. Richardson, *Bearing Witness while Black* (New York: Oxford University Press, 2020), 5.

12 John Durham Peters, "Witnessing," *Media, Culture & Society* 23, no. 6 (November 2001): 707–23, https://doi.org/10.1177/016344301023006002.

13 "Bid, n.," in *Oxford English Dictionary Online* (Oxford: Oxford University Press, 2009), www.oed.com.

14 This phrasing is deliberately similar to Rubenstein's description of the narrative of emergency claims. See Jennifer C. Rubenstein, "Emergency Claims and Democratic Action," *Social Philosophy and Policy* 32, no. 1 (2015): 101–26, https://doi.org/10.1017/S0265052515000096.

15 Rubenstein.

16 Henry Jenkins, Sam Ford, and Joshua Green, *Spreadable Media: Creating Value and Meaning in a Networked Culture*, Postmillennial Pop (New York: NYU Press, 2013).

17 Sarah J. Jackson, Moya Bailey, and Brooke Foucault Welles, *#HashtagActivism: Networks of Race and Gender Justice*, illustrated ed. (Cambridge, MA: MIT Press, 2020); Richardson, *Bearing Witness while Black*; Axel Bruns, *Gatewatching and News Curation: Journalism, Social Media, and the Public Sphere*, Digital Formations (New York: Peter Lang, 2018).

18 James Kinsella, *Covering the Plague*, AIDS and the American Media (New Brunswick, NJ: Rutgers University Press, 1989).

19 Simon Watney, *Imagine Hope: AIDS and Gay Identify* (New York: Routledge, 2000), 107.

20 Alexandra Juhasz, *AIDS TV: Identity, Community, and Alternative Video*, illustrated ed. (Durham, NC: Duke University Press, 1995), 3.

21 For discussion of this activism online, see Cait McKinney, "Crisis Infrastructures: AIDS Activism Meets Internet Regulation," in *AIDS and the Distribution of Crises*, ed. Jih-Fei Cheng, Alexandra Juhasz, and Nishant Shahani (Durham, NC: Duke University Press, 2020), 162–82.

22 Watney, *Imagine Hope*, 11.

23 See Nicola Gavey, "Fighting Rape," in *Theorizing Sexual Violence*, ed. Renée J. Heberle and Victoria Grace (New York: Routledge, 2011), 96–124; Karina Hagelin, "Gossip as a Site of Resistance: Information-Sharing Strategies among Survivors of Sexual Violence" (master's thesis, University of Maryland, 2018), http://drum.lib.umd.edu; Allyson Mitchell, "The Writing's on the Wall: Feminist and Lesbian Graffiti as Cultural Production," in *Turbo Chicks: Talking Young Feminisms*, ed. Allyson Mitchell, Lisa Bryn Rundle, and Lara Karaian (Toronto: Sumach Press, 2001), 221–32.

24 Richardson, *Bearing Witness while Black*, 31.

25 Richardson, 32.

26 John Fiske, *Media Matters: Race and Gender in U.S. Politics*, rev. ed. (Minneapolis: University of Minnesota Press, 1996), 127.

27 Izzy Star, "LA Riots EBS Message (SSTEAS Reupload)," YouTube video, 1:03, uploaded February 3, 2020, https://youtu.be/YzoAtEx9CIA. This video was originally shared by a controversial YouTube account, SSTEAS, that often posted Emergency Broadcast System videos. The dusk-to-dawn curfew, enforced by the California National Guard, U.S. troops, and federal law enforcement, went into effect at 12:15 a.m. on April 30, 1992, and concluded on May 4, 1992.
28 Richardson, *Bearing Witness while Black*, 46.
29 Simone Browne, *Dark Matters: On the Surveillance of Blackness* (Durham, NC: Duke University Press, 2015).
30 Mia Fischer and K. Mohrman, "Black Deaths Matter? Sousveillance and the Invisibility of Black Life," *Ada New Media* (blog), October 31, 2016, https://adanewmedia.org.
31 Fischer and Mohrman.
32 Issie Lapowsky, "For Philando Castile, Social Media Was the Only 911," *Wired*, July 7, 2016, www.wired.com.
33 Salvador Rodriguez, "How Facebook Live Is Becoming the Social 911 for People Who Can't Trust the Police," *Inc.*, July 7, 2016, www.inc.com.
34 Lapowsky, "For Philando Castile, Social Media Was the Only 911."
35 Throughout this book, I have capitalized "Black"; Richardson does not capitalize this in her work with "black witnessing," so I have retained her terminology here.
36 Richardson, *Bearing Witness while Black*, 5.
37 Richardson, 7.
38 Lapowsky, "For Philando Castile, Social Media Was the Only 911."
39 Jackson, Bailey, and Welles, *#HashtagActivism*.
40 Jackson, Bailey, and Welles, *#HashtagActivism*. See also Deen Freelon, Charlton D. McIlwain, and Meredith D. Clark, *Beyond the Hashtags: #Ferguson, #Blacklivesmatter, and the Online Struggle for Offline Justice* (Washington, DC: Center for Media and Social Impact, School of Communication, American University, 2016).
41 Jackson, Bailey, and Welles, *#HashtagActivism*.
42 Jackson, Bailey, and Welles, 199.
43 Kara Weisenstein, "Meet the Women Behind the Viral Protest Art All Over Instagram," *Mic*, June 19, 2020, www.mic.com.
44 Rasul Mowatt, "Black Lives as Snuff: The Silent Complicity in Viewing Black Death," *Biography* 41 (September 2018): 777–806, https://doi.org/10.1353/bio.2018.0079; Richardson, *Bearing Witness while Black*.
45 Jackson, Bailey, and Welles, *#HashtagActivism*.
46 Jackson, Bailey, and Welles.
47 Moy Bailey, *Misogynoir Transformed: Black Women's Digital Resistance* (New York: NYU Press, 2021).
48 Jackson, Bailey, and Welles, *#HashtagActivism*, 59.
49 "2 Officers Shot in Louisville Protests Over Breonna Taylor Charging Decision," *New York Times*, September 23, 2020, www.nytimes.com.

50 Ryan M. Milner, *The World Made Meme: Public Conversations and Participatory Media*, The Information Society Series (Cambridge, MA: MIT Press, 2018); Limor Shifman, *Memes in Digital Culture* (Cambridge, MA: MIT Press, 2013); Whitney Phillips and Ryan M. Milner, *The Ambivalent Internet: Mischief, Oddity, and Antagonism Online* (Malden, MA: Polity, 2017).

51 Aja Romano, "'Arrest the Cops Who Killed Breonna Taylor': The Power and the Peril of a Catchphrase," *Vox*, August 10, 2020, www.vox.com.

52 Ellie Bate, "Lili Reinhart Apologised for Her 'Tone Deaf' Topless Instagram Post Demanding Justice for Breonna Taylor," *BuzzFeed*, July 1, 2020, www.buzzfeed.com.

53 Romano, "Arrest the Cops Who Killed Breonna Taylor."

54 Romano; Kalhan Rosenblatt, "Twitter Memeified Justice for Breonna Taylor: But Can a Joke Make Change?," *NBC News*, June 19, 2020, www.nbcnews.com.

55 Rosenblatt, "Twitter Memeified Justice for Breonna Taylor."

56 Rosenblatt.

57 Lauren Silverman, "Facebook, Twitter Replace 911 Calls for Stranded in Houston," *NPR*, August 28, 2017, www.npr.org.

58 Cade Metz, "How Facebook Is Transforming Disaster Response," *Wired*, November 10, 2016, www.wired.com; Gregory Asmolov, "Crowdsourcing and the Folksonomy of Emergency Response: The Construction of a Mediated Subject," *Interactions: Studies in Communication and Culture* 6, no. 2 (July 2015): 155–78, https://doi.org/10.1386/iscc.6.2.155_1; Muhammad Imran et al., "Using AI and Social Media Multimodal Content for Disaster Response and Management: Opportunities, Challenges, and Future Directions," *Information Processing and Management* 57, no. 5 (September 2020): 102261, https://doi.org/10.1016/j.ipm.2020.102261; Megan Finn, *Documenting Aftermath: Information Infrastructures in the Wake of Disasters* (Cambridge, MA: MIT Press, 2018).

59 John Fiske, *Understanding Popular Culture*, 2nd ed. (New York: Routledge, 2010).

60 Gerard Goggin, "Adapting the Mobile Phone: The iPhone and Its Consumption," *Continuum* 23, no. 2 (2009): 233, https://doi.org/10.1080/10304310802710546.

61 Siva Vaidhyanathan, *Antisocial Media: How Facebook Disconnects Us and Undermines Democracy* (New York: Oxford University Press, 2018).

62 Cade Metz, "How Facebook Wants to Save the World," *Wired UK*, February 4, 2017, www.wired.co.uk; Caitlin Dewey, "Why Facebook's 'Safety Check' Deployed in Paris—but Not in Beirut, Garissa or Ankara," *Washington Post*, November 16, 2015, www.washingtonpost.com; Omar Mohammed, "Facebook Is Being Criticized for Not Activating Safety Check during the Côte d'Ivoire Attack," *Quartz Africa*, March 14, 2016, https://qz.com.

63 "Crisis Response | Social Impact Partnerships at Facebook," Facebook, accessed December 13, 2020, https://socialimpact.facebook.com.

64 Nick Statt, "Facebook Launches Crisis Response Hub to Help Users during Disasters and Attacks," *The Verge*, September 14, 2017, www.theverge.com.

65 Finn, *Documenting Aftermath*.

66 Vaidhyanathan, *Antisocial Media*, 107.

67 Finn, *Documenting Aftermath.*

68 Finn, 133.

69 Carla Gray, "Looking Out for the Uber Community during an Emergency," Uber, September 24, 2018, www.uber.com.

70 "Airbnb Open Homes—Disaster Relief," Airbnb, accessed December 13, 2020, www.airbnb.com.

71 Alex Rosenblat, *Uberland: How Algorithms Are Rewriting the Rules of Work* (Berkeley: University of California Press, 2018); José van Dijck, Thomas Poell, and Martijn de Waal, *The Platform Society: Public Values in a Connective World* (New York: Oxford University Press, 2018).

72 Sigal Samuel, "How to Help People during the Pandemic, One Google Spreadsheet at a Time," *Vox*, March 24, 2020, www.vox.com.

73 Dean Spade, *Mutual Aid: Building Solidarity during This Crisis* (Brooklyn: Verso, 2020), 19.

74 Dean Spade, "Solidarity Not Charity: Mutual Aid for Mobilization and Survival," *Social Text* 38, no. 1 (March 2020): 131–51, https://doi.org/10.1215/01642472-7971139.

75 Lana Swartz, *New Money: How Payment Became Social Media*, illustrated ed. (New Haven, CT: Yale University Press, 2020).

76 Robert Soden, "Crisis Informatics and Mutual Aid during the Coronavirus Pandemic: A Research Agenda," *Items* (blog), June 2, 2020, https://items.ssrc.org.

77 Cait McKinney, *Information Activism: A Queer History of Lesbian Media Technologies*, annotated ed. (Durham: Duke University Press, 2020).

78 Elizabeth Ellcessor, "The Care and Feeding of 9-1-1 Infrastructure: Dispatcher Culture as Media Work and Infrastructural Transformation," *Cultural Studies*, 2021, https://doi.org/10.1080/09502386.2021.1895249.

79 Aimi Hamraie, "Solidarity Chat 10: Embry Wood Owen," *Contra** (podcast), June 19, 2020, www.mapping-access.com.

80 Leah Lakshmi Piepzna-Samarasinha, *Care Work: Dreaming Disability Justice* (Vancouver, BC: Arsenal Pulp Press, 2018).

81 Matthew Green, "How PG&E's Power Shutoffs Sparked an East Bay Disability Rights Campaign," *KQED*, November 6, 2019, www.kqed.org.

82 Ashley Shew, "Let COVID-19 Expand Awareness of Disability Tech," *Nature* 581, no. 7806 (May 2020), https://doi.org/10.1038/d41586-020-01312-w.

83 Matthew Green, "Coronavirus: How These Disabled Activists Are Taking Matters into Their Own (Sanitized) Hands," *KQED*, March 17, 2020, www.kqed.org.

84 Aimi Hamraie, "Solidarity Chat 6: Dasom Nah," *Contra** (podcast), June 12, 2020, www.mapping-access.com.

85 Diana Budds, "Can a Neighborhood Become a Network?," *Curbed*, June 23, 2020, https://archive.curbed.com.

86 Nathan Schneider, "How to Build Mutual Aid That Will Last after the Coronavirus Pandemic," *America Magazine*, April 1, 2020, www.americamagazine.org.

87 Rubenstein, "Emergency Claims and Democratic Action," 114.

88 Rubenstein, 119.

CONCLUSION

1 I first saw this unattributed post shared on a friend's Facebook wall in summer 2020, and later through multiple other people and groups. Attempts to pin down its original author or date failed.

2 Silvia Lindtner, Shaowen Bardzell, and Jeffrey Bardzell, "Reconstituting the Utopian Vision of Making: HCI after Technosolutionism," in *Proceedings of the 2016 CHI Conference on Human Factors in Computing Systems*, CHI '16 (New York: Association for Computing Machinery, 2016), 1390–1402, https://doi.org/10.1145/2858036.2858506.

3 Elise Schmelzer, "Mental Health Professionals Replace Police on Some Denver 9-1-1 Calls under New Program," *Denver Post*, September 6, 2020, www.denverpost.com.

4 Gilbert Caluya, "Pride and Paranoia: Race and the Emergence of Home Security in Cold War America," *Continuum: Journal of Media and Cultural Studies* 28, no. 6 (December 2014): 808–19, https://doi.org/10.1080/10304312.2014.966406; Carol A. Stabile and Carrie Rentschler, "States of Insecurity and the Gendered Politics of Fear," *NWSA Journal* 17, no. 3 (2005): vii–xxv, www.jstor.org; William V. Pelfrey, Steven Keener, and Michael Perkins, "Examining the Role of Demographics in Campus Crime Alerts: Implications and Recommendations, Implications and Recommendations," *Race and Justice* 8, no. 3 (July 2018): 244–69, https://doi.org/10.1177/2153368716675475.

5 Jim Newell, "Old People Elected Trump. Will They Make Him a One-Term President?," Slate Magazine, September 16, 2020, www.slate.com.

6 David M. Perry and Lawrence Carter-Long, "The Ruderman White Paper on Media Coverage of Law Enforcement Use of Force and Disability" (white paper, Ruderman Foundation, March 2016), https://rudermanfoundation.org.

7 Liat Ben-Moshe, *Decarcerating Disability: Deinstitutionalization and Prison Abolition* (Minneapolis: University of Minnesota Press, 2020); Talila "TL" Lewis, "Disability Justice Is an Essential Part of Abolishing Police and Prisons," *LEVEL* (blog), October 7, 2020, https://level.medium.com.

8 Ben-Moshe, *Decarcerating Disability*, 283.

9 Sara Ahmed, *The Cultural Politics of Emotion* (New York: Routledge, 2004), 69.

10 Katie Oliviero, *Vulnerability Politics: The Uses and Abuses of Precarity in Political Debate* (New York: NYU Press, 2018), 6.

11 Oliviero, *Vulnerability Politics*.

12 Leah Lakshmi Piepzna-Samarasinha, *Care Work: Dreaming Disability Justice* (Vancouver, BC: Arsenal Pulp Press, 2018), 53.

13 Mara Marin, *Connected by Commitment: Oppression and Our Responsibility to Undermine It, Connected by Commitment* (New York: Oxford University Press, 2017).

14 Eva Feder Kittay, "The Ethics of Care, Dependence, and Disability," *Ratio Juris* 24, no. 1 (2011): 54, https://doi.org/10.1111/j.1467-9337.2010.00473.x.

15 Kittay, 54.

16 Andreas Chatzidakis et al., *The Care Manifesto: The Politics of Interdependence* (Brooklyn: Verso, 2020).

17 Chatzidakis et al., 123.

18 Chatzidakis et al., 46.

19 Steven J. Jackson, "Rethinking Repair," in *Media Technologies: Essays on Communication, Materiality, and Society*, ed. Tarleton Gillespie, Pablo J. Boczkowski, and Kirsten A. Foot (Cambridge, MA: MIT Press, 2014), 232.

20 Angela Y. Davis, *Abolition Democracy: Beyond Empire, Prisons, and Torture* (New York: Seven Stories Press, 2005), 39.

21 Lily Irani, "San Diegans Shouldn't Be Lab Rats for Innovation," *Voice of San Diego*, September 24, 2019, www.voiceofsandiego.org.

22 Ejeris Dixon, "Building Community Safety: Practical Steps toward Liberatory Transformation," in *Beyond Survival: Strategies and Stories from the Transformative Justice Movement*, ed. Ejeris Dixon and Leah Lakshmi Piepzna-Samarasinha, annotated ed. (Chico, CA: AK Press, 2020), loc. 306.

23 Dixon, loc. 102.

24 Oakland Power Projects, "Maybe You Don't Have to Call 911?," in Dixon and Piepzna-Samarasinha, *Beyond Survival*, loc. 1894.

25 Ejeris Dixon and Leah Lakshmi Piepzna-Samarasinha, "Introduction," in Dixon and Piepzna-Samarasinha, *Beyond Survival*, loc. 112.

26 Audrey Fraizer, "Reclassifying Emergency Dispatchers," *Journal of Emergency Dispatch*, July 16, 2020, https://iaedjournal.org.

27 James N. Gilmore and McKinley DuRant, "Emergency Infrastructure and Locational Extraction: Problematizing Computer Assisted Dispatch Systems as Public Good," *Surveillance & Society* 19, no. 2 (June 2021): 187–98, https://doi.org/10.24908/ss.v19i2.14116.

28 Hunter Knapp, "Managing an Administrative Emergency: Establishing FEMA as an Independent Agency," *Colorado Natural Resources, Energy and Environmental Law Review* 31, no. 1 (2020): 231–64; *An Independent FEMA: Restoring the Nation's Capabilities for Effective Emergency Management and Disaster Response, Hearing before the Committee on Transportation and Infrastructure House of Representatives*, 111th Cong. 32 (2009); Dara Khosrowshahi, "Getting Serious about Safety," Uber, April 12, 2018, www.uber.com.

29 Aarian Marshall, "Uber's New Features Put a Focus on Rider Safety," *Wired*, September 26, 2020, www.wired.com.

30 Gwendolyn Wu, "San Francisco Teams up with Uber, Location Tracker on 911 Call Responses," *San Francisco Chronicle*, April 22, 2019, www.sfchronicle.com.

31 Aarian Marshall, "Uber's New Features Put a Focus on Rider Safety," *Wired*, September 26, 2020, www.wired.com.

32 "How to Use Signal Encrypted Messaging," *Wired*, August 18, 2020, www.wired.com.

33 Elaine Scarry, *Thinking in an Emergency* (2010; repr., W. W. Norton, 2012).

INDEX

Page numbers in *italics* refer to figures.

ABOUT THE AUTHOR

ELIZABETH ELLCESSOR is Associate Professor in the Department of Media Studies at the University of Virginia. She studies access and disability in relation to digital and historical media cultures and technologies. She is the author of *Restricted Access: Media, Disability, and the Politics of Participation* and the co-editor of *Disability Media Studies*.

www.ingramcontent.com/pod-product-compliance
Lightning Source LLC
Chambersburg PA
CBHW020253030426
42336CB00010B/744